THE UPPER ROOM DISCIPLINES 1994

THE UPPER ROOM
# Disciplines
# 1994

*Coordinating Editor*
Glenda Webb

*Consulting Editors*
Rita B. Collett
Lynne M. Deming
George R. Graham
Charla H. Honea
Janet R. McNish
John S. Mogabgab
Tom Page
Robin Philpo Pippin
Mary Lou Redding
Beth A. Richardson

UPPER
ROOM BOOKS
NASHVILLE

# The Upper Room Disciplines 1994

© 1993 by The Upper Room. All rights reserved.

Cover photo © Nancy Anne Dawe
Cover deisgn by Jim Bateman

*Revised Common Lectionary* copyright © 1992 by the Consultation on Common Texts (CCT). Used with permission.

Scripture quotations not otherwise identified are from the New Revised Standard Version of the Bible, © 1989 by the Division of Christian Education, National Council of the Churches of Christ in the USA. Used by permission.

Scripture quotations designated RSV are from the Revised Standard Version of the Bible, copyrighted 1946, 1952, and © 1971 by the Division of Christian Education, National Council of the Churches of Christ in the USA. Used by permission.

Scripture quotations designated NIV are from the *Holy Bible, New International Version*. Copyright © 1973, 1978, 1984 International Bible Society. Used by permission of Zondervan Bible Publishers.

Scripture quotations designated TEV are from the *Good News Bible*, The Bible in Today's English Version - Old Testament: Copyright © American Bible Society 1976; New Testament: Copyright © American Bible Society 1966, 1971, 1976.

Scripture quotations designated NKJV are from The New King James Version. Copyright © 1979, 1980, 1982, Thomas Nelson Inc., Publishers. Used by permission.

Page 387 constitutes an extension of this copyright page.

**ISBN 0-8358-0674-X**
**Printed in the United States of America**

# CONTENTS

One of my favorite stories in the Bible is the one about the man at the Beautiful Gate in Acts 3:1-10. In this story, Peter and John are on their way to the Temple to pray when they come across a man who is crippled and who must beg for his livelihood. The man asks Peter and John for money. But Peter tells him, "I have no silver or gold, but what I have I give you." With that Peter tells the man to walk in the name of Jesus Christ. Indeed, the man jumps up and enters the Temple with them, "walking and leaping and praising God." All who see the man recognize him as the one who was crippled. They are filled with wonder and amazement.

Although this story happened almost two thousand years ago, it feels familiar. This very scene will be replayed today many times all around the world. People who cannot provide for themselves must ask others for food or money. I witness it at least several times each week in the city where I live. This story feels familiar because it deals with issues that are still with us today.

But the real reason I think this story seems familiar is that it illustrates a dichotomy at the heart of many problems in our society—the contrast between quick fixes and deep needs. In the story, the man at the Beautiful Gate asks for the money he needs to live that day, but he does not ask for the healing that could change his life. Without the hope of medical treatment and after what was probably years of begging, it seems natural that the man would have given up any hope of healing. In a society without advanced medical treatment or a social safety net, begging was one of the few ways he could provide for himself. But Peter and John were able to avoid a quick fix and address his deeper need for healing.

While medical technology has improved and the government now funds disability income, our society grapples with quick fixes and deeper needs just as much as society in the time of the early church. We live in a society that specializes in quick fixes, sometimes ignoring deeper needs.

Interest in quick fixes is pervasive, spreading even into our spiritual lives. In some ways in my spiritual life, I identify with the man at the Beautiful Gate. Like the beggar who asked Peter and John for alms, sometimes I sit before God and ask for spiritual alms. I ask for instant answers to my prayers or deliverance from all kinds of adversity. It is more difficult to focus on deeper concerns that need radical healing. I am also learning that it takes a great deal of energy and time to discern where these places are.

While some might argue that spending a few moments every day with a Bible reading and a meditation is a quick spiritual fix, I would argue otherwise. For me daily Bible reading and reflection give me the opportunity to think about deeper concerns in my life and the life of the world as well as to discern how I might respond faithfully to these situations. This daily time apart is not a quick fix. Rather, it is part of a long journey where there are no guarantees of immediate answers or deliverance from difficulties. When I have doubts about the journey, often I hear God's reassurance in Peter's words: "What I have I give you." When we read the Bible, we see again and again that what God has God gives, moving beyond quick fixes to address people's deeper needs.

Wherever we are on our spiritual journey, this edition of *The Upper Room Disciplines* is meant to provide a map. Based on the Revised Common Lectionary, *Disciplines* is a collection of daily meditations by writers from a broad range of backgrounds. The combination of challenging scripture readings and fresh perspectives on those readings invites us into uncharted territory in our spiritual lives.

On that journey, daily contact with the Word means daily assurance that what God has God gives us. Assurance of God's generosity and abundant love frees us from requesting quick fixes and encourages us to consider our deep needs as well as the deep needs of the world in which we live. May *Disciplines* give you that daily assurance.

George R. Graham
Editor, *alive now!* magazine

# IN LOVE AND MERCY, GOD-WITH-US

January 1–2, 1994          **George Donigian**✝
**Saturday, January 1**          Read Matthew 2:1-10.

Consider the personalities in this passage. Foremost is Herod the Great, king of Israel. Herod could be passionate and compassionate, generous and orderly. Accounts of Herod's kingship also record many cruelties and the use of power to destructive purposes. Fearing intrigue, Herod murdered family members whom he feared as rivals. Herod stands as one with horrifying might and authority.

The magi, anonymous as they are in Matthew and the basis for many legends, seem the stuff of innocent wisdom. Because of their anonymity in the Gospel, fictional names and background accrued to the magi acknowledge the substance of their lives. After study and devotion, the discipline of intellect and religious affection, the magi initiated a pilgrimage to an unknown place in search of one to be born. Their strength reveals itself in their meeting with Herod the Great. They do not flinch before the king, despite the fear evidenced by those who heard the magi's question about the new king of the Jews. Their persistence typifies the extraordinary quality of faith in difficult circumstances.

Now consider the character of Bethlehem. Unlike Herod the Great, Bethlehem has little power or might. The birthplace of King David, Bethlehem is identified with a noble past, but now the city is lowly. Lowly Bethlehem becomes the holy place of Jesus' birth.

**Prayer:** *Gracious God, in an age of cruelty and corrupt power, keep us from destructive acts of self-hatred. Encourage us that, like the magi, we may continue our trek. Like Bethlehem, grace us that from the least of our selves we may become holy places. Amen.*

---

✝Editor, Children's Department, Division of Church School Publications, General Board of Discipleship of The United Methodist Church, Nashville, Tennessee; clergy member of the Virginia Annual Conference.

**Sunday, January 2**                    Read Matthew 2:11-12.

Christmas makes us aware that consumable gifts go in and out of style. Despite the example of gifts given by the magi, many of us find ourselves in an economic never-never land in which we struggle spiritually and emotionally against the guilt implied by the question, "Did you have a good Christmas?"

Continuing the discipline of their journey, the magi found the newborn king in Bethlehem. The magi worshiped and paid homage to Jesus. Then they opened their treasure chests and offered gifts. Isaiah 60:1-6 and Psalm 72 inform our reading of Matthew 2:1-12. The passages speak of kings bearing gifts and describe gifts of gold and frankincense. Matthew names three esteemed gifts: gold, frankincense, myrrh. All are fit for a king. The gifts have significance in the life of Jesus and in the life of each Christian, but the act of opening one's treasure chest— one's innermost secrets, one's commodities, one's gifts— remains the act celebrated in our Christmas giving. Good news becomes real in the opening of our selves to Christ Jesus.

The magi avoided Herod after their act of devotion and returned to their home country "by another road." They did not fall victim to injustice but received the grace of God through a dream. I imagine the magi speaking to one another on their way home. Their studies have been fulfilled. They delight in this fulfillment and despite the murderous intent of Herod, the magi recognize the gift of a Savior to all people. The light of that star in the East bears witness to the Light of the world; the magi know, and their knowledge cannot be contained.

**Prayer:** *Grace and peace and joy, glory and honor and blessing be given to you, O Lord, at all times and in all places. Amen.*

# GOD'S PASSION: A NEW CREATION

January 3–9, 1994
**Monday, January 3**

**Helen R. Pearson**✠
Read Genesis 1:1-5.

The Genesis creation story is a statement of religious faith, not historical or scientific fact. To ask the "why," "when," and "how" questions takes us away from the dynamic, mysterious unfolding revelation of God. We cannot know what God was doing until that first created day, nor can we know the origin of the chaos and darkness. But what we do know, by faith, is enough—God simply started creation.

Brooding and hovering over the indistinguishable shapeless mixture of everything that existed, the breath-wind of God moved. Through the formless void and over the watery deep, the constant sigh of God's vivifying and birthing spirit welled forth From uncreated darkness, God spoke light into being, pronounced it good, and separated it from the darkness; and creation thus became a process of separation.

The separation of light and darkness defined boundaries and made visible the need for naming and identifying the new realities of God's creation, but they are not opposites that explain good and evil. Rather, light and darkness are the two coexisting integrated sides of the first day created and named by God. Calling them evening and morning, God lives and dwells and continues to create in both without contradiction.

**Prayer:** *Creating God, enliven us as we seek ways to nurture and sustain that which you have given us. Bless us to be worthy co-creators as we praise and glorify your name. Amen.*

---

✠Dean for Community Life, Candler School of Theology, Emory University, Atlanta, Georgia; ordained clergy, United Church of Christ.

**Tuesday, January 4**          Read Genesis 1:1-5.

We are familiar with the scriptures where God dwells in supra-brilliant light and those where darkness means death, Satan, hell, sin, and evil. The scriptures about darkness as God's dwelling place are most often considered exceptions to be explained away. This was not so for the writers of the Old and New Testaments. For them, darkness was a place of God's abode: night was often the time of God's visitation in dreams and visions, dark clouds were the manifestation of God's presence and guiding activity, and shadows were places of divine protection. Perhaps we have lost our sense of the sacred within the mysterious darkness of the unknown and now find it difficult to imagine goodness where there is no light. Instead of turning *from* darkness as a place of death, let us turn *toward* darkness as a source of life, regeneration, rest, renewal, imagination, and healing.

Eulalio Baltazar, a Philippine theologian, has called darkness "the envelope of Divine glory." At creation, darkness enveloped God's presence, and it was out of darkness that God first spoke. Darkness was the birth-bearer of light; and from that point on, the darkness of night midwifed the saving acts of God in the central events of our Judeo-Christian religion: the awesome night of Passover and exodus, the silent night incarnating Jesus' birth, the intimate night of the Last Supper, and the wondrous night of God's redemptive act, Jesus' resurrection.

In darkness, God's strong, abiding presence continues the invisible work of salvation with us. God's shalom, discovered in the night of our souls, blesses us; and we can begin the day with rested minds, renewed hearts, regenerated imaginations, and restored vision. Thanks be to God!

**Prayer:** *God of pillared clouds and shadowed wings, shelter us in the good night of your most amazing day. Amen.*

**Wednesday, January 5**                    Read Psalm 29:3-8.

God bent the heavens with a thunderous voice; and as far as the Israelites were concerned, all creation responded. No natural phenomenon awakened their hearts more with awe than did the mysterious claps of thunder from above. Like the wind-breath of God at the first creation, God's voice in the thunder could not be seen, but it could be felt and heard and experienced.

At the sound of God's majestic voice from the darkness of a storm, nature spun and whirled and danced. The cedars split, the mountains and land trembled and quaked. The lightning flashed flames of fire, the oaks whirled, and all the forests were stripped bare. The voice in the thunder, followed by awe-evoking activity, made God known to the Israelites and communicated to them what God was like. God's voice was an event by which God's will was accomplished. This sovereign God, whose speech rumbled forth creation and ruled over the mighty flood waters of chaos, was acting still. God's voice and mighty acts were a rehearsal of God's continued involvement in the Israelites' deliverance.

In Hebrew, *dabar* is a term that means both "word" and "deed." God's voice, or word, was always followed by a divine deed. What had not existed before was articulated and set forth in time. The power of the word is the power of creation. With our word, each of us has the power to create what has never existed before. Our words can bless or curse, hurt or heal. To love, to cherish, to hate, to anger, to forgive, to worship—the effect of these words when voiced into deed are unknown; for once spoken, they can never quite be reclaimed or undone. Let us be mindful of what new creation the word we speak brings into being.

**Prayer:** *Incarnate Word, empower us to make of our lives the image of your word and deed. Amen.*

17

### Thursday, January 6 (Epiphany)
Read Mark 4:4-8.

John the Baptizer stepped into history as a voice crying out in the wilderness, proclaiming a new day of the Lord. His words spun into deeds that set him apart as a man of intense passion. John's eyes were riveted on the future. The approaching kingdom of God, where he would meet the one who was more powerful than he, was the place of his hope. To repent for the forgiveness of sins, to confess all, and to be baptized by water was the way to enter this particular future. This was the way to the one who was yet to come. Repentance was urgent, but it was also difficult. It meant a reversal of the old in order to begin life anew.

Some biblical scholars claim that at the same time John was preaching, the Judean wilderness also became a place of refuge and a center of hope for a religious sect. They believed the long-expected messiah would first appear in the wilderness. When they heard a prophet, a new Elijah, was baptizing in the wilderness nearby, they were certain the messiah's coming was upon them. They went to John, expecting to find the Anointed One. Instead, they witnessed the baptism of a carpenter from Nazareth of Galilee. They were so intent on what they expected to find that they missed God's Epiphany.

**Suggestion for meditation:** *If you had been in the crowd that day, would you have recognized Jesus as the Messiah, for whom you had been waiting? Do you ever miss Jesus' presence right now because you are so intent on preparing for something greater in the future? Is repentance for the forgiveness of your sins an urgent personal matter?*

**Prayer:** *Merciful God, forgive our sins so that we may boldly and truthfully proclaim your epiphanies in the future. Amen.*

**Friday, January 7**                    Read Mark 1:9-11.

Jesus came from Nazareth of Galilee to be baptized by John in the Jordan. For those who were watching, it looked like all the other baptisms John had performed. Only Jesus saw the heavens torn apart and experienced the Spirit's descending like a dove on him. Only Jesus heard the voice from heaven that claimed him as a beloved son. Only Jesus received the assurance that God was pleased, and only he knew that something strange and wild and hopeful had happened. Only Jesus knew that when he came up out of the water, he was a new creation, that nothing would ever be the same—not with him and not with the world.

Looking back, we might think it would have been easier for Jesus if everyone in the crowd had known what had happened. But this is not the way the Gospel writer of Mark tells the story. There were no witnesses to testify on Jesus' behalf. Jesus had to go alone—first into the wilderness and then into his public ministry. No one else knew *this* baptism ushered in a new age or that the dove-spirit that rested on Jesus was the same Spirit that hovered like a bird over its nest at the first creation. No one else knew that Jesus was now God's speech made into servant and deed, that Jesus was God's greatest confession of love among us, that Jesus was God's prayer made manifest in human form, that Jesus was God's answer to the question of who God is. No one else knew.

But we know. As Christians looking back, we know who Jesus is. We have received the good news. However, we must guard against amnesia. We must remember and rehearse Jesus' baptism. Likewise, we must find ways to remember our own baptism—to remember whose we are—and to be thankful for our new creation.

**Prayer:** *Spirit God, descend on us so that we will not forget who you are in and through Christ Jesus. Amen.*

**Saturday, January 8**                    Read Acts 19:1-7.

Paul was in Ephesus when he came upon some disciples. Not known for his shyness, Paul asked if they had received the Holy Spirit when they became believers. They were not even aware there was a Holy Spirit. "Into what then were you baptized?" was Paul's very direct question. Hearing that John had baptized them, Paul told them what John had said about Jesus, and they were baptized—this time in the name of the Lord Jesus. Only after Paul laid his hands upon them did the Holy Spirit give them power to speak in tongues and prophesy.

John's baptism for repentance required a change of heart and attitude. Baptism in the name of Jesus was different. Through Jesus, invisible God became visible; and a new thing, a new humanity, a new creation was begun. When the mysterious wind of the Spirit began to blow, hearts were changed. Eyes and ears too. New possibilities broke forth for all those who were baptized with the Holy Spirit. It was the Holy Spirit that brought persons face to face with Jesus, God's gesture of peace and love—the good news in action.

The disciples whom Paul baptized discovered a truth that also deserves our attention. Before the Holy Spirit became a doctrine of the church, it was first a human experience. Persons who received this gift knew that something had happened in their lives that had never happened before. The Spirit was highly contagious. It caught on. Unless we too participate in the experience of the Holy Spirit, the doctrine remains lifeless words of someone else's testimony. Perhaps we need to hear again Paul's question, "Into what then were you baptized?"

**Prayer:** *Breathe on me, breath of God. Baptize me with your Spirit. Let not my heart forget your wondrous love. Amen.*

**Sunday, January 9**          Read Psalm 29:1-2, 10-11.

The prelude to this enthronement psalm was a procession up the slope of Mount Zion by pilgrims celebrating the New Year Festival. It was in the Temple, at the autumn feast of ingathering, where the people poured out their praise and thanksgiving to God. God, whose mighty acts of salvation had delivered and sustained them throughout their history, was their sovereign king. Enthroned on high, God was all-powerful, all-knowing, majestic in holiness, and creator of the entire universe. God, who had spoken from above at creation, continued to speak new realities, new conditions, and new possibilities into existence. When spoken, God's word was sufficient.

In response to God's event-filled voice, the people worshiped God. Falling down before God, all those who were gathered in the Temple shouted a single word in one unanimous voice: *Glory*! The psalm reports that their praise turned to prayer as they petitioned God to give them strength and to bless them with peace. God, as speaker of mighty deeds, was also a listening Presence who heard the people in their own speech—honoring sighs too deep to be shaped into words.

To the Israelites, God was beyond them, among them, and within them—all at the same time—speaking, listening, acting, waiting, being, loving, creating. Most of all, God was creating. Creating, not because that was the only thing God could do. Creating, not in order for God to have something to love. God created and is still creating because that is God's passion. A new creation, you and I—here we stand together. We are God's passion. And if we look closely at one another, we may see God's epiphany. *Glory*!

**Prayer:** *Passionate God, cradled in the arms of your love may we embrace one another as your new creation. Amen.*

## ECHOES OF LOVE

January 10–16, 1994
Monday, January 10

Larry J. Peacock✢
Read Psalm 139:13-18.

A wise spiritual director told me to lay aside all the books I had brought to read on a week-long retreat and begin by reading and praying Psalm 139. It was a wise word to me—and a good one for us this week. God's love for us permeates verses 1-18. God searches us and examines us. God knows us and forms us even while each of us is in our mother's womb. This week's scripture echoes this awesome and incomprehensible love of God.

Begin with praise. There are external and objective reasons to praise the Creator of the universe, but the poet is wonderfully personal in this psalm. The psalmist reflects on being created, formed, knit together in the womb by God. Such awareness elicits praise. "A wonder am I" (v. 14, JB). All of me is created to be wonderful. We are God's delight, the apple of God's eye (Psalm 17:8). Indeed, everything that God has created is wonderful. We are all "fearfully and wonderfully made" (v. 14) and connected to the source of creation. The appropriate posture is one of praise.

God touches not only the beginning of life but all the days of one's life. The hint of predestination in the thought that our days are written already in God's book is more likely the psalmist's reflection that all one's days have been and are under the scrutiny and care of an amazing God. So the psalmist concludes with reverential wonder at the greatness of God, who though personal and loving is still beyond grasp and comprehension.

**Suggestion for meditation:** *In a period of silent prayer repeat either, "I am God's delight" or "A wonder am I." End your prayer time with a word of praise and gratitude for God who created you and continues to form you.*

✢Co-pastor, Malibu United Methodist Church, Malibu, California; author, retreat leader, and publisher.

**Tuesday, January 11**                    Read 1 Corinthians 6:12-20.

"Do you not know that your bodies are members of Christ?" Thus Paul addresses a group of believers who seem to have forgotten that they are "fearfully and wonderfully made" by the loving touch of the Creator. This group in the Corinthian fellowship was pushing Paul's theme of freedom in Christ beyond its intentions. They were separating the body from the spirit, and by elevating the spiritual they claimed it did not matter so much what the body did. By their devious reasoning, how much one ate and who one slept with were no major concern to the wider community. After all, they argued, "All things are lawful."

Paul calls the minority back to wholeness. Our bodies, minds, and spirits are connected within the human personality and linked to the body of Christ. Our Monday behaviors and Saturday night flings are connected to our Sunday prayers. Our body, mind, and spirit are part of the gift of God and under the rule of the risen Christ. The body is not merely physical; it is the temple of God. God delighted in making us with bodies—bodies that run and dance, make love and enjoy good food, skip and jump, hug and laugh. So Paul advises us to glorify God by taking care of our bodies, shunning sexual immorality, and honoring the precious gift of our relationships.

**Prayer:** *Loving God, we see the pain of broken relationships, we read the reports of sexual abuse even in the church family, and we know the temptations that abound. Keep us in your loving embrace so that our thoughts may be pure, our eyes may see you in all and in each, and our hearts may be filled with your joy. Loving God, help us to glorify you in our thoughts, words, and deeds. Amen.*

**Wednesday, January 12**                    Read Psalm 139:1-6.

I climbed the hill behind the retreat center and found an isolated spot to sit and pray. The high desert country was quiet, except for a few birds and a few flies that buzzed. There in the silence, in the depths of my being, I heard God call my name. I felt known and loved. God had listened to the complaints that I had just reeled off and now called my name, assured me of love, gently chided me, and encouraged me to go back and continue the ministry to which I had been called.

Like the psalmist, I discovered that it is an awesome and somewhat frightening thing to be known by God. God's complete knowledge staggers the psalmist—God knows our rising, sitting, and lying down; God knows the words before we speak them; God even knows the thoughts we harbor. Such knowledge is both comforting and discomforting to the psalmist and is often so to us. God's hand is always there to guide us and hold us (vv. 5, 10). Such knowledge is wonderful. Yet sometimes we do not wish all our thoughts known, all our deeds seen, all our words heard. It is like being hemmed in, "behind and before" (v. 5). Even if we wished to hide our error and sin, God searches for us (vv. 1, 7). But thank God that the One who searches us, who knows us inside and out, is also the One who loves us with a love that goes to the depths of our despair, to the farthest corners of our darkness, to the silent places of our hiding, and to the pinnacles of our joy.

Such knowledge is wonderful beyond compare. Even as we are known, faults and all, so are we loved. We are known by name and loved by the Holy One, who formed us in the beginning. So again we take our place in worship and take the posture of praise.

**Prayer:** *Tender Friend, you know me and love me. Place your hand upon me and let me feel your blessing throughout this day. Bless my rising to activity, my sitting with others, and my lying down to rest in peace. And let my life be a blessing to others. Amen.*

**Thursday, January 13**                    Read John 1:43-51.

Nathanael would fit right into much of contemporary North American society. His first words are skeptical, "Can anything good come out of Nazareth?" (v. 46) He echoes the doubts of many U.S. citizens. Can Washington, D.C. produce significant change? Can politicians keep their hands clean? Can any leader lead us in compassion for the homeless and justice for the poor and oppressed?

Philip takes a skeptical yet searching Nathanael to see Jesus. Jesus knows Nathanael like God knew the psalmist. Jesus sees through the cynicism and sees one without deceit or guile. Here is one like the trickster Jacob of the Old Testament, who is capable of seeing the truth.

Such knowledge of himself is astounding to Nathanael. "Where did you get to know me?" he asks. Again Jesus uses a reference to the Old Testament and knows that when Nathanael was sitting under the fig tree he was meditating on peace and the One who was to bring the reign of peace (Mic. 4:4). Nathanael is amazed that Jesus could see the depths of his heart, know the longing in his prayer. Yet he catches the messianic hints in Jesus' words and sees in Jesus the One who is promised, the One who will transform all people. He confesses his faith, and Jesus tells him that he shall see even more, shall see into the heights of heaven.

To be known and loved is a transforming experience. It calls us from skepticism to belief, from caution to action, from despair to hope. Jesus knows us, loves us, calls us, and leads us to the realms beyond.

**Suggestion for meditation:** *Imagine yourself sitting under a tree, deep in prayer, when Jesus comes, calls you by name, and asks to sit with you. Open your heart to him.*

**Friday, January 14**                    Read 1 Samuel 3:1-10.

God's call comes to each of us. It may come as a sudden experience like Paul's on the road to Damascus or as a persistent beckoning like the four calls to Samuel. God often speaks in the language of everyday events. Our conversations with others, the walk to the mailbox, a night rich with dreams, even the seemingly chance encounter may hold a clue to God's call. God works in and through many events.

Sometimes God calls us to do something we feel inclined toward. Other times God invites us to walk out in faith, trusting in God's empowerment. Usually a call carries a summons to be of service to others. Always a call involves listening and obeying.

But listening is not always easy. Evidently, the art of listening to God was neglected in Eli and Samuel's time. Seldom was the word of God heard. They were out of practice, so Samuel did not know that it was God calling the first three times. Finally, Eli reached back into his memory and remembered that God used to call. His two sons had forgotten how to listen, but maybe now this young boy, Samuel, would hear again the voice of God and bring a message back to the people. Thus the word of God that Samuel heard "came to all Israel" (1 Sam. 4:1).

We need to recover the art of listening. "If we go on listening, we feel God pulling us, drawing us into another current, a larger, deeper, stronger one than our usual little force."*

God calls each of us. God is continually drawing us into the deeper current.

**Suggestion for meditation:** *Remember a time you felt God's presence, heard God's call. Give thanks. End your prayer time by repeating, "Speak, Holy God, your servant is listening." Take a few moments to listen in silence.*

* Ann Ulanov and Barry Ulanov, *Primary Speech* (Atlanta: John Knox Press, 1982), p. 9.

**Saturday, January 15**      Read John 1:43-51.

*Follow me.* Two words, simple and direct, spoken by Jesus, which have the power to change the course of a person's life and even alter the course of human history. *Follow me.* A St. Francis leaves the comfortable life and becomes a fool for Christ, befriending the poor, loving all creatures and creation. *Follow me.* A Mother Teresa sees the face of Christ in the dying of India and discovers a shift in her vocation that has captivated the world. *Follow me.* A Martin Luther King, Jr., hears a new call in the action of a Rosa Parks, who refuses to sit in the back of the bus, and thus becomes a drum major for justice and a prophet to the nation.

*Follow me.* According to the scripture, from this call Philip becomes a disciple and evangelist—for God's call usually involves ministry on behalf of the loving God, in service to all God's creation. Philip searches for Nathanael and tells him, "We have found him about whom Moses . . . and also the prophets wrote." Philip carries the good news of Jesus Christ to Samaria (Acts 8:5) and opens the word to the Ethiopian eunuch (Acts 8:26-40). *Follow me.* Philip's own world is changed forever. He is a follower, a listener, a disciple. And the people that he meets are affected forever because he is a channel of God's love, a minister of the word, a teller of the good news.

In the days of Samuel, "The word of the LORD was rare" (1 Sam. 3:1), but now in Jesus Christ, the word of God is alive and active. It searches for us, finds us, and calls us again and again to "follow me."

**Suggestion for meditation:** *Philip tells Nathanael, "Come and see." Imagine in your mind's eye that a friend is taking you to Jesus. See Jesus waiting for you, beckoning you to come and sit awhile. Tell Jesus you want to follow him. Ask for his guidance. Listen for his response. Let him give you a blessing before you go. Thank Jesus. Thank your friend.*

**Sunday, January 16**                    Read 1 Samuel 3:1-10.

Priestly tasks and prophetic calls are woven in this passage. Eli is preparing Samuel for priestly duties. No doubt he is instructing him in the performance of the rituals and the offering of appropriate sacrifices. Samuel learns to care for the ark, to keep the lamps lighted, and to counsel the community of faith. He sleeps near the ark; thus, he is constantly in the presence of God. We would say he is being formed, shaped, trained for Christian service.

Yet the prophetic word weaves its way into this priestly path. The remark that visions were not widespread at the time lets us know that prophets have been rare. Whereas priests were usually born into or given to the priestly role, prophets were usually called in dreams or visions. Though Samuel was preparing to be a priest, he is called to the prophetic office. His first word from God is against his mentor, the priest Eli. Such is often the hard task of the prophet.

All week we have considered the echoes of love—the confirmation and fuller development in the New Testament of various Old Testament themes. We return now on this holy day to the ways we have been formed in love and for love. Though we are not all priests, we can live out a priestly care for others and a reverence for things that are holy. Though we are not all prophets, we can speak on behalf of the poor, work with the forgotten, and challenge the principalities and powers. Though we are not Samuel, we can keep close to God through worship, prayer, scripture study, and service. With open hearts and sensitive spirits, we can be ready when God calls us by name.

**Prayer:** *Holy God, on this day of worship keep me near, hold me in your tender embrace, and open my ears and heart to receive your word. Amen.*

## GOD'S URGENCY

January 17–23, 1994                          **José P. Bové**✛
**Monday, January 17**                    Read Jonah 3:1-5, 10.

God had not given up on Nineveh or on Jonah! The prophet had fled from God and ignored the divine call—God had some nerve, ordering Jonah to go convert the enemy. It wasn't until Jonah's last in a series of adversities, finding himself inside a large fish, that he finally realized God was trying to tell him something.

God's second urgent call to Jonah, "Get up, go to Nineveh, that great city, and proclaim to it the message that I tell you," expresses God's patience with the sinner. The capital of Assyria stood for everything that was despised by Israel, but God wanted to bring about the salvation of those hated by God's own people.

Jonah did go to Nineveh, and he preached to its citizens about the impending punishment coming to them; and to his great surprise, Nineveh repented of its sins. God was moved to compassion and spared the city. In spite of himself, Jonah had carried out his mission well.

The Book of Jonah may have been written during the period following the return of the Jews from the Babylonian captivity. Judaism, with its emphasis on religious exclusivism, was taking root in the hearts of the former exiles and the generations that followed. The chosen people were forgetting God's mission for them to be a light unto the whole world.

Let us be open to God when God calls us to be agents of reconciliation.

**Prayer:** *Dear God, bring us back to you when we try to escape. Amen.*

✛Diaconal Minister of Education, First United Methodist Church, Lakeland, Florida.

**Tuesday, January 18**                    Read Psalm 62:5-8.

Most, if not all of us have had our seasons of despair, tribulation, and loneliness. For many of us, dear companions in our journey of faith have provided comfort and support; and to a large extent, serenity has filled us. Thanks be to God for those souls! However, there is a depth in the human spirit that only God can reach. The psalmist recognizes in God the ultimate source of hope as he exclaims, "For God alone my soul waits in silence."

*Rock, fortress, salvation, refuge* are descriptive words used in reference to God throughout the psalms. Many of our hymns include these words in the texts as reminders of God's strength and closeness in times of trouble.

The psalmist also declares that "on God rests my deliverance and my honor." I like the inclusion of the phrase *my honor.* It tells me that God is concerned for my personal integrity as a human being as well as for my deliverance from trouble.

Recently, I attended the quadrennial organizational meeting of my denomination's General Commission on Christian Unity and Interreligious Concerns in San Francisco. I cherish the corporate worship experiences in the mornings and evenings. One of these—a service of anointing—stands out in my mind. As members of the group anointed each other and imparted mutual blessings, we sang a hymn with the wonderful message of peace and assurance that God alone suffices when we are dismayed. Its haunting melody in a minor key and the serenity of the lyrics filled my soul and reaffirmed to me that all is well as long as I have God.

Calmly and gently we are urged to put our trust in God at all times. *Solo Dios basta*—God is enough.

**Prayer:** *O God, for you alone my soul waits in silence. Be with me and fill me with your presence. You are all I need. Thank you for this wonderful truth. Amen.*

**Wednesday, January 19**                    Read Psalm 62:9-12.

Bring to mind the figure of Francis of Assisi (1182-1226) as you read these verses from Psalm 62. This young man renounced a life of high social status when he fully realized that God was calling him to embrace poverty and simplicity and to depend only on the Creator for basic sustenance.

The same attitude toward social status that Francis displayed as a priest we see in the psalmist as he declares that in the sight of God both those of low and high estates are "lighter than a breath" when placed on a balance. Should we come upon material wealth, we are admonished not to make it life's main priority. How reassuring it is to know that God does not expect us to practice those things that the world deems important! God relieves us of much excess baggage when we are willing to put first things first.

The psalmist leaves us with a closing lesson as he impresses upon us that both power and love belong to God and that we are rewarded according to our faithfulness. The life of the Christian is one of faithfulness to the calling to be *faithful*. This is a verity that sometimes gets lost as we expect from God what we believe we deserve. The person of Jesus Christ stands before us as the model we are to emulate in our complete submission to the God who calls us to put God first in all.

Yesterday we emphasized the presence of God as the source to meet all our needs, whatever they might be. Let the words above remind us of the quality of life we are called to live as lovers of God in Jesus Christ.

**Prayer:** *Lord, with Francis of Assisi we pray: Make us instruments of your peace. Amen.*

**Thursday, January 20**          Read 1 Corinthians 7:29-31.

Events in the church at Corinth created much mental anguish for the apostle Paul, among them disputes among leadership factions, immorality, the corruption of the Eucharist, materialism, and heresies. In spite of his anger at the new church, Paul sought to correct them sternly, yet with love. It is a wonder that First Corinthians 13 could have emerged out of the apostle's pen after the frustrations the Christians at Corinth created for him!

We conclude that Paul never married. His letters contain many admonitions that Christian men not marry if at all possible, in order to spend their time and effort practicing and propagating the gospel. Thus, their loyalties would not be divided between their Lord and their domestic responsibilities. The verses that precede today's scripture reading (vv. 25-28) give us Paul's viewpoint on female chastity as well as his directions for unmarried and married men. In the second part of verse 28 we can detect Paul's bias against marriage—bachelor Paul minces no words! As a whole, these four verses give us a good preamble to verses 29-31 and help us understand Paul's urgent tone.

The apostle himself was a product of the early church's belief in the impending and immediate second coming of Jesus with all the physical upheavals it would bring upon the present order. Paul is admonishing the young church at Corinth to be primarily concerned with single-minded devotion to those matters of the Lord and not with possessions. In no way is he calling them to cease caring for other persons, including spouses. Whether married or single, we are urged to be in the world, yet not belong to the world.

**Prayer:** *We pray for your guidance, dear God, in determining what is eternal and what is transient. Help us to choose wisely as your faithful servants. May others be able to meet the loving Christ in us. Amen.*

**Friday, January 21**                    Read Mark 1:14-15.

Mark the evangelist does not take time to explain John's arrest; he will treat that crucial New Testament event later in his Gospel. In his usual characteristic style of *movement*, Mark simply states that "Jesus came to Galilee" to begin his preaching of the advent of the kingdom of God—the reign of God—and the requirements necessary to be a citizen of such a kingdom. Mark's "came" thus sets before us the expediency of the moment with a minimum of transition—typically Mark!

The phrase *kingdom of God* carries with it an inherent urgency because this is a kingdom open to all, yet demanding in its divine nature. *Kingdom of God* is synonymous with the arrival of Jesus himself. He gives his followers several commands if they are to be recognized as citizens of this kingdom: repent, change directions, and adopt a new state of mind ("believe in the good news") that fits the order Jesus was establishing as a way of life.

Jesus urges us to live a life of inward community with God as we allow our minds, hearts, and wills to be in complete harmony with that in us which is the image of God. As members of this kingdom we live in it in the present as well as in the future as we proclaim it through a personal witness that inspires others to want to establish God's order. We are thus called to labor with God in bringing about the ultimate Christian hope for the world!

**Prayer:** *God, the reality of your kingdom overwhelms us in its simplicity and its expectations. Help us to be in tune with it as children created in your image and as followers of the Christ. We pray in Jesus' name. Amen.*

**Saturday, January 22**                    Read Mark 1:16-18.

It is interesting that Jesus' first four disciples were two sets of brothers who were fishermen. These men made a living fishing in the Sea of Galilee—really a lake 7½ miles wide, 12¾ miles long—well known as a fishery. Their financial position, although not extravagant, allowed them to meet their needs in a relatively comfortable way. Fishing was quite a demanding occupation, but Galilean fishermen worked at their trade diligently. They certainly were not lazy!

Why did Jesus call fishermen first and promise them nothing but to "make you fish for people"? It is probable that Simon and Andrew would recall the similar Old Testament figure of speech (Jer. 16:16), so that Jesus' words were nothing new to them. The difference, however, would lie in the fact that this time the actual calling came from a man directly challenging them and not from a prophet who had lived over 400 years earlier.

Simon (Peter) and Andrew have been subjects of many pieces of great art, among these Duccio di Buoninsegna's *The Calling of St. Peter and St. Andrew*, painted between 1308 and 1311 in Siena, Italy as part of an altar panel for the cathedral. Many regard this painting as one of the greatest creations of the Byzantine School, in spite of its rudimentary and almost naive treatment of the subject matter. The dramatic three main figures, however, convey the message of the work quite dramatically: an austere Jesus with his right hand extended in an invitation and with eyes that communicate the urgency of the moment; an impetuous Simon holding the net with the left hand but responding affirmatively with the lifted right one; and a pensive Andrew, holding the net bursting with fish, the source of his livelihood, with both hands, not quite convinced he is ready to take the risk.

**Prayer:** *Dear brother Jesus, give us a visionary spirit and a loving heart to respond to your urgent call to follow you. Amen.*

**Sunday, January 23**                    Read Mark 1:19-20

Just a few steps away from where Simon and his brother, Andrew, have been casting their nets, Jesus encounters another set of brothers: James and John, sons of Zebedee, himself a fisherman who perhaps had built up a lucrative trade for himself and his sons.

Later in his Gospel, Mark refers to these two brothers as *Boanerges*, Aramaic for "sons of thunder" (Mark 3:17). We must take a look at this interesting epithet. Was such a name indicative of their past lives? Were they known as hot, impulsive men, noted for their passionate outbursts? Had they been identified with the Zealot movement of their day, a political anti-Roman force? It is likely that these two brothers were men of fiery, eloquent speech delivered with strident, thunderous voices.

These two are called by Jesus not so much for the dignity they would provide their future apostolic office as for the potential he saw in them. These "sons of thunder" were to learn that the higher the calling to serve their Lord, the harder the discipline fitting them for it. Through experiences in which these brothers participated in a very unique way—the Transfiguration (Mark 9:2-8), the raising of the daughter of Jairus (Mark 5:21-42), the Passion at Gethsemane (Mark 14:32-42)—they were prepared for apostleship in the post-Ascension church in Jerusalem.

God urgently calls us to a life that challenges our basic nature and our impulses. As God purifies us, we surrender our human instincts to a heavenly design. The process is not an easy one, and we usually rebel.

**Prayer:** *Deal with me both gently and roughly, dear God, that I may envision both the loving Father and the disciplining Master who seeks to bring forth in me the attributes for a life of discipleship today. Amen.*

January 24–30, 1994      **J. Brendonly Cunningham✢**
**Monday, January 24**      Read Deuteronomy 18:15-16.

*A promise of genuine prophecy*

The Book of Deuteronomy is a farewell address to the Israelites, who are about to cross over the Jordan to enter the promised land. Many were second-generation Israelites, born in the wilderness. They had not experienced slavery nor had they known freedom.

Moses' concern was how the Israelites would live in a free land as free people. He devoted much time to instructing them how to be obedient to God so that they would be prosperous as well as free. Moses knew he would not enter the promised land with the Israelites. Inasmuch as Moses would not be with them, he tried to assure them that God would send another prophet like himself to give them genuine prophecy and guidance.

The prophet was very important to the people. It was the prophet to whom the divine will of God was made known. It was the prophet who communicated with God on behalf of the people and then advised the people of God's desires for them. It was the prophet who predicted future blessings or curses. It was expedient that this prophet be genuinely of God and not be a soothsayer or a diviner. The good news is that Israel would never be without a genuine prophetic voice. The people would know the prophet to be genuine because prophecies would come to pass.

Every generation needs to hear a prophetic voice, a voice that offers hope and justice for all.

**Suggestion for meditation:** *How do you experience prophetic voices of today? Which voices do you trust: the voices of politicians, preachers, physicists, and astrologers, or a still small voice within?*

✢United Methodist pastor; consultant in spiritual formation and personal growth, Austin, Texas.

**Tuesday, January 25**          Read Deuteronomy 18:17-19.

*Called to make a prophetic promise*

Moses had been the prophetic voice for the Israelites for forty years. He tarried and toiled with them in the wilderness. When water was not available to them and they were thirsty, Moses turned to God; and God provided water from a rock. When they were without food, Moses turned to God; and God provided quail and manna. When they were confused about God's will for them as a freed people, Moses went to Mount Sinai and dwelled with the Lord for forty days. He returned with the commandments of God written on two stone tablets so the people would know how to live in harmony and with respect for one another. These people had not experienced the responsibility of freedom. The time was fast approaching when Moses would no longer be with them. He assured them that God would raise up a genuine prophetic voice among them, one such as Moses had been.

The Gospels present Jesus going through a similar process with the disciples when the time for him to go to the cross was near. Jesus tried to prepare the disciples for his departure. He wanted them to know that it would become their responsibility to continue the work he had begun. That prophetic voice lies with the church today, making Christians people with a promise. We have been called the salt of the earth because we bring hope in hopeless situations. Christians offer joy in the midst of sorrow and promise life even when facing death. The Christian call is a call to make a prophetic promise. It is the tradition of our faith.

**Suggestion for meditation:** *God continues to raise up daughters and sons who seek to reflect the life of Jesus and present his teachings as prophetic promises. Do you have a story to tell about God's activity in your life that will make your prophetic promise seem trustworthy?*

**Wednesday, January 26**                    Read Psalm 111.

*God's love expressed through redemptive acts*

A sincere "thank you" is becoming a thing of the past in today's fast-moving society. However, in Psalm 111 the writer begins a trinity of hallelujah psalms as an expression of gratitude to God. The mind, heart, and body all give praise at the contemplation of this holy presence. The psalmist rejoiced in remembering stories told to him by his ancestors about how God fed the Israelites with quail and manna during their sojourn in the wilderness. The Israelites believed God did this because they were God's chosen people. The psalmist rejoices and gives thanks for the land of Canaan as his heritage. Several times the psalmist mentions the covenant given at Sinai as something for which to give thanks. The psalmist is excited because God's love has been expressed through these redemptive acts.

The last verse notes, "The fear of the LORD is the beginning of wisdom." The fear of the Lord does not refer to being fearful but rather to being completely *trustful* as a child learns to trust her mother. The child, likewise, is sad when he is not in a loving relationship with his mother. It is good to be sad when we are not in a loving relationship with God.

The Christian tradition remembers and celebrates the incarnation, the birth, the crucifixion, and the resurrection of Jesus as God's redeeming gift of salvation. This gift requires a response in order for the covenant to be binding.

Thanksgiving is not only an act of worship but also the act of living. To live thankfully is to be aware of that holy presence within us that connects us with all that is good.

**Suggestion for meditation:** *Think about past experiences in your life when God's redemptive acts were expressed on your behalf, when justice did not prevail because mercy intervened.*

**Thursday, January 27**                    Read 1 Corinthians 8:1-13.

*Love makes us one another's keeper.*

Paul's letter to the church at Corinth was a response to the question of whether Christians could eat meat that had been offered to pagan gods. It was perfectly good meat, and it was common knowledge that idols had no real existence. Much of the meat sold in the marketplaces had come from animals sacrificed in pagan temples. Some of the worshipers used portions of the meat consecrated to gods to give a banquet in honor of the god. The banquets were often held in social halls where no worship was involved. Christians wanted to attend these celebrations and saw no reason why they should not. Paul was concerned about the influence this practice could have on weaker members. He responded, "Knowledge puffs up, but love builds up." Paul wanted them to understand that love for one another would not allow those who were knowledgeable and stronger to eat the meat because of that influence on the weaker members. When you "sin against members of your family, and wound their conscience when it is weak, you sin against Christ." Many members were still caught up in the law and had not allowed grace to liberate them. They were still on their pilgrimage at this point, and that was all right. Our love for God really is expressed in our love for one another.

Here we get a reflection of "Love your neighbor as yourself" (Mark 12:31). Let us receive and love people as they are where they are. We may have more insight and freedom, but our greater commitment is to love and build one another up without threatening others' faith. Divine laws lead to insight and wisdom; they are not the end of the journey. With new insight comes new freedom, but none frees us from loving and being responsible for one another.

**Suggestion for meditation:** *"Our love for God really is expressed in our love for one another." What does this mean for you in your current life situation?*

**Friday, January 28**                    Read Mark 1:21-22.

*Anointed to teach with authority*

Jesus had waited to be about his Father's business since he was twelve years of age. At about age thirty he started his ministry in Capernaum, a town by Lake Galilee, in order that the light of God would first shine upon darkness as Isaiah promised (Isa. 9:2). Galilee had been invaded and its people looked upon as a people whom God had forsaken. Jesus started there. That Sabbath, Jesus and his newly called disciples went to the synagogue, as was the custom. For a person with a message from God, what better place to go to deliver that message than to the church? Ordinarily the scribes would have read the lesson and quoted various authorities as they attempted to explain the lesson. But Jesus had his authority from God. When he was baptized, he had heard God call him God's beloved Son with whom God was pleased (Mark 1:11). Jesus had the victory of the wilderness temptations behind him (Mark 1:12); he was anchored in God. He spoke as a voice of God and not as a scribe. The people were astounded because Jesus seemed to know exactly what he was talking about.

Is it not interesting that people are surprised when one speaks with authority? We seem to have settled for being entertained with business as usual, and we do not really expect to hear from God. One of the reasons I appreciate Psalm 23 so much is that the psalmist wrote as one who had authority, as one who had experienced God as a shepherd. Jesus' relationship with God made him an authority on the scripture.

**Suggestion for meditation:** *What is unique about your relationship with God that enables you to speak with clarity and authority? Will your relationship and experience with God support your story as one anointed to tell your story?*

**Saturday, January 29**                    Read Mark 1:23-24.

*Satan challenges divine authority.*

The world in which we live is comprised of both good and evil. Evil never gives way to good but must be overcome by it; even then it puts up a good fight. You may relate to this theory by remembering bad habits you have overcome. The habits did not just fade away like a dream. Through a commitment to overcome them, you persisted; and today they are at least in the background of your life, if not totally gone.

The man who entered the synagogue was possessed by an evil spirit, a demon, according to the scripture. This man was aware of Jesus and shouted, "What do you want with us, Jesus of Nazareth? Are you here to destroy us?" (TEV). The *us* meant that the demon and the man were a team; they belonged together. There was an acknowledgment that Jesus did have the power to destroy them.

We do not talk much about demons in our culture today. We do acknowledge positive and negative thoughts. These negative thoughts, when nourished and supported, have destructive power over us. We imagine many negative things about ourselves and others that never existed. Many people are falsely accused and relationships destroyed because people entertain and nourish negative thoughts that become evil and destructive. These evil thoughts will not leave voluntarily; they will slowly take over your life. Our pulse accelerates, our blood pressure goes up, our head hurts, our joints stiffen, and many other physiological things happen when negative thoughts abide within us. Let us be as wise as the demon-possessed man and realize that God has power to destroy these negative thoughts that trouble us.

**Suggestion for meditation:** *Reflect on negative thoughts you are willing to have come out of you in order that you may be healed. Prepare to be healed.*

**Sunday, January 30**                    Read Mark 1:26-28.

*Healed by the authority of God*

The demonic referred to Jesus as "Holy One" or "Holy Messenger" (v. 24, TEV). Jesus was not ready for his identity to be publicly revealed. He rebuked the spirit saying, "'Be silent, and come out of him' . . . And the unclean spirit, convulsing him and crying with a loud voice, came out of him." This man was healed by the authority of God. The people marveled that Jesus had power over the demonic spirit. They were excited about what had happened in the synagogue at Capernaum, a place that was once considered to be abandoned by God. Immediately Jesus' fame spread.

This story allows us to see that evil puts up a good fight before leaving one's life. The person is affected painfully by the absence of this negative addiction even as healing takes possession of the body and the mind. A greater insight might be to note how easy it is to become satisfied and make peace with evil and accept it as a way of life. The demon-possessed man had become accustomed to living with this evil spirit and claimed it as a part of his very being. Prayers were said and scriptures read, and then it was back to business as usual. But this Sabbath was different. Jesus read the scripture with authority; and hearing this voice, the man could not remain silent. The demonic spirit no longer had complete power over this man; at last he was in the presence of one greater than this spirit. This presence was great enough to destroy the demon and even the man. But the spirit of God compelled the man to speak out. He spoke out of order, but he spoke and Jesus did the rest. Whatever is destructive within us must come out, and we have the responsibility to speak out for help.

**Suggestion for meditation:** *If you want to be healed from negative thoughts and fears, prepare to encounter the pain of letting go; plan to endure a few convulsions, but also prepare to receive the love of God and be healed.*

## A NEW SET OF PRIORITIES

January 31–February 6, 1994       **Ben Witherington III✢**
**Monday, January 31**       Read Isaiah 40:21-31.

Many of us have had the unusual sensation of watching a familiar landscape dotted with people and things shrink into nothingness as we gaze out the window of an airplane gaining altitude. One can understand then how the psalmist felt when he said that the God who made the universe sits above the circle of the heavens, looks down, and sees earth's inhabitants as though they were grasshoppers. He wishes to convey the awesome power of God not only in God's power of creation but also in God's ability to change human history: God raises up and brings to nothing the rulers of this world. This same all-powerful God is also all-knowing. The vast number of the stars and creatures have not escaped God's notice.

In verses 27-31 the psalmist reminds God's people that a person is quite incapable of hiding anything from such a God— not one's deeds or words, not even one's thoughts. While we might be tempted to think that such an awesome God surely would not be very interested in the mundane affairs of small creatures like us, the psalmist insists this is not so. Rather, the psalmist reminds us that we must not make the mistake of assuming that since God is so great, God will not bother with creatures so small. The real problem is the size of our faith, not the magnitude of God.

**Prayer:** *O great holy God, help us to remember that you not only observe but also care about our every move. You are working in our very midst changing history, for you are not content to create or observe only, but always you must be redeeming as well. Amen.*

✢Professor of Biblical and Wesleyan Studies, Ashland Theological Seminary, Ashland, Ohio.

**Tuesday, February 1**                    Read Isaiah 40:28-31.

From a human point of view it might seem that being God is a wearying job. To the contrary, verse 28 suggests that God never grows tired and never ceases to give strength to the faint and power to the powerless. Sometimes young people seem to have boundless energy, but God is forever energetic. God keeps seeking, strengthening, and working out the divine plan.

When we read verse 31, we should not forget the preceding verses which remind us of God's great power, knowledge, will to save, and ever-present activity in our midst. This tireless God will renew the strength of those who "wait for the Lord." Thus, the secret of strength and resolve to meet the challenges of this or any day come from being plugged into the eternal power source.

Some people believe only abstractly that God is all-powerful, and they fail to take time to rely on this powerful God to help them in their daily lives. Still others wait on the Lord but then squander the resources the Lord provides. But those who use what God gives in an appropriate way can mount up like a great bird of prey and soar over the sea of their troubles. This was good news to God's people languishing in exile, and it is good news for us as well. God keeps on going and keeps us going.

**Prayer:** *Almighty and everlasting God, give us the patience to wait upon you, the perception to know what is right, the power to will what is right, the purpose and resolve to do what is right, and the persistence to see these tasks through to the end. Amen.*

**Wednesday, February 2**          Read Psalm 147:1-11, 20c.

When I first became a minister, I fell into the trap of thinking that it was my job to please all my parishioners. But difficulties soon set in. I had to deal with alcoholism, suicide, family feuds, prejudice, and many other serious problems. Tough decisions had to be made, and some hurt people's feelings.

Gradually it dawned on me that I could neither be all that my church members wanted me to be nor could I please them all. By reading scriptures like the one for today, I realized that my job was not to please the people and help God but to please God and help God's people to the best of my ability.

In verses 10-11 we read that God takes pleasure not in the things that humans often marvel at, such as the grace of a racehorse or the speed of a track star. Rather, God's pleasure is in those who revere God, in those who hope in God's steadfast love. It is all too easy to set our hopes on humans, whether on our own abilities or on those of others. But when we make it our goal to please God and to count on God's enduring love, we are fulfilling the purpose of every child of God. That purpose, said John Calvin, is to know God and enjoy God forever. The psalmist would have agreed heartily.

**Prayer:** *Lord God, help us set our hearts on you, knowing that that above all else pleases you. You who heal the brokenhearted and bind up the wounded and gather the outcasts, please use us to help others so they too will see that devotion to you is the source and purpose of our very being. Amen.*

**Thursday, February 3**　　　　Read 1 Corinthians 9:16-18.

The United States is a country that preaches that "you don't get something for nothing." The Corinthians would have understood this ethic. Numerous social relationships in Roman Corinth were based on the assumption of reciprocity—you scratch my back and I'll scratch yours.

Into this environment came a man determined to offer the greatest gift of all time to whoever would hear and receive it—for free! Paul was determined to make the Corinthians see that he was not offering them goods in exchange for services rendered or for money. Thus, he refused to accept the offer of patronage in Corinth; he preached the gospel free of charge.

Paul was a man under authority, and he felt a strong compulsion to preach the gospel. He felt that one could hardly boast about something one *had* to do, since it would not then be a matter of choice. Thus, he preached the gospel without accepting the remuneration, lest the Corinthians think he was like many other ancient teachers who advertised themselves as available for hire. In this he said he could boast, could even expect a reward from God, because it was doing something extra, something for free.

It is worth pondering when we last did something freely, with no thought of return. It is also worth asking when the last time was that we shared the gospel freely with someone.

**Prayer:** *Lord Jesus Christ, free us from our inhibitions about sharing your love and good news with others. Teach us to look for opportunities for giving with no thought of return, as you did throughout your life and even in your death. Amen.*

**Friday, February 4**                    Read 1 Corinthians 9:19-23.

The term *public servant* is often bandied about without reflecting on what the term really means. One of the more common images of a politician is that of an ego-driven, self-seeking person who uses people in order to get something for him/herself.

It is fair to say that Paul had an image problem in Corinth. He saw himself as a public servant who would do anything ethically and legally possible and make any sacrifice necessary to win both Jews and Gentiles to Christ. Many in Corinth saw this behavior as an indication that Paul was like their self-serving, disreputable politicians. In their view, a person who tried to be all things to all people was surely suspect. In their mind, both Paul's teachings about free grace and his servant-like behavior were suspicious. Corinthians had always worshiped gods who expected sacrifices in exchange for answered prayers. What kind of God leads people to be servants of each other and offers salvation free of charge?

Paul was a person who believed that God had indeed turned the world's normal system of evaluating things upside down. He believed in a God who chose the foolish to shame the wise, the weak to shame the strong, the poor to shame the rich, and a crucified manual laborer from Nazareth to save the world! In short, Paul believed that when one became a Christian one gave oneself to a lifetime of service and gave up being worried about evaluating oneself according to the world's system of values. A sense of self-worth comes from being like Christ who "though he was rich, yet for your sakes he became poor, so that by his poverty you might become rich" (2 Cor. 8:9).

**Prayer:** *Gracious Lord, teach us not merely how to give up things to serve you but how to live like you. Forgive us when we allow the world's standards to mold us and so neglect the high calling to which you call us all—to be like Christ. Help us to be less self-conscious about what others think of us and more conscious of what your will is for us. In your name we ask it. Amen.*

**Saturday, February 5** Read Mark 1:29-34.

In a world full of charlatans, a world lacking much real medicine, Jesus was indeed the Great Physician. Today's story speaks of Jesus' healing Simon Peter's mother-in-law on the Sabbath. This act of compassion would have raised many eyebrows, because various early Jewish teachers argued that doing good on the Sabbath, including healing someone whose life was not in immediate danger, was forbidden because it was a form of work (Mark 3:1-6). Jesus, however, had a different view of the day of rest. For Jesus, the Sabbath was to be a day of restoration of health and happiness, and what could better restore health than healing?

This story also tells us that Jesus was not worried about another Jewish convention of the time, that of being made ritually unclean by touching those who were ill or even dead. Jesus believed that only what comes out of a person's heart defiles a person (Mark 7:15). Thus, Jesus reached out his hand to the woman and raised her from her sickbed. Her response was one of gratitude as she served Jesus and his disciples.

Good news travels quickly, and the story indicates that many who had been afraid to approach Jesus on the Sabbath came after sundown to be touched and healed. A close examination of the healing miracles in the Gospels will show that Jesus performed these acts purely out of compassion, not in order to impress anyone.

This story raises these questions for us: Are we willing to set aside customs and conventions in order to reach out to the sick, the homeless, and others in need? Are we prepared for the time when God will unexpectedly present us with an opportunity to perform an act of compassion?

**Prayer:** *O Great Physician, teach us how to be healers in our own immediate setting, being open even today to perform an unplanned act of mercy if you preser t us with an opportunity. Teach us to be like the Wounded Healer, who died on the cross to bring wholeness and holiness to all. Amen.*

**Sunday, February 6**                    Read Mark 1:32-39.

It is a remarkable fact that in the Gospel of Mark Jesus saw the most essential task of his ministry to be preaching, not healing. He did not set out to heal, but people brought the sick to him and he had compassion on them. Jesus said, "Let us go on to neighboring towns, so that I may proclaim the message . . . for that is what I came to do."

Notice that Jesus settled on this plan after getting up very early to pray for guidance. He had spent the previous evening healing those who came to him. It seems clear that Jesus sought to avoid gaining a reputation as a wonder-worker, because he knew that such a reputation would hinder or even prevent him from completing his main mission during his ministry—proclaiming the good news of the inbreaking dominion of God. His priority—preaching before healing—was made clear to him through prayer.

At first blush, this might seem a cold way to evaluate things. We might ask how preaching mere words can be more important than healing the sick. Jesus, however, believed that healing people would help them temporarily in the present, but preaching the word of God about eternal life would benefit them forever. It was a matter of a good thing and something even better, and Jesus sought to keep the priorities of his life's work in order.

From time to time it is worthwhile to take stock of our lives not only to evaluate what we have done but to ask the question: What is God's best for me at this time? Doubtless we can do many good things, but the question remains: to which one should I give priority? Certainly, Christ's example in this story makes us realize that time alone in prayer can help us prioritize our lives according to the values of the kingdom.

**Prayer:** *God of grace and God of glory, give us the wisdom to seek your will for our life's work, the patience to wait for your direction, and the courage to order our lives according to your will. Amen.*

## TRANSFORMED AND TRANSPARENT

February 7–13, 1994        **Stefanie Weisgram, O.S.B.**✢
**Monday, February 7**        Read Psalm 50:1-6.

In our psalm today, the Mighty One speaks, calling forth the earth and calling forth each of us. We are called to judgment and to hear God's words. God wants to make it clear that empty worship is worthless, that it is not acceptable. God wants true prayer and true morality from us. We can pray and sacrifice all we want, but words and promises will be empty and meaningless unless our prayer and our sacrifice also inform our lives.

But if we want our prayer and our sacrifice to inform our lives, then we cannot mouth empty words or compartmentalize our lives by separating what we say from what we do. Rather, how we live, how we act, must fulfill the promise we speak in our prayers. We must live lives of integrity. In this way we will be transformed from empty rattles or clanging cymbals into prisms through which God may shine.

Bringing our prayers and our lives together can be difficult. It seems impossible to recognize our lack of integrity or even where to begin. How can we become so whole in prayer and life that we are transparent enough for God to shine through? But in the psalm we see that God shines forth for all the earth. And God also shines into our lives so that, bit by bit, we can see more clearly how to make our prayer and our lives one.

**Suggestion for meditation:** *Often, God shines forth in ways I do not recognize. How can I be more aware today of God shining into my life? of God shining through my life?*

✢Member of a Benedictine community of women in St. Joseph, Minnesota; college librarian and theology teacher who also volunteers in Guatemala at a monastery library open to the public.

**Tuesday, February 8**                    Read 2 Kings 2:1-12.

Moses was one of God's great mediators with Israel, and Elijah was another. It was Moses who made the covenant with God and who received the law from God. Elijah carried on the covenant and led the people in keeping the commandments. He was their guide and their source of security in relating to God. Elijah, taken up by a chariot and horses of fire, also left no trace. Both Moses and Elijah left successors to lead the people in constancy and loyalty to God. And both men appear together with Jesus at his transfiguration (Mark 9:4).

When we remember the prophets, we often think of their crusty side, their righteous indignation, their calling down the wrath of God in dramatic episodes. We forget their more tender side, their doubts, sometimes even their sense of justice for the needy. We would do well to remember Elijah's great despair and then his finding God in the still small, undramatic voice (1 Kings 19). We would do well to remember Elijah's calm walk into the unknown as he traveled to meet the fiery chariot. True, he had Elisha to keep him company, but he did not invite companionship, he only accepted it.

This example can speak to us today. We do not await fiery chariots, but we all will pass on to the unknown. We too sometimes know doubt or despair; we too look for and find God in unexpected places. While many of the prophets left writings that have inspired generations, Elijah left no writings. We know of him from biblical "hero-legends." What about us? We need not leave memorials, but will we leave stories of our constancy, our trust in God?

**Prayer:** *God of constancy and surprise, be known to us today in unexpected ways. Be known through us, and let us all know and share your constancy. Amen.*

**Wednesday, February 9**     Read 2 Corinthians 4:3-6.

Today's reading brings us closer to seeing the source of our transformation—God's glory in the face of Christ.

Paul does not want to speak of himself but of Jesus Christ as Lord. When he speaks of himself he speaks of his ministry for the gospel and of himself as the community's servant for Jesus' sake. What Paul actually *preaches* is Jesus Christ as Lord. This is all that matters because Jesus Christ is the likeness of God. Through Christ we will know God. But first we must open ourselves to God's light, because it is this light's shining into our hearts that enables us to see God's glory in the face of Christ. We must be open to God's light before we even begin to preach or to witness to the gospel in our lives. Otherwise, we are in danger of obstructing the gospel message.

One way we obstruct the gospel message is by separating our words from our actions. We must reflect what we say in what we do, or we speak empty words. We must live the gospel daily and not simply talk about it. When our lives have integrity between word and action, we can be transparent and God's light can shine through us, enabling both us and others to see God's glory in the face of Christ.

What bears recalling here is that while we easily see the glory of Christ in the resurrection, this glory cannot be separated from the glory of the cross. Becoming transparent to God's light and Christ's glory also means coming to terms with our own cross, whatever it might be.

**Suggestion for meditation:** *In my life, how do I daily preach Jesus Christ as Lord? If I get in the way of the gospel message, how can I get back on track? How can I live and preach the gospel so that my words and actions are one?*

**Thursday, February 10**                    Read Mark 9:2-3.

After six days, Jesus led three of the disciples apart—after six days. What happened six days before this? Jesus had spoken of how he was to suffer, to be rejected, and to die. His followers would also have to take up their crosses. What must have been going through the minds of the disciples as they recalled these heavy words? They had expected the coming of the kingdom but were told to expect suffering and death.

Jesus took Peter, James, and John and led them apart up the mountain. For anyone familiar with the Hebrew scriptures, going up a mountain meant the possibility of encountering the divine presence. And seeing or hearing God usually led to painful missions as with Abraham or Moses or Isaiah. (See Genesis 22; Exodus 3; Isaiah 53.) Perhaps the disciples were too disturbed by what they had heard six days earlier to be expecting a divine encounter, but suddenly Jesus was transfigured before them.

What an awesome experience it must have been. This was how the disciples must have hoped to see Jesus in the coming kingdom: radiant with glory. For them this was a preview of what was to come. This was what Paul later described as the glory of God shining in Christ's face; and Peter, James, and John saw it firsthand before anyone else. They had heard Jesus' teaching about suffering and death and the demands of discipleship. Now these three disciples had a glimpse of the glory to come.

Nearly two thousand years later, how do we feel when we experience the painful demands of discipleship? when we fail to see God's glory shining from the face of Christ among us? when we fail to allow it to shine through us?

**Prayer:** *Transfigured Christ, be present to us and lead us apart for a moment. Let your glory shine into our darkest places and make us transparent with your love. Amen.*

**Friday, February 11**                     Read Mark 9:4-6.

Peter has a way about him of being half comic and half on target with his reactions. Perhaps this ability is what makes him both appealing and easy to identify with when we see him in action. This time he is in the midst of a full-fledged epiphany, an experience of the divine, a preview of the glory to come; and he breaks into the moment with his outlandish idea of putting up tents so Jesus, Moses, and Elijah can stay around.

But perhaps Peter is not reacting so simply after all; perhaps something more complex is behind his offer. Yes, Jesus has been transfigured before them. Yes, Jesus reflects the glory of God. But this is a preview. The glorified state comes only with the resurrection, and the resurrection comes only after the cross. There is just no escaping the cross, not even by keeping Jesus on the mountaintop with Moses and Elijah, if that was Peter's intention .

Then again, perhaps Peter wants to prolong this experience because it is a moment of consolation. If Jesus must go to Jerusalem to suffer and die, and if Peter cannot understand why this must be, perhaps this momentary comfort can last at least a little longer. Aren't we often just like Peter? We also want to avoid what we do not understand, to avoid our own crosses, even when we know that ultimately they can lead to our salvation. "No pain, no gain" is not our idea of salvation, is it? It is natural to want to keep Jesus close and transfigured. But epiphanies do not last forever. We must come down from mountaintops; and like the disciples, we must go where Jesus goes, be transformed into his image, and let him shine through us.

**Suggestion for meditation:** *What are the mountaintop experiences in my life that can encourage me in times of confusion? How can God encourage others through me?*

**Saturday, February 12**                    Read Mark 9:7-8.

Today we read of the divine claim on Jesus, the claim that establishes Jesus' identity. Jesus is the Beloved Son. God claims him, not just as faithful follower or true worshiper or loyal prophet. God claims Jesus far more intimately as son. That in itself must have amazed the disciples. But God goes further. God claims Jesus as beloved. That must have been even more amazing. God says Jesus belongs to him intimately.

This is more than a stamp of approval. This is more than a sign of friendship, a recognition of good work, or an award for faithful service. This is a sharing in God's life and glory, a being known and loved by God at a deeper, more intimate level. The transfigured state shows that glory, but the voice from the cloud confirms strongly the love of God for this beloved son.

And then the voice continues: "Listen to him!" (verse 7). We might understand it as, "Hear what he has to say, and take him seriously." Or "Listen to him, and know you can believe him." All of these messages could be what the disciples understood as well as what we might understand today. It could also be understood in the context of the difficult news from six days earlier when the disciples learned of what Jesus was to suffer and of the cost of their discipleship. Perhaps it said to them that after this moment of consolation (a consolation they needed), they must listen to Jesus even when the teaching is painful.

This message is no easier for us today than it was for the disciples. We too need consolation. We too need to listen, even to the hard, painful teachings of Jesus.

**Prayer:** *Jesus, Beloved Son, open our hearts to hear what you have to say, to hear that we too are beloved, that we too must accept the cross that will transfigure us. Amen.*

**Sunday, February 13**                    Read Mark 9:9.

Jesus and his three disciples came down from the mountain, returning to what they had left behind, forging ahead to what awaited them. Peak experiences are good and necessary, but we always return to the daily. Mountaintops can offer consolation, encouragement, and hope; daily life is the setting in which we carry out our roles, whatever they might be. The peaks are where we experience the transfigured Christ. Daily life is where we become transparent so Christ can shine through us. Obviously we need both the mountaintops and daily life. We need both hope to sustain us and reality in which to live out that hope in transparency.

And as they came down the mountain, Jesus charged them to tell no one. How confusing this must have been. To have an experience of the glory of Christ and then to be changed with silence . . . until after Jesus had risen from the dead—in other words, until after the suffering and death and resurrection, which is the inevitable, inescapable cost of discipleship. They were back face to face with the conundrum they wanted to escape: behind this glimpse of glory lies the cross. But behind that cross also lies glory, lasting glory. So the disciples must carry on courageously.

Where does this leave us? Are we puzzled like Peter, James, and John? Do we want to return to the mountaintop, prolong the vision, avoid the cross? Are we hope-filled and ready to move forward alongside Jesus? Perhaps we are a little of each of these. But move on we must, and so we do. We move on to our work, our leisure, our prayer, our lives as Christians with all the demands, sorrows, and joys. All of these are the essential elements of daily life. When we face them with hope and faith, God removes the obstacles within us and makes us transparent. And in our transparency, God shines forth.

**Prayer:** *God of glory, transfigured Christ, show yourself to us and through us. Amen.*

## GOD'S PRESENCE IN THE STORMS

February 14–20, 1994
**Monday, February 14**

**William L. Sachs✛**
Read Genesis 9:8-17.

Summer storms rise with little warning on the Chesapeake Bay. One afternoon several fishermen found themselves in a sudden storm. They hastily got underway but could not outrace the storm. Wind and rain beat upon them, and the boat rocked as waves slapped the hull. Lost in the storm, with no ability to guide the boat, the fishermen feared running aground. Then, as suddenly as it began, the storm abated. Visibility returned, the wind slackened, and the weary men got their bearings and returned to dock. Outside the harbor the men glimpsed a rainbow and murmured appreciation.

For Christians, life entails many mysteries. One of them is the mystery of suffering. It is expressed by the question, "Why do bad things happen to good people?" The book by this title captures a prevalent perception. Innumerable instances of human suffering with no justification exist. Storms cross every life and create havoc.

The other mystery is the power of God's promises. Even though we are unable to explain suffering, we are mystified by God's love. In a way we cannot grasp but only accept, this love breaks through the gloom that enshrouds us. No matter how tumultuous the storm, only God's love endures.

**Prayer:** *In your compassion, merciful God, break through the storms of our lives with the light that gives us direction and brings us peace. Amen.*

---

✛Assistant rector, St. Stephen's Episcopal Church; adjunct faculty, Union Theological Seminary, Richmond, Virginia.

**Tuesday, February 15**                     Read Psalm 25:1-10.

Repeatedly today, evidence of abuse comes to light. Numerous people have acknowledged the harm that has been done them or that they have done. In the intimate aspects of life, horrible realities have appeared. The prevalence of abuse has been shocking.

Abuse is an inhumane injury that leaves a tremendous scar. When abuse occurs, the perpetrator often is someone who is known and trusted and who has taken advantage of that responsibility. The result is a loss of the victim's ability to trust anyone or anything. Abuse is a monstrous evil.

Psalm 25 affirms that God is worthy of trust, and those who "break faith without cause" (NEB) will come to shame.

During Lent, in the face of human evil divine promise stands in clear relief. Those who have experienced abuse can come to trust God's promise. Divine love can overcome even this deep pain. God's grace reaches out to them and wants to help them learn to trust.

A victim of childhood abuse confided that she felt estranged from Christianity for years. Male imagery tainted the church for her until, on a whim, she joined a friend at a Bible study group. In that setting, a bond grew and several persons revealed that they also had been victims. Under careful leadership, the group members resonated with God's word and with one another. They became a community whose bond was God's love. They learned to trust by being led to a healing place. There they came to know the meaning of grace.

**Suggestion for prayer:** *Pray that victims of abuse may realize their personal worth and find the means to trust. Pray for those who abuse others, that their pain and hatred may be broken.*

## Wednesday, February 16 (Ash Wednesday)

Read Psalm 51:10-17.

Tom's problems began with minor pranks at school and spats with his family. These instances seemed normal to childhood, but Tom moved on to destructive behavior. Lying, stealing, and cheating became common, as did fits of anger. Then he abandoned his family and began habitual drug use. Tom moved from childhood in a stable home to adulthood at society's margin.

Everything came to a head one Sunday morning when an intoxicated Tom disrupted worship at his family's church. He was taken for treatment to an alcohol and drug abuse center, where a remarkable change took place. Sober for the first time in years, Tom began to gain perspective. For years he had not understood that his life had become distorted. Now Tom felt overwhelming remorse. Why had he lived destructively? How could he climb out of this deep hole?

Sometimes the gospel enters our lives as a cold blast of truth. Sometimes we are like travelers stranded by a blizzard, trying to seal the windows and doors to keep out icy reality. But truth is a wind we cannot withstand; it collapses our facades. Our ability to deny cannot sustain us. A painful moment of truth awaits us.

This crisis of truth becomes the basis of triumph. Conversion requires an abandonment to truth. God's grace follows, leading us from despair to hope. Admitting our need for God's love, we are forgiven and accepted. Ash Wednesday is the day of confession and the start of conversion. It is the day when scripture's promise becomes our own: "A wounded heart, O God, thou wilt not despise" (NEB).

**Suggestion for meditation:** *How do you need to be reconciled and healed? To whom, and how, have you done wrong? Consider those things you wish to confess, remembering that our remorse invites God's grace. By that love we become free.*

**Thursday, February 17**                    Read Joel 2:12-13.

In the close proximity of an airplane, a chance encounter is quite likely. As my flight circled its destination, the woman in the next seat asked my profession. Hearing I was a minister, she seemed energized. "I've tried every religion," she claimed, listing churches, seminars, and groups she had attended. The result was that she felt confused, and she wondered where to turn next.

For decades some people assumed that religion would wane. Now they puzzle over the diverse expressions of spiritual life. The search for truth compels people to move from one group to another. Spirituality has become a lively interest, and publications on the subject abound. The spiritual awakening is encouraging, but there is danger of confusion and preoccupation with "correct" beliefs, identifying God's love with doctrines or forms of prayer. We may be suspicious of those whose spirituality differs from what we revere.

"Rend your hearts and not your garments" (NEB). The doorway to God's love in Christ is not a particular belief. Like the many species who populate God's creation, human beings are diverse. We become one by expressing our faults, by accepting God's love, and by reconciling with one another. To rend our hearts, breaking them open to God, is the true spiritual way.

**Prayer:** *Gracious God, who is ever ready to hear our prayers, whose love for us knows no boundaries; rend our hearts to accept that love, in whose truth our journeys end, and we find life. Amen.*

**Friday, February 18**

Read Mark 1:9-15;
1 Peter 3:18-22.

On the campus of a private university, an entire floor of one building is devoted to an elaborate ballroom. Beautifully decorated with impressive chandeliers, it would seem to be the setting for a formal dance to mark college graduation or to honor a distinguished faculty member. But dances have never been held there. This Christian college does not allow dancing on campus. This church school is making a statement that certain behavior is "unbefitting a Christian person."

We long for something that distinguishes us as Christians. We must have some means of conveying to the world that our lives uphold our baptisms. Regardless of the denomination or whether a person is baptized as an infant or an adult, there should be a discernible difference in a follower of Christ. Our lives have been renewed by water and the Holy Spirit, and we should see ourselves as people set apart.

First Peter 3:21 offers us a healthy perspective on where Christian identity lies. We think that the identity of baptized persons lies in following a higher morality. But while we receive a higher calling, we cannot expect moral and spiritual perfection. In this life we remain pilgrims seeking to follow God. Despite dedicated efforts, we sometimes fall short. Then, seeking God's forgiveness, we remember both our humanity and our calling.

Baptism leads us not to moral superiority but to spiritual clarity. Striving to do God's will, we attain spiritual insight, grow in love, and gain vision to live as baptized persons whom God sustains.

**Suggestion for meditation:** *When were you baptized? What vows did you make, or did your parents make, on your behalf? Consider what was promised and what living today as a baptized person might mean. How have you been set apart from the world?*

61

**Saturday, February 19**     Read 2 Corinthians 6:1-10.

Christianity makes an astonishing claim: by our faith the reign of sin ends, and the day of deliverance dawns. The heart of Paul's message lay in this startling announcement. To live as Christians meant to live as people who had been healed, forgiven, and reconciled. Those who claimed the love of God showed its gifts in their lives. To realize God's grace and to live God's love were the challenges Paul addressed.

And there were severe challenges. Second Corinthians 6 records the hardships Christians endured. They were "flogged, imprisoned, mobbed; overworked, sleepless, starving" (NEB). Yet they persevered with "truth, . . . patience and kindliness; by gifts of the Holy Spirit" (NEB). Members of the Christian community faced relentless suspicion and systematic persecution. Often tempted to betray their faith, they remained resolute. Despite human frailties, they remained resolute. Facing incredible danger, they trusted in Christ's promise that the "hour of favour has now come" (NEB).

We Christians in the United States are not persecuted for our faith. Instead we are tempted away from it by the claims rampant in our society. Many products offer us comfort. Programs and seminars promise health and assurance. With so many offering so much, it is difficult to know whom to trust. Where can we find our day of deliverance?

Paul knew that deliverance comes not through what we gain but through what we give. Christ releases us from fear and want as we learn to serve.

"We recommend ourselves" (NEB) by behavior, by striving to live as Christ commands. That striving is the dawn of deliverance.

**Prayer:** *God, who is present in our daily strivings, keep us clearly fastened upon your kingdom as our end and your love as our means. Do not let us be diverted by temptations, but keep our commitment to you clearly expressed in our lives. Amen.*

**Sunday, February 20**     Read Matthew 6:19-21;
1 Peter 3:18*a*.

Every few years our family has a yard sale, and each time we are amazed that it is possible. How could we have forgotten so much that we had bought? How could some things have deteriorated so badly? We become embarrassed that we have tossed so much aside. We live modestly, yet we manage to accumulate an amazing amount of material goods.

Our materialism acts as a treadmill, pulling us onward but taking us nowhere. Every item in a yard sale at one time seemed like a treasure. Everything on those tables was desired and sought. Somehow the product never matched its promise. Gadgets were used a few times, then broken or lost. Clothing faded and became a reminder of an earlier era. Yesterday's treasure became a remnant and then a curiosity, pushed aside by updated versions.

Lent is a time to reconsider our notion of treasure. Much of what once seemed necessary proves to have only passing worth. Even those items that are necessary eventually reach the scrap heap. Actually the real treasures in most homes are the photographs that record relationships, which outweigh any material possession.

Genuine treasure is not a commodity. It is a relationship to God and to others in which we give and receive love. In this reality no possessions are exchanged. Rather, a bond is built and sustained, becoming eternal. That bond will never tarnish and can withstand considerable stress. The love of God is the one treasure our hearts need never lose. It is life.

**Prayer:** *Keep us responsible, God, in using material goods. May we accept them as transitory gifts that we must share. Give us devotion to responsible living as participants in that human community, which is the supreme gift of your creation. Amen.*

## BOUND TO GOD IN COVENANT

February 21–27, 1994            **David Lowes Watson✚**
**Monday, February 21**          Read Genesis 17:1-7.

This passage is one of the most awesome in the whole Bible. The God of the cosmos, with its billions of planets and stars and galaxies, is inviting a human being into a covenant relationship.

It is difficult to grasp the significance of this today. In our self-centered culture we tend to think of God as a divine customer service agent, available to us on call, but otherwise dispensable. One glance at a star-studded sky, however, and we are jolted back to reality. We are not the center of the universe; we are not God's only creation. We live on a middle-sized planet that orbits a middle-sized star in a middle-sized galaxy. Not only are we a miniscule part of a vast creation; we are also just plain average.

Yet somewhere, somehow, this average little planet has gone terribly wrong. It has turned away from its Creator and is caught up in suffering and evil and sin. The wonder is that the God of the universe is taking steps to put things right on planet Earth. It is a dramatic divine initiative, and it should take our breath away.

**Suggestion for meditation:** *Astronomers estimate that among the billions of planets in our galaxy, the Milky Way, there are some 600 million that may well have life forms like ours. To count these planets at the rate of one per second for eight hours a day would take more than fifty-seven years. And the Milky Way is just one of billions of galaxies!*

✚Professor of Theology and Congregational Life and Mission, Wesley Theological Seminary, Washington, D.C.

**Tuesday, February 22**                    Read Genesis 17:1-7.

The word *covenant* has become seriously devalued in the modern world. People use it as a social convenience, to make a relationship more meaningful or a business arrangement more dependable. In church life it is often used as a pastoral accessory, inducing people to churchly commitment through their prayers, their presence, their gifts, and their service. We even invite members to make "short-term covenants," hoping to secure their more active participation in our programs and activities.

We should beware of such blasphemies. The Hebrew word for covenant came from an old Akkadian word meaning a shackle, or a fetter. When God invited Abram into covenant, it was a binding agreement. It could not be negotiated or terminated, neither could it be short-term. It was for all time, and it could only be kept or broken.

If that seems unduly restrictive, look at the conditions of this covenant. The God of the universe asks for Abram's loyalty and in turn promises to make him Abraham, "the ancestor of a multitude of nations" (v. 5). Restrictive is hardly the word. This is the opportunity of a lifetime.

By the same token, when God invites us into covenant, there can be no hesitation or haggling. The opportunity is no less momentous for us than it was for Abraham, and the conditions are just as clear: Put on the handcuffs and throw away the key. No trial period to see if we like it. No escape clause in case we change our mind. When we are asked to share in the divine cosmic initiative to heal this planet, our answer can only be Yes–or No.

**Prayer:** *O God of all creation, I am humbled that you have called me into covenant. If you will have me in your service, I will accept your conditions unconditionally. Amen.*

65

**Wednesday, February 23**          Read Genesis 17:15-16.

Among the delights of the Hebrew Bible are its vivid accounts of conversations with God. The Creator of the cosmos talks freely and openly, reacts with disarming candor to what people have to say, and encourages them to respond in kind. Thus, when God promises to make Abraham the ancestor of a multitude of nations by giving him a son, we read that the old man "fell on his face and laughed." God understands. In the next chapter we read that his wife Sarah found the idea no less amusing; after all, she was ninety years old and her husband was one hundred. Again, God understands. For God knows that this covenant promise will come to pass, their geriatric mirth and incredulity notwithstanding.

The scriptures make clear that all of God's promises to Abraham were fulfilled. He was indeed fruitful. He did become the progenitor of a multitude of nations. Yet all of this lay in the future. At first, the only sign that he and Sarah had of God's covenant faithfulness was their son, Isaac. And miraculous though this was, it was only the beginning.

This is always the pattern of God's covenant-making. We are invited to set out on a journey that requires our trust and obedience. Yet for the most part, God's promises remain just that: promises. Some of them are fulfilled, quite often miraculously, but only in sufficient measure to deepen our faith and temper our obedience.

Immature disciples become impatient with this and begin to doubt, even when confronted with God's miracles. But seasoned disciples know that *all* of God's promises are trustworthy. How do they know? Because, as they honor their covenant with God, God honors them by granting them an ever-deepening faith.

**Prayer:** *O God of Abraham and Sarah, help me to remember that you will always have the last laugh. Amen.*

**Thursday, February 24**     Read Psalm 22:23-31.

To grasp the significance of these verses, we must read the psalm in its entirety. We are exhorted to rejoice in the power of the God who rules over nations, yet in the opening verse we have the very words Jesus uttered from the cross: "My God, my God, why have you forsaken me?" We find the Lord extolled for hearing the cries of the afflicted, yet this follows a bitter litany of woe and despair.

We can note two things about these apparent contradictions. First, there is no reserve on the part of the psalmist. He cries out in pain and anguish that God has abandoned him and allowed him to be mocked and scorned. We should take note of this outburst, because we too are in covenant with God; and we too will experience God's abandonment. The psalmist is telling us that when this happens, it is altogether appropriate to let God know how we feel. When we suffer, God understands our anger and resentment and does not expect us to "grin and bear it."

The second thing we can note is that when the psalmist has raged and protested against God, he can still praise God. Indeed, praise seems to pour out all the more because of the preceding lament. For the psalmist knows that abandonment is never God's final word. God can be trusted. God's people will be vindicated. The poor shall eat and be satisfied. And one day all the families of the nations shall sing and shout their praises.

**Suggestion for prayer:** *Feel free to rage and protest before God in the midst of pain and suffering. Jesus did. Then remember to praise the God of our covenant, whose saving righteousness will always prevail.*

**Friday, February 25**                    Read Romans 4:13-25.

*The righteousness of faith.* These words are at once the bedrock and the shipwreck of Christian discipleship.

The bedrock of our discipleship begins with faith in Jesus Christ. This is the precondition of our covenant relationship. To continue in this relationship, however, our faith must be lived out in obedience to Christ. As we obey, our faith is strengthened; and as our faith is strengthened, we find ourselves empowered to do more for Christ, even the ridiculous and the impossible.

The shipwreck occurs when we think we can sustain our covenant relationship without being obedient. We become more concerned about our belief in God than in obeying God's law. We seek to deepen our relationship with Jesus without doing what Jesus commanded us to do (see Matthew 25). Paul reminds us, however, that Abraham's covenant faith was strengthened by doing God's will, not merely by trusting God's promises, which in any event he and Sarah initially found laughable.

How do we avoid this shipwreck? First of all, by acknowledging that our very faith is a gift from God. Just think how vigorously we resisted God's covenant invitation before finally accepting it. And when we did accept, it was probably with ill grace: "Very well, Lord, have it your way. I'm tired of the hassle." We are due no credit at all.

Then we must realize that, as with all of God's gifts, our faith is meant to be used. If we live it out in obedient service, our relationship with Christ will deepen. But if we fail to serve Christ, our faith will diminish. Many Christians face shipwreck because the rope of their faith has rotted from lack of use.

**Prayer:** *Most gracious God, help me to live out the faith you have given me in obedience to your will, so that my anchor may hold firm in the storms of life. Amen.*

**Saturday, February 26**                    Read Romans 4:13-25.

Jesus was handed over to death for our trespasses and raised for our justification. In this sacrificial offering, as Jesus explained to his disciples on the eve of his execution, God has made a new covenant with humankind, sealed with Jesus' body and blood. (See Luke 22:19-20.)

We stand in awe that the God of the cosmos should enter into a covenant relationship with the inhabitants of this very average planet. The awe becomes unspeakable that God should take human form in order to redeem planet Earth from its waywardness. But when the cost of this redemption proves to be the suffering and death of the Son of God, the unspeakable awe becomes deeply mysterious.

It should now be clear why the utilitarian use of the word *covenant* in our culture (see Monday's reflection) becomes such blasphemy in the life and work of the church.

"God, I covenant to read my Bible each day for a month."

"God, I covenant not to miss Sunday school this fall."

"God, I covenant to give to world hunger during Lent."

How dare we insult the covenant-making God by so demeaning the word! This new covenant means all or nothing. It cost the Son of God his life.

There are many insights into the divine insanity of the cross, but one must surely speak to us at the end of a century of human holocausts and planetary abuse. On the cross, God identifies with the sin, evil, suffering, and death of our planet and asks us to trust that these are not the stuff of eternity. The crucified God makes this new covenant altogether trustworthy.

**Suggestion for meditation:** *Whatever the cost of your discipleship, remember the cost to God of your redemption.*

**Sunday, February 27**                    Read Mark 8:31-38.

In this passage, Jesus explains why it is so important for his disciples to be in a covenant of obedience. The path will not be easy. Their discipleship will be demanding. At the outset, therefore, they must be willing to surrender everything, including their lives if need be.

Christian disciples today must likewise surrender everything to Christ. We must willingly accept the work he gives us to do and readily go wherever he sends us.

The passage also reminds us that the world into which Jesus sends us is not neutral territory. The forces in opposition to the coming reign of God will do everything they can to divert us. They will even seek to sabotage our work through our very loyalty to Christ, as Peter discovered in this blunt and almost brutal exchange with Jesus.

The operative word, therefore, is that we *bind* ourselves in covenant with God. In a moment of strength, we must shackle ourselves to Christ, firmly and irrevocably, so that we remain secure in our inevitable moments of weakness. Far from enslaving us, these shackles give us perfect freedom: the freedom of belonging to the God who loves us more than any human mother, who can be trusted more than any human father, and who died on the cross that we might live.

**Prayer:** *I put myself wholly into thy hands: put me to what thou wilt, rank me with whom thou wilt; put me to doing, put me to suffering, let me be employed for thee, or laid aside for thee, exalted for thee, or trodden under foot for thee; let me be full, let me be empty, let me have all things, let me have nothing, I freely and heartily resign all to thy pleasure and disposal.\* Amen.*

\*From John Wesley's Covenant Service of 1780.

## THE LAW OF THE LORD

February 28–March 6, 1994                     **Chan-Hie Kim**✢
**Monday, February 28**                     Read Exodus 20:1-7.

Contemporary Christians tend to strongly reject any legalistic coercion or demand on their own conduct and behavior, particularly when it touches on religious and moral issues. We have a natural instinct to defend ourselves from any demands at all. Christians are so aware of Jesus' impatience with Pharisaic legalism that any moral codes or ethical demands are seen as contrary to Jesus' teachings.

However, the basic demand to obey God's will and law is the foundation of our Christian faith. By voluntary obedience to the law of the Lord, we find joy in our life. We are not asked to be slaves to God's law but servants of it.

The preface to the Ten Commandments reminds the Israelites that they entered into a covenant relationship with God when they were freed from the bondage in Egypt. It may sound as if God is imposing another kind of bondage on the Israelites, but the preface is rather a declaration of liberty the Israelites will enjoy by having a new covenant with God.

The law of God is a promise of salvation—salvation from our own sinful selves. And it is also a promise that we will no longer be slaves to ourselves.

**Prayer:** *Put your yoke of law on us, O Lord, that we may carry it and enjoy it in our daily life. Amen.*

---

✢Associate Professor of New Testament Greek and Director of Korean Studies, School of Theology at Claremont, Claremont, California.

**Tuesday, March 1**                    Read Exodus 20:8-11.

The Sabbath is a day of rest. It is also a holy day because the Lord blessed it and made it holy—so says the writer of the Book of Exodus.

However, the Sabbath is not simply a day of rest; it is a day that we must dedicate to God. Refraining from work is not enough; we should dedicate the day to the Lord by attending worship services and doing other services for the glory of God.

This may sound like a foolish and old-fashioned admonition. We have many Christian sisters and brothers around us who feel that it is boring to participate in a worship experience every Sabbath. They prefer to spend their days of rest watching games on television or playing golf and other sports and recreational activities. Surely these things are all a necessary part of our life—indeed God might encourage us to do so.

But pause a moment and reflect on the commandment, "Observe the Sabbath and keep it holy" (TEV). Keeping something—a day—holy means in a sense setting it apart from everyday activities we call secular. We distinguish sacred objects or holy days from what we do in our ordinary days. The Sabbath belongs to such a category. It is a day we dedicate to God for our well-being and welfare. By resting and meditating on the grace and mercy of God, we give God our sincere thanks for our life and world.

**Prayer:** *Forgive, O Lord, our disobedience to your commandment to rest on the Sabbath and keep it holy. Amen.*

**Wednesday, March 2**                    Read Exodus 20:12.

In the animal world, offspring that reach adulthood often totally sever their relationship with their parents. But human beings are different. Unlike most animals, humans maintain family connections, particularly with respect to parents. While it is sadly true that the love some parents feel for their children is expressed in unhealthy ways that often lead to child abuse, God's plan for family relationships is that they become stronger and stronger as both children and parents mature together. Usually, as children grow older, they better understand the love their parents have for them—love that had been understood earlier as a kind of parental control or power play. But this tendency is a natural one on the part of children. The fifth commandment reminds us of the kind of sacrificing love parents can have for their children.

In the Confucian cultural world, filial piety is one of the most highly valued virtues. If people treat their own parents contemptuously or mistreat them by not caring for them, they are usually excommunicated from their community and family circles; sometimes they are treated as criminals. The act of neglecting or ignoring parents is regarded as the most serious violation of the moral codes.

In a society like ours that seems to become busier every day, it is imperative that we recall the fifth commandment daily and find special ways of letting parents know of our love and care. The honoring of parents is but one way God's law helps build loving relationships among the families of the earth.

**Suggestion for meditation:** *Think of how you can honor your parents today—even if they are no longer living.*

**Thursday, March 3**     Read Exodus 20:14.

Adultery is a common, very serious disease in our society to-day. The most deplorable situation is that even ordained clergy who are to dedicate themselves to the highest ideals of the Christian life often do not take the seventh commandment seriously.

We live in a permissive society. Because concern that had been given to moral injunctions and ethical demands has shifted to political, economic, and ecological dimensions, we pay less attention to the personal moral life. Since we have to deal with so much evil in our world today, we forget to take care of our own individual moral lives. Since people are crying for justice and food, since our natural environment is being exploited by greedy corporations, and since there is no end to war in the foreseeable future, we seem to have no time to pay attention to our own personal evil. We are caught up more in fighting against global evils. Is the individual moral life any less important than these urgent global issues? By no means!

Statistics show that more than fifty percent of divorces in America occur because of the infidelity of spouses. If adultery is such a blatant cause of the breaking up of families with the potential emotional damage to children, then adultery becomes as serious a problem as economic, political, and ecological issues. The peace of family life can help our world remain strong in its struggle to avoid destruction caused by other evils.

**Suggestion for meditation:** *Am I faithful to my spouse? Do I take personal moral issues as seriously as other social issues?*

**Friday, March 4**                    Read John 2:13-22.

The Gospel of John places the story of Jesus' cleansing of the Temple at the beginning of Jesus' ministry. However, the synoptic Gospels place the story toward the end of his ministry. The difference is interesting. The synoptic Gospel writers understand the incident as a culmination of his lifelong ministry.

The Temple is not to be a place of profit-making, but "a house of prayer for the people of all nations" (Mark 11:17, TEV). This declaration from the prophecy of Jeremiah (7:11) is quite fitting here. Jesus' ministry has never been limited to the Jewish people alone but has been for all the nations of the earth.

But when we take a close look at John's recording of the story, we notice an additional dimension in the Temple cleansing. Here Jesus is not simply driving out money-changers and other merchants but the innocent animals like sheep and cattle as well. It is an announcement of the end of the religion that is centered around the Temple and the cult of animal sacrifices. We now need to worship God in spirit and not with animal sacrifices.

Like prophets of old who abhorred animal sacrifices that were unaccompanied by genuine obedience to the law of God (e.g., Amos and Micah), Jesus calls for our absolute commitment to God's will shown in God's law.

It is shocking to read that Jesus used violence in cleansing the Temple. But as John reminds us through Psalm 69:9, Jesus' act was out of his passionate devotion to God's Temple as the place of worship. Do we also not need righteous indignation in confronting the evils of the world? Perhaps we, too, may need to lift up our whip to cleanse our community and world. Anger for the sake of righteousness and justice is much needed today.

**Prayer:** *O Lord, may I have anger for your sake. Amen.*

**Saturday, March 5**                    Read 1 Corinthians 1:22-25.

The Christian faith is viewed sometimes as absurd or contradictory by the standard of common wisdom and understanding. How can the Messiah be crucified—a total defeat by the enemy? It is certainly not only offensive but blasphemous to the Jews. The Christ is supposed to be a hero and a liberator who would save the Jews from the bondage of the Romans rather than be a victim of the conquerors.

At the same time the crucified Christ is nonsense to the Greeks, the Gentiles. To proclaim a "victim" as a "victor" does not make sense at all in the eyes of the people who treasure wisdom more than anything else. Irrational logic has no room in the mind of the Greek.

Yet, Paul proclaims that "the crucified Christ" has done more work than any human wisdom has accomplished because God makes human wisdom and pride foolish. What humans consider to be nonsense is the very wisdom of God. Our way of looking at things is totally rejected by God. "God's foolishness is wiser than human wisdom" (TEV). Our logic does not seem to be acceptable by God. God uses the weak, the poor, the powerless, and the foolish of the world to accomplish his will. God turns our logic completely upside down. In this circumstance how can we boast in God's presence?

The Christ who took the form of a human being, mingled with the outcasts of society, and suffered shameful crucifixion, is the very person who shook the world and put it in a totally different order than was known previously. He gave us a new value system and showed us a new world—a world no one had ever seen before.

**Prayer:** *Thank you, O Lord, for the Christ—our wisdom and power in time of trial. Amen.*

**Sunday, March 6**                    Read Psalm 19:7-14.

Here we read a great song praising the law of the Lord. The psalmist praises it because it is perfect, trustworthy, always right and just. God's law gives us new strength and wisdom. It provides us with happiness and understanding.

But is it really "more desirable than the finest gold" (TEV) as the psalmist sings? Is it worth sacrificing our financial gain? Is it so precious that it is worthy of sacrificing even our own lives?

The law of God that is given to us not only in the Ten Commandments but also revealed throughout the books of the Torah and Prophets certainly declares the will of God toward us. The saints and missionaries of old and of the present gave up their lives for the sake of the law because it *does* give meaning to life and it *does* show us the right direction for our lives. God's law surely is the most precious wisdom we could ever seek. And we should seek it at any cost.

The law of the Lord gives us true knowledge and shows us true beauty because it reveals the nature of the foundation of creation to us and reveals the nature of the Creator of the beauty we see in all creation—both natural and human. God's law enables us to put our world back in the order in which it was originally created. Without God's law, human life will experience chaos. God's law, then, surely deserves our absolute trust. It gives us the assurance that God will never fail us or desert us.

**Suggestion for meditation:** *How can I obey the law of God without becoming legalistic?*

## FROM DEATH TO LIFE

March 7–13, 1994                           **Steve Harper**✝
**Monday, March 7**                       Read Numbers 21:9.

Lent. So often we think of it exclusively as a time to give up something. We make vows of self-denial during this season, and we engage in appropriate repentance. Like an expert tree trimmer, Lent reminds us there are "dead limbs" in our spiritual life that need removing.

However, our texts this week reveal the ultimate purpose of Lent: life. We prune the deadness so new life can emerge. We confess sin so we can receive forgiveness. We let some things go so we can have time and space to take up other things. Lent is about moving from death to life. Every text this week is life-giving.

But life is not easy or without pain. It is not simple and effortless. Lent challenges us to take the deepest possible look at our lives, a look so deep that only God can reveal it to us.

As we make the journey from death to life this week, we will note God's provision, personhood, process, priority, and price. We will see our perversion of God's plan also. We are Easter people who get there by the way of the cross. Life comes through many little deaths.

**Suggestion for meditation:** *Consider not only what you are giving up for Lent but what you need to take up for Lent.*

✝Executive Director of A Foundation for Theological Education; founder of Shepherd's Care ministry to ministers, Lexington, Kentucky.

**Tuesday, March 8**              Read Numbers 21:4-9.

*God's provision*

God knows. God cares. God acts. These affirmations combine to form the word *providence*. It is God's nature to provide for our needs.

In the Old Testament we see two great elements of God's provision. First, it is *universal*. Everyone who was bitten could "look at the serpent of bronze and live."

Orthodox Christianity affirms the reality of hell, but no one has to go there. God's provision for salvation, like the bronze serpent, is lifted up for everyone. Lent tells us that no one is doomed; no one is stuck; no one is without hope. God provides the way. All we have to do is look for it.

Second, God's provision is *specific*. The Israelites were snake-bitten; their provision was a bronze serpent. Our problem is sin; our provision is a Savior. Our issue is lying; God's provision is truth telling. Our weakness is a short temper; God's provision is greater patience. God's provision always relates to the need at hand.

Lent forces us to get specific. God deals in particulars. Vague, undefined generalities are not the means of healing grace. We move from death to life by recognizing specific aspects of ourselves that cause us to fall short of who God intends us to be. We come alive in relation to particular needs.

Universality and specificity combine to form the word *grace*. God writes no one off, but God calls all of us to look specifically at the "deadness" in our lives. In such moments of honest confession, healing can occur.

**Suggestion for meditation:** *Select an area of need in your life. What does God know about it? Why do you believe God cares about it? How is God at work to help you deal with it?*

**Wednesday, March 9**          Read Psalm 107:1-3, 17-22

*God's personhood*

"Sometimes I feel like I'm bothering God when I pray about my needs," she said as we talked about petitionary prayer. It was a joy to remind her that meeting needs is what God delights to do most.

The movement from death to life is rooted in the heart of God. The phrase "steadfast love" is the repeated phrase not only in these lectionary verses but also in four other places in this psalm. The writer wants to drive home the point that the nature of God is the surest proof that we can be delivered from any and all evil.

God does not redeem and restore us out of a formal sense of duty or a cold sense of obligation. Lent reveals the God who renews us out of a heart of intense desire. Lent introduces us to the God whose essential nature is *love*. God's person is not One who "has to" but One who "wants to."

I continue to be amazed at how many people still have not experienced this truth. They would rewrite the psalm, replacing *steadfast* love with *conditional* or *uncertain*. Still others would question the word *love* itself. For all who experience God this way, Lent is a wonderful season to fall in love with the God who loves you!

On the other hand, Lent is a difficult time if we do not know God loves us. We draw back from exposing our deepest needs to a God who might respond punitively. So it is the person of God that makes Lent work or not work. That is why it is essential to see that God's personhood is love, *steadfast* love.

**Prayer:** *"O Love that wilt not let me go; I rest my weary soul in Thee."* * Amen.

*From the hymn, "O Love That Wilt Not Let Me Go" by George Matheson.

**Thursday, March 10**                    Read Ephesians 2:1-3.

*Our perversion of God's will*

Make no mistake—sin is real. Life lived "following the course of this world," "following the ruler of the power of the air," and "following the desires of the flesh and senses" has perverted God's design. Lent peels back the layers of rationalization and pseudosophistication to reveal our fallen nature as "children of wrath."

We often are acculturated to think so highly of ourselves that we sometimes try to relegate these words of Paul to a premodern age. But the simple fact is that Lent makes no sense apart from perversion. If there is no death, one does not need to be led toward life. If there is no sin, one does not need a savior.

Thus, the movement from death to life begins when we declare the reality of sin and confess our need for help. This is precisely the starting point of the various twelve-step programs that have helped millions find deliverance from all sorts of evils. From the Christian perspective, we accept the same view of powerlessness and relate it to salvation in Christ.

We must never apologize for being in the transformation business for the simple reason that all people everywhere need to be changed. The Bible calls that radical change *conversion* and the subsequent changes *sanctification*. Lent affords the days for considering where and how we need to be changed.

Change is personal and corporate. It is private and public. It is needed in souls and systems, individuals and institutions. Perversion is not a sign that we are doomed so much as it is the sign that we are diagnosed. Healing is imminent.

**Prayer:** *Teach me, O God, to confess my need quickly and completely, knowing you are more ready to forgive than I am to ask for forgiveness. In Jesus' name. Amen.*

**Friday, March 11**                    Read Ephesians 2:4-10.

*God's process*

When I was a child, the Greyhound Bus Company used this slogan: "Take the bus, and leave the driving to us." The point was that the trip was too long and hard to do it yourself, so the thing to do was to climb on board and let Greyhound take you there.

That is close to the message of Lent. The movement from death to life is too difficult to accomplish by yourself. The way of deliverance is the way of *grace*. Jesus in effect said the same thing, "What is impossible for mortals is possible for God" (Luke 18:27).

*Impossible*—we don't like that word. We would much prefer Jesus' words to read "harder" or "more difficult." But that is not what he says, and it is not what Paul means in the epistle reading. Salvation is "not the result of works"—period.

But in reality, that is the best news we can ever hear. If it were possible for us to do it ourselves, we would soon create such a maze of legalism and subjectivism that no one would know which plan to follow. Take away grace, and egotism runs wild. In no time, self-styled gurus and self-salvation programs would suffocate us.

So, God establishes the only process that can work the same for everyone—the way of *grace*. We are unable to boast. But neither are we subjected to endless lists of "do's" and "don'ts." Our journey from death to life is often long and hard. It is good that we do not make the journey alone.

**Suggestion for meditation:** *What does the word* impossible *evoke in your mind and/or emotions? Why? How does faith look different when grace becomes the controlling idea? Where do you need to "leave the driving to God"?*

**Saturday, March 12**                    Read John 3:14-15.

*God's priority*

With these words we come full circle. The snake-bitten Israelites become the "whoever" people of every age. The movement from death to life is the journey from poison to paradise. It is the single most important issue that every human being faces. Time is of the essence; eternity is at stake.

Lent is the "continental divide" of the Christian faith. Depending on what we do with it, life goes one way or the other. Lent is the North Star that God has placed in the world to make navigation through life possible. Lent is the priority, the message to be "lifted up" for all the world to see.

But notice! The priority is a *person*. In Christianity, the gospel is not a concept; it is the Christ! The Word does not remain word; it becomes flesh. The meaning of Lent is not information to be processed but rather Incarnation to be embraced.

"What will you do with Jesus?" is *the* most important question of all time. The deliverance we need is through the One whom we follow; the One who said, "I am the way, and the truth, and the life" (John 14:6). Nicodemus was privileged to hear the words of this Gospel lesson from Jesus himself. We are privileged to have access to the same salvation offered to Nicodemus that night on the hillside.

Theologians and saints have said it for two thousand years: Our faith is Christ-shaped. Lent is the amazing news that God has made salvation the priority and has become our savior in Christ.

**Prayer:** *Truly, God, this is the greatest story ever told. In this moment, I accept it to be eternally true. Thank you, Jesus. Amen.*

**Sunday, March 13**                    Read John 3:16-21.

*The price*

Dietrich Bonhoeffer warned the Christian world not to fall prey to "cheap grace." The movement from death to life must inevitably pass through the cross. A high price has been paid for our redemption. Jesus died for us, so that we can live for him!

By its very nature, Lent keeps us focused on the price. When Easter comes in a little while, we will have plenty of time to celebrate the victory. Lent forces us to calculate the cost.

In this week's Gospel lesson, the cost is calculated in human terms; Jesus had to die. The cost is calculated in ironic terms. Many preferred their darkness to God's light. The cost is also calculated in potential terms: even if only a few respond, the price is worth it!

We started the week with a serpent on a pole. We end it with a savior on a tree. The message from start to finish has been "look up!" The movement from death to life is by fixing our eyes on Jesus and following him wherever he leads us.

Lent's message is one of guidance and hope. There is a way out for any and for all. It is a message of gratitude and commitment. The price has been paid! Lent provides us with forty days to hear this message, embrace its abiding relevance, and move forward with Christ as our savior and Lord. Our response to and during Lent must be, "Thanks be to God, who loves us, who leads us, and who lifts up the only Son for all to see!"

**Prayer:** *Heavenly Father, thank you for sending us your Son. Thank you that through Christ we can indeed be your daughters and sons, with complete access to all that you are and heirs to all that you have. It is still the most amazing story on earth. Amen.*

## CHANGING OUR HEARTS FROM THE INSIDE OUT

March 14–20, 1994 **Thomas R. Hawkins✝**
**Monday, March 14** Read John 12:28-33.

Too often Lent becomes a time when we narrowly preoccupy ourselves with our own weaknesses and failings. We act as if we can change ourselves by the sheer force of our own efforts. Consequently, we spend more time looking at ourselves than looking at Jesus. Yet it is by looking at Jesus that we are saved.

In John's Gospel, Jesus proclaims three times that when he is lifted up, he will draw all men and women to him (3:14-15; 8:28; 12:32). This prediction echoes an incident in Numbers 21:4-9. Fiery serpents had bitten the people of Israel, and many were dying. So Moses made a bronze serpent and lifted it high on a pole. When the people looked up to see it, they were healed.

Our lives are healed when we look up to see Jesus lifted high on the cross. Lent is less a time to work on our own lives than it is a time to gaze upon Jesus and allow him to draw us into a closer, more loving relationship.

And as Jesus draws us heavenward, we see the world from God's perspective. God lifts us beyond our own lives to gaze with compassion upon the world Christ loves, died for, and calls us to serve.

**Prayer:** *Gracious God, remind us that we cannot save ourselves by our own efforts. Teach us to use this week as a time for you to draw us to you so that we might see our lives and the world from your perspective. Amen.*

✝Associate Dean for Programs at McCormick Theological Seminary, Chicago, Illinois; United Methodist clergy, Southern New England Conference.

**Tuesday, March 15**                    Read Jeremiah 31:31-34.

Just a few weeks after my wife and I discovered that we were expecting a child, we heard our son making his first sounds. The doctor amplified the baby's heartbeat, and we could hear its regular, pounding beat. A few weeks later, we saw that same heart beating and throbbing as we looked at the ultrasound pictures the lab technician gave us. It seemed as if his tiny body were wrapped around a huge heart, as if his heart were at the center and his whole body was growing outward from it.

Jeremiah's promise of a new covenant suggests the same image. The process of growing in faithfulness to God begins at the level of our hearts. The heart represents the center of our whole self. A change at the center gradually extends outward. God changes us from the inside out.

Jeremiah contrasts this new covenant that begins at the center, in our hearts, with the old covenant that Israel had accepted on Mount Sinai. The difference is not in the content but in the process. The old covenant had tried to change Israel from the outside in.

Israel could not bear God's direct address and instead wanted Moses as a mediator (see Exod. 20:18ff). As a result, Israel's heart had not been in what it was called to be. It had failed to keep its covenant with God. But in the new covenant, God dwells in the inmost being and addresses each person directly.

In Jesus Christ, we are invited into this new covenant that Jeremiah promised. When we welcome God's spirit into our hearts, we invite God to transform us from the inside out.

**Prayer:** *O God, you have created our hearts, and they are restless until they rest in you. Come, dwell in our hearts and transform us from the inside out. Amen.*

**Wednesday, March 16**                    Read Psalm 51:1-9.

Persons often associate this psalm with David's prayer for forgiveness after the prophet Nathan confronted him regarding his sexual misconduct with Bathsheba. David, or the psalmist speaking in his voice, acknowledges his guilt and pleads for forgiveness and mercy. Once again, we encounter the image of God's transforming action as something that begins in the heart.

The psalmist requests that God restore personal wholeness by granting wisdom in the inward heart. Cleansing from sin begins at the level of one's heart. The process by which our sins are washed away must begin there because our heart is the place from which our willing and thinking originate. We are purged of sin and changed from the inside out. New life works its way outward from this transformation at the center of who we are.

A friend of mine whose hobby is gardening likes to quote the saying, "No fruit without roots." Unless his garden has well-tended soil with the right nutrients, even the best varieties of plants cannot produce a good crop. Helping his plants develop a healthy root system and providing those roots with the right nutrients are crucial to a good crop of fruit or vegetables.

The same is true of human beings. Unless a change begins in the roots of who we are—in our minds and our wills—then our lives will not bear serious and lasting fruit. Unless our roots are cleansed and renewed, our limbs and fruit cannot be wholesome and life-giving.

**Prayer:** *O God, wash and cleanse us from our sin. Enable us to nourish the roots of our lives that we may bear good fruit. Amen.*

**Thursday, March 17**                    Read Psalm 51:10-12.

Both Jeremiah and the psalmist use the metaphor of the human heart to speak of our relationship to God. When we pray these verses, we are making three requests of God.

First, we are asking God to transform our whole selves. In the Hebrew scriptures, the heart is the locus of the will and the intellect. Even today, we still speak of memorizing something "by heart." And when we say, "My heart is just not in this task," we mean that we lack the will to do it.

When we pray for a "clean heart," we are asking God to renew both our minds and our wills. We need a new perspective on our lives and our world. We need a new capacity to act and to speak in ways faithful to that perspective. This transformation begins with God's action at the center of our lives—in our hearts.

Second, we are asking God to grant us the power to make the changes that come as a result of having a new heart. We need a "new and right spirit" that is nourished by the Holy Spirit. When we practice those disciplines that allow us to be open to the power of God's Spirit, we can sustain a new orientation to our lives.

Third, we are praying for joy. Some people work so hard to change themselves that they lose all joy and enthusiasm for life. When we lack joy, we need to ask ourselves whether we are trying too hard to change ourselves rather than looking to the One who, when lifted high on the cross, will transform us as he draws us to him.

**Prayer:** *O God, create a clean heart in us. Keep us ever aware of your Spirit's presence, and remind us that we are transformed not through our own efforts but by allowing ourselves to be drawn to you. Amen.*

**Friday, March 18**                    Read Hebrews 5:5-10.

Suffering is not something that any of us seek or want. It is, however, something that happens to all of us. Not even Jesus was exempt from it. Echoing the Gospel accounts of Jesus' agony in Gethsemane, Hebrews argues that Jesus achieved perfection not by avoiding pain but by learning obedience through it.

These are strange words for North Americans, who go to almost any extreme to avoid suffering. Our national motto could be the television commercial that announces "We haven't got time for the pain."

But in fact, our hope for personal wholeness lies not in escape from painful situations in our lives but rather in learning to be obedient to what these moments have to teach us. The obedience meant here has its roots in the original meaning of the verb to obey, which means "to listen to."

A friend was so successful as a solitary research biologist that her company promoted her to a management position. Suddenly, she was less successful. She faced one interpersonal problem after another. For the first time in her life, she met with failure. She was tempted to resign. Instead, she sought help and learned that many of her difficulties stemmed from behaviors rooted in the unresolved problems of her own childhood and family of origin.

Rather than avoid her suffering, she decided to listen to what it was trying to tell her. As a result, she grew, learned, changed. Like Jesus, my friend learned that perfection is not a passionless state free from pain. Instead, it is growth through listening to and learning from life's inevitable problems.

**Prayer:** *Loving God, be with us in our painful problems, that we may listen to and learn from them. Amen.*

**Saturday, March 19**                    Read John 12:20-27.

Like the Greeks who came to Philip and Andrew, we also say, "We wish to see Jesus." Yet seeing Jesus is no simple matter. John's Gospel indicates that Jesus does not directly answer the Greeks. Instead, he announces that the hour of his glorification has come. A few verses later, a heavenly voice proclaims that God's name is glorified in Jesus. Yet some in the crowd hear only thunder.

God's presence, power, and purpose are not always easily revealed in our lives. More frequently, they are shrouded in mystery and only indirectly understood.

A few years ago I had some problems with my vision. In reading about how our eyes work, I ran across what one book called the field/ground character of our vision. We can focus on either the field or the ground, but not on both at the same time. If I look through the screen window above my desk and focus on the trees, the screen's wire mesh fades from view. But if I focus on the wire mesh, then the trees go out of focus. I can clearly see one or the other—either the field or the ground—but I cannot simultaneously hold both sharply in my vision.

This same dynamic applies to our efforts to see Jesus. In John's Gospel, Jesus refuses to show himself to the world. Rather, he holds before us the mystery of his Passion and invites us to follow. We are most likely to see Jesus not when we search directly for him. Instead, we find Jesus when we take up our cross and follow his example of discipleship.

**Prayer:** *Gracious God, help us to learn that we are most likely to see you when we are not looking for you. Empower us to take up our cross and discover you in our discipleship. Amen.*

**Sunday, March 20**                    Read John 12:20-27.

The Greeks at the feast of Passover may have come to Philip and Andrew because they too bore Greek names. Philip and Andrew were Galileans, and Galilee was a region where Greeks had lived alongside Jews for generations. They may have felt that Philip and Andrew were Jews who would understand and would welcome these Greek outsiders.

Philip and Andrew did not ask any questions or judge whether it was appropriate for these foreigners to ask how they might see Jesus. Instead, they told Jesus so as to bring them into Jesus' presence. We might ask how we respond to those who come to us seeking Jesus. How do we bring them to Christ? How do we point them to the truth?

Let us assume that the Greeks in John's Gospel did come to Philip and Andrew because they identified with their Greek names. Is it possible that the starting point for helping people see Jesus is identifying with them in their struggles and in their humanity?

Sometimes we are tempted to ask people questions about their lives or to give them advice about what they ought to do. Instead, we might follow Philip and Andrew's example. We help people see Jesus by walking with them in their journey, inviting them to walk with us in ours, and pointing to the One who guides both their journey and our own.

Such hospitality is a catalyst for forming partnerships in the gospel. John's Gospel invites us to reflect on how we create a welcoming place in our lives and in our congregations for strangers seeking meaning in their lives.

**Prayer:** *God, you often come to us as a stranger and outsider. Help us to welcome you in that form and at those moments. Through our words and deeds, may we invite the stranger in our midst to see Jesus. Amen.*

## PRAISE AND PASSION

March 21–27, 1994 **Mary Lou Santillán Baert✠**
**Monday, March 21** Read Psalm 118:1-2, 19-29.

This royal psalm of thanksgiving begins by extolling the goodness of the Lord. The psalmist was in distress, surrounded by oppressive forces. Salvation came when he was rescued by "the right hand of the LORD" (vv. 15-16). The psalmist is not alone; those around him join in his praise and thanksgiving. They witness in amazement what mighty work the Lord has done for this one who has suffered greatly and has been rescued.

The psalmist knows from personal experience that God's goodness and love endure forever. This ordeal has made the psalmist aware that the Lord is on his side, that the Lord has never deserted him, that the Lord's mercy is everlasting, that the Lord will rescue him from his distress and not let him die.

Now the psalmist can tell others about God's mighty acts. The salvation experienced is so important and so powerful that the psalmist links it to the salvation of the whole community, which has joined him in this litany of praise and thanksgiving.

How many times has the Lord rescued us from distress, illness, death, oppression? How many times have we joyfully witnessed to "the right hand of the LORD"? How many times have we cried out to someone to open the gates of the church that we and the company of believers might enter with praise and thanksgiving for the gift of salvation?

**Prayer:** *Almighty and loving God, grant us vision to see your powerful hand at work in our lives. Amen.*

---

✠Elder in the Rio Grande Conference, pastor of St. Luke's United Methodist Church, Dallas, Texas.

**Tuesday, March 22**                    Read Mark 11:1-11.

The time for the Passover celebration was drawing near. Jesus sent two of his disciples into Bethphage to fetch a colt upon which he was to ride into Jerusalem. Many pilgrims had assembled just outside the city of Jerusalem. They gathered leafy branches from the fields, which the Gospel of John identifies as palms. Loud hosannas rang out as the people removed their garments and laid them in the path that Jesus would travel into the city of David. They cried out, "Blessed is the coming kingdom of our ancestor David!" No one recognized who Jesus really was. Did they understand the "save us" they were raising with their voices? Do we know what we are saying when we too sing our hosannas?

Earlier Jesus and his disciples had been in Jericho. As they were leaving that city, Bartimaeus, a blind man, sitting by the roadside shouted out to Jesus when he heard of Jesus' approach. "Jesus, son of David," he exclaimed. It is surprising that a blind man could sense the presence of the living God in Jesus.

Outside of Jerusalem people were emotional and excited as they followed Jesus, but in the Gospel of Mark, it seems that Jesus entered the city and the Temple alone. What did the city of Jerusalem represent to the crowd? Was it the majestic, triumphant, glorious city where God dwelt? Or was it the city of death, violence, disorder? Was it indeed the city that "kills the prophets and stones those [messengers] who are sent to it"? (Matt. 23:37)

And what about our cities? What does it mean to follow the Christ all the way into the city? Would we follow him into the inner city?

**Suggestion for meditation:** *What does it mean for God to enter our city? In what ways could it mean the end of old structures and an opportunity to meet God in new and fresh ways?*

**Wednesday, March 23**                    Read Isaiah 50:4-9*a*.

I would never choose to suffer voluntarily, especially since I have experienced pain and abuse needlessly, simply because of who I am—a Mexican American.

Therefore, two words for a time were not very popular in my vocabulary: *sufriente*, suffering and *siervo*, servant. Suffering seemed so unfair, useless, and crippling. And being a servant seemed so menial, so humiliating, so lowly.

In this the third of the Servant songs, the prophet Isaiah portrays the Suffering Servant as one whom God has blessed with gifts and graces. The servant has submitted his will and entrusted his life completely to God and thus has not been confounded. God has given him a tongue that brings comfort to the weary. God has also enabled him to be a good listener and has strengthened him to turn his back when others try to strike him.

The Suffering Servant is so confident of God and so trusts the power of God's love that he does not ask, "Why is this happening to me?" Rather, he lays down his life that others may live. He fulfills his calling through suffering and by doing so in silence, unlike Job, who cursed the day he was born or like most of us who meet suffering with complaints, swearing, bitterness, and "why me?"

What can we do with our suffering? How can God make it a blessing for us and for others?

To suffer is no disgrace for the servant, for his trust is in the Lord, who will vindicate him.

When I discovered and finally understood how God could transform my suffering and servant experience into gifts, joy overwhelmed me, and I blessed God.

**Prayer:** *Show us, O merciful God, how to release our pain into your love that it may bless others. Amen.*

**Thursday, March 24**                    Read Psalm 31:9-16.

The intense feelings, frustrations, and confidence in God of one who felt mortally threatened are expressed graphically in this long lament. The psalmist leaves nothing unsaid. He has experienced pain, brokenness, and loneliness because of his physical condition.

The psalmist cries out in distress. His strength fails; his eyes burn with so much crying. His physical condition is such that he is a "horror to his neighbors." Even those who see him on the street turn away from him and flee. He feels forsaken and forgotten. "I have passed out of mind like one who is dead." Physically, mentally, socially, emotionally, and spiritually the psalmist is a broken individual.

But then his confidence returns as he remembers the goodness and faithfulness of the Lord. The psalmist comes to the realization that God can be trusted, even with his life. Thus he declares, "You are my God." The Lord is in control even though seeming to be silent and powerless. Salvation comes as the psalmist encounters God through a personal relationship with God. Thus, the psalmist is able to offer his praise and thanksgiving to the God who responds and meets his need. The psalmist knows now that salvation has been available all along and that it has become a reality in his life. Once he had been on the brink of despair, but the Lord heard his cry. His adversaries and their taunts are powerless at last.

The psalmist bursts forth in a song of thanksgiving as he recounts his personal experience and bears witness to God's faithfulness. It is a moving picture of one who self-surrenders to God, trusts God completely, and witnesses to the God who saves.

**Prayer:** *Faithful God, help me to trust you with my life in sickness and in health, in fullness and in emptiness. Amen.*

**Friday, March 25**                    Read Philippians 2:5-11.

What is success? Is your idea the same as that depicted in the advertising media? They tell us that if we are to be "with it," we must use particular products, be seen in certain circles, engage in special activities, associate with the "right" people.

Yet in today's Bible passage, the paradigm of success is modeled by the one who took a towel and a basin and washed his disciples' feet, by the one who emptied himself and took the form of a slave, by the one who lay down his life in order to offer life to all, even to his enemies.

If Paul, in writing to the church at Philippi, is quoting an early Christian hymn, was this the church's understanding of Christian discipleship? Was this the lifestyle the church advocated for all believers? Was this how the early church grasped the meaning of the life, personhood, and work of Jesus Christ?

The Gospels portray Jesus as the great worker of miracles, wonders, and signs. He gives sight to the blind, makes the lame walk, feeds the hungry, frees those possessed by demons, cleanses the lepers, rebukes the winds and the sea, and raises the dead. But here in this epistle, Paul's deep amazement arises from Jesus' humiliation, his lowliness, his powerlessness, his humility, and his obedience and suffering even unto death, not his power and charisma.

How tragic that some commit murder so that they or their children may become "número uno," Number One—success at any price, it seems! Are you spending (wasting) your time trying to save your life in order to be "with it"? What prevents you from considering servanthood as your lifestyle now and as long as you shall live?

**Prayer:** *Spirit of God, descend upon my life that I may joyfully and willingly empty myself and take the form of a servant. Amen.*

**Saturday, March 26**                    Read Mark 14:1-71.

The plot thickens! The religious leaders move quickly to trap Jesus and to do away with him once and for all. They choose not to understand or accept him. He is a troublemaker, a Sabbath breaker, a friend of harlots and publicans. The central figure of Mark's Gospel has been Jesus and all that he did, but now the evangelist focuses not so much on what Jesus did as on what was done to him.

An unnamed woman enters the house of Simon the leper in Bethany, where Jesus is a guest. She breaks open an alabaster jar of ointment and pours it over Jesus' head. Judas Iscariot takes steps to betray Jesus. Two disciples make the necessary preparations for the celebration of Passover. As they eat this last supper together, the twelve are surprised to learn that one of them is a betrayer. In Gethsemane, Peter, James, and John fall asleep while Jesus struggles to accept God's will. Then Judas comes, not with a sword in hand but with a friendly kiss. Jesus is arrested and convicted. Peter denies Jesus and afterwards cries bitterly.

What a long day and night it must have been for Jesus! And how lonely he must have felt as death was a few hours away. Except for Judas, his disciples and friends did not necessarily turn against him; they just fled the scene and disappeared.

We often feel that we are strong in our faith, that we would never betray Jesus or deny our faith. We are so confident, so sure of ourselves. So were the disciples, some even boasting that they would go to the death for him. It was not an outsider who betrayed Jesus, but an insider, one who had lived with him, eaten with him, been in mission with him, prayed with him, listened to him, loved him, participated in the covenant meal with him.

**Prayer:** *Forgiving God, grant that we may leave your table to go and sin no more. Amen.*

**Sunday, March 27**                    Read Mark 15:1-47.

Jesus stands before Pilate with no one to defend him. The questioning begins. "Are you the king of the Jews?" The Roman ruler wants to know. The only response he gets is, "You say so." Pilate tries again and is amazed that Jesus will not defend himself, even when the chief priests continue to harass him. Pilate tries again to question him, but Jesus will answer no more questions. Jesus is not a pretender to anybody's throne; he is King because God has made him Lord.

Pilate cannot deal with silence, so he turns to the crowd. Jesus had been rejected already by his own people, the Jews, and now he is rejected by the Gentiles, Rome, and the crowd. The crowd clamors for blood, and Pilate offers them an innocent victim. He who is condemned to die is the only calm and confident one in the crowd. Jesus seems like the weak one, the powerless one, the humiliated one. All fail to see that he is the real monarch, the true ruler, the rightful sovereign. His authority was undergirded by love.

Pilate pronounces the sentence. Mocking soldiers lead Jesus away to be crucified. The inscription on the cross reads, "The King of the Jews."

The question for us becomes then, "Who is Jesus indeed?" Whose answer do we use? The preacher's, our parents', a teacher's, a friend's—or our own, born out of our personal relationship with him?

Such a death on the cross moves a centurion to confess what Jesus' followers should have proclaimed, "Truly, this man was God's son!" The silent presence of the women also witnessed to their love and faith. Jesus died and was buried, but that is not the end of the story. To be continued.

**Prayer:** *O Lord God, instill in us the desire not only to love your kingdom but to witness to the living Christ and to bear the cross. Amen.*

March 28–April 3, 1994        **K. Cherie Jones**✢
**Monday, March 28**        Read John 12:1-11;
       Isaiah 42:1-9.

Tucked in near the end of today's reading is an unnerving statement: "So the chief priests planned to put Lazarus to death as well."

Remember the story of Lazarus in John 11? Following the death of Lazarus, Jesus stood before his tomb and summoned him back to life. In this event, Jesus proved he was no common miracle worker; for at his command, one who was dead was transformed to life. Some believed in Jesus because of this transformation, but others felt threatened. Indeed, this was the action that finally prompted the religious authorities to plot Jesus' death.

Later, Lazarus was included in the plot because his very presence—alive, breathing, entertaining guests—bore astonishing witness to the transformational power of Jesus. The crowds came to see not only Jesus but Lazarus as well. The authorities simply could not let that continue, so they planned to put Lazarus to death also.

Jesus' transformational work continues. He stands before our tombs where we experience death (emotional, psychological, spiritual) and summons us to life. As this occurs, we may become a threat to some because we bear witness to the One who gives life to the dead. But we can be assured of his presence and grace to sustain us.

**Suggestion for meditation:** *When have I experienced the power of Jesus transforming me from death into life? When have I experienced suffering or alienation because of these transformations? How have I experienced the presence and grace of Jesus in those moments?*

✢International Director, the Walk to Emmaus, a program of The Upper Room, Nashville, Tennessee.

**Tuesday, March 29**                    Read John 12:20-36;
                                              Acts 10:34-43.

In today's lesson, Jesus again tells us the requirements for discipleship (vv. 25-26). Discipleship involves death to self-interest and brings us eternal life. We are also called to follow Jesus. The requirements are stringent and go against both our nature and our culture. Who among us truly dares to follow him?

Just before Christmas, 1990, the Reverend Viktor Mdolo and his wife, Gloria narrowly escaped death when attacked by members of a rival tribe outside their black township of Katlehong, South Africa. They were recognized because Viktor had delivered the message at the funeral of a fellow Xhosa tribe member. They endured a harrowing few hours before they were finally safe.

Several months later, Viktor and other clergy began meeting together, without politicians present, to work for peace in their beleaguered township. Katlehong was in chaos. Water and electrical services had been cut off. Teachers were on strike. Violence was escalating; one woman observed, "When you get up in the morning, you do not know if you will live to see the sunset." Once the clergy had developed a plan for dealing with these issues, they would invite the political leaders to assist them. When asked if this was dangerous work, Viktor replied that three clergy had been assassinated recently for similar work.

Viktor knew from experience how quickly life can be extinguished. Yet he was willing to risk his life because he was convinced that Jesus went before him in Katlehong.

His witness challenges me to think about my own responses to Christ. Am I willing to let go of my life in order to live eternally? Am I willing to follow Jesus wherever he goes? Are you?

**Suggestion for meditation:** *What does it mean to me to "hate [my] life in this world?" Into what community situations am I being asked to follow Jesus?*

**Wednesday, March 30**                    Read John 13:21-32.

There is a telling scene in the film *In Remembrance*. In this portrayal of the Last Supper, Jesus announces that the disciple who will betray him is the one whose hand is on the table. As the camera pans each disciple, one has a look of surprise, another a look of concern, yet another a look of questioning. And each disciple has a hand on the table. The visuals, whether reflective of the literal truth or indicative of the spiritual truth, imply that each one was capable of betraying Jesus.

Each disciple knew in some way that the seeds of betrayal are buried in each heart and that the bonds of loyalty can be weak even in the strongest of relationships. At that point, it was simply not clear to them who would betray Jesus. Each one was suspect.

Yet Jesus did not abandon them. He showed loyalty and compassion by staying at the table with them. Each one of these disciples, even Judas, was given to him by the heavenly Father as an answer to prayer (see Luke 6:12-16). In the midst of their questions about themselves and one another, Jesus refused to abandon them. Even knowing Judas's plans, Jesus washed his feet (John 13:5-20) and offered him bread to give him strength to change his mind (v. 26). As Ray Anderson in *The Gospel according to Judas* notes, "The grace of being chosen and loved by God counts more than the sin of betrayal."* Jesus will not let go of his own.

Our hands are on the table too. We are capable of betrayal through actions, words spoken and unspoken, and attitudes. Yet Jesus does not leave our table. He has called us and will not let us go.

**Prayer:** *Jesus, my hand is on the table, yet you stay with me. My loyalty fluctuates, but you do not let me go. I am grateful. Amen.*

---

*Ray S. Anderson, *The Gospel according to Judas* (Colorado Springs: Helmers & Howard Publishers, 1991). Used by permission.

### Thursday, March 31 (Maundy Thursday)

Read John 13:1-17, 31*b*-35.

The little drama reduced us to tears. Near the end of a long day on retreat near Johannesburg, South Africa, a group of women acted out a skit about Christian service. Following a reading from today's text, six women—black, white, colored—stood in a semi-circle, softly singing a Zulu song. In their midst, a middle-aged black woman sat in a chair while a young white woman knelt before her and gently washed her feet. It was at once a profoundly spiritual and profoundly political moment.

On the night in which he was betrayed, Jesus once again turned expectations upside down by taking the role of the lowliest servant in the household in order to wash the disciples' feet. He offered two reasons for his actions.

The first was simply that he must cleanse them and they, however uncomfortable they felt, were to receive his ministering. "Unless I wash you, you have no share with me" (v. 8). The initiation, the action, belongs to Jesus. We, the church, respond to this divine initiation and are anchored in his cleansing action. This attitude of receptivity was not easy for Simon Peter, nor is it easy for us, yet it is foundational for our relationship with Jesus Christ.

Second, Jesus modeled an attitude of humility and service that they were to emulate. "So if I, your Lord and Teacher, have washed your feet, you also ought to wash one another's feet" (v. 14). We are challenged to set aside our notions of power and position, just as he did. We follow Jesus into the arenas of need in our families, neighborhoods, and world. Following him will turn expectations upside down. Our ministry may produce as much discomfort and questioning as the disciples experienced with Jesus.

**Prayer:** *Gracious God, I am your child, and you know me completely. Cleanse me from sin. Show me how I can participate with you today in ministry. Amen.*

## April 1 (Good Friday)

Read John 19:17-30;
Psalm 22.

*And carrying the cross by himself, he went out.*

I remember vividly that morning so many years ago. I stood near the waiting room window and watched the sun rise over the Hollywood hills. Earlier, hospital employees had taken my father to the operating room. As we said good-bye, the look of fear on my father's face mirrored the fear in my soul. At age twenty, I had to seriously consider for the first time that my strong and energetic father was mortal. I felt alone and frightened. The only prayer I could utter was one word—*please*—over and over.

In John's account of the final leg of the journey to the cross, Jesus walked alone. There was no Simon of Cyrene to ease his burden. He was surrounded by guards and onlookers, but he carried his cross by himself. However, in the certainty of God's companionship, he could attend to his mother's care, say with assurance that he had finished his task, and give up his spirit.

Even though I felt alone that bright morning, I was not alone. My mother and sister were in the room, family friends were on their way to join us, and my friends at the university were praying for us. Each one was a means of grace to me, reminding me of the presence and provision of the Holy One in the midst of my fears.

During this experience, I learned—again—that in moments of isolation that envelop each of us at one time or another, the promise is that through the presence of the Holy Spirit, God is our companion. The challenge for us is to remember the promise and to trust the One making the promise.

**Prayer:** *O God who is my companion, you promise to walk with me through all my days. When I feel alone, help me to remember your promise and to trust in your faithfulness. In the blessed name of Jesus, I pray. Amen.*

103

## April 2 (Holy Saturday)

Read John 19:38-42;
Psalm 31:1-4.

Four days after we graduated from high school, one of my closest friends was killed in a car wreck. Her death was a horrible shock for my friends and me. In the weeks following Heather's death, I wrestled with trying to understand the meaning of life and death. And my Christian faith, nurtured throughout my life by family and churches, came under question as well. Where was God when the man ran the red light and sideswiped her car? Midway through the summer, I decided to trust God with Heather, with my life, and with my grief—a point of conversion for me. The next day my grandfather died, and the task of grieving took a new turn.

That summer of death and grief was a turning point for me. My faith put down deeper roots and became more personal than it had been. I began the disciplines of daily prayer and study and became more active in my church. The crucible of that summer gave me the opportunity to make choices about my response to God.

For Joseph of Arimathea and Nicodemus, Jesus' death was an opportunity to make choices about their discipleship. Up to that point, both had been fairly secret about their faith. Both had prestigious positions that might have been jeopardized by their relationship to Jesus. Yet his death was a catalyst that forced them to reevaluate their loyalty to him. Without their intervention, his body would have been consigned to a common grave. When faced with the choice of remaining secret disciples or being identified as followers of Christ, they chose to go public with their loyalty.

Times of crisis can help us reevaluate our loyalties and respond to God's invitation to a deeper relationship.

**Prayer:** *Lord Jesus, daily you summon me to follow you, and daily I must respond. Give me the courage to continue choosing to follow you, even as you continually choose me. Amen.*

### Sunday, April 3 (Easter)
Read Psalm 118:1-2, 14-24;
John 20:1-18.

My given name, "Cherie," is uncommon. Thus it is frequently mispronounced and/or misspelled, which I have come to expect. However, my name is part and parcel of who I am, and I expect those who know me well to both pronounce and spell it correctly. I assume that my family and friends will get it right. The pronunciation and spelling of my name helps me identify whether I am dealing with a friend or a stranger.

Early on the first day of the week, Mary Magdalene went to Jesus' tomb and discovered it was empty. Later, as she stood weeping, a man engaged her in conversation. She did not know his identity until he spoke her name, "Mary!" She had looked at him; she had talked with him, but she did not know it was Jesus, the Good Shepherd, until he said her name with the tone and inflection he had used so often. "Mary!" Neither Mary's knowledge of the Hebrew scriptures nor her remembering Jesus' own prophecies about his death and resurrection identified him for her at this point, only her name spoken in the early morning—"Mary!"

So it is with us. We must study and meditate on the scriptures to receive the written record of the self-revelation of God. We must pursue our theological reflection and seek after God with our minds. But knowledge of scripture and theological reflection can take us only so far. At some point, we each also must experience the Holy One at a personal level as the One who knows my (your) name and pronounces it correctly. This intimacy unveils for us the presence of the Risen Savior.

**Prayer:** *On this holy day, Lord Jesus, you called Mary by name, and she recognized you. Today you call me by name, and I respond with praise and adoration. Blessed is your name! Amen.*

## WHERE THE LIVING CHRIST IS FOUND

April 4–10, 1994                          **John Clifford✝**
**Monday, April 4**                       Read Psalm 133.

We recall the scene from some of the latter stages of the football season as the last seconds tick off the clock: the winning coach suddenly is doused with water or sports drink, but as he shakes himself off, he is smiling. His team has pulled hard together all year and now has achieved more than most folks imagined they could. This victory is one of immense satisfaction.

See! We really are not that far removed from the psalmist's description of how "good and pleasant" it is to have brothers (and sisters) dwelling in unity! Oil dripping from head to chin to collar, the signs of plenty and blessing and accomplishment, are foreign ideas only momentarily.

The joy of each such occasion is palpable. As we enter these Great Fifty Days, from Easter to Pentecost, our first theme is joy, and our second theme is the way we discover and share it.

Where is Christ found alive today? Where was he discovered after the resurrection? Where the people of God gather together; live together in unity; and work, celebrate, pray, and sorrow together, we continually discover how truly good God is.

**Prayer:** *O God, bring us together with one another in the hope and joy of the resurrection, that we may be your light to all the world. Amen.*

✝Pastor, First United Methodist Church, Mart, Texas.

106

**Tuesday, April 5**                              Read John 20:19-23.

We have all heard the traffic reporters say it and perhaps have had a guilty twinge as we listened: "Accident at this location, traffic backed up behind it, onlooker slowdown from the opposite direction." Yes, we all want to get a good look at the scene. Perhaps we daydream of being a hero on the spot, or perhaps we wonder what will happen to the parties involved. Like moths to a flame, we are drawn to the places where the action is.

Just so in Jerusalem that evening of the first day. For the disciples, the action all week had been around Jerusalem—a parade into the city, a moving Passover with Jesus, a cataclysmic rush to judgment and the cross and a tomb, and that first-day-of-the-week surprise of the empty tomb and Jesus' appearance to Mary Magdalene.

What would you do? Ten of the disciples (and a number of Jesus' other friends and followers) did what comes naturally. They gathered in a secure room near the scene to hash over the week's events. What was real? What was just hopeful dreaming? They could at least encourage one another.

And then Jesus appears. For this, they are not prepared—except in one way: they have gathered in his memory. They have locked out the world, wanting no intrusion on their remembrances. They have come together to reflect. Suddenly those "onlookers" are becoming swept into the events of the day in unimagined ways. And in this crowd, joy and excitement become the theme, as Jesus speaks and bids them peace.

**Prayer:** *Jesus, bring us into the fellowship where you are to be found and make us bearers of your peace. Amen.*

**Wednesday, April 6**                    Read John 20:24-25.

I have a problem getting in my exercise. I would prefer to get it playing tennis, but that limits me. It is quite difficult, and very little fun, to play tennis alone. And doubles is more fun than singles, especially when you are just getting back into shape.

Thomas was out exercising his sorrow in solitude, it seems, when Jesus appeared on the evening of the day of resurrection. We do not know what Thomas was doing—John does not fill those gaps in the story for us—but we are told that he cannot believe the others got their spirits "in shape" so quickly.

In his skepticism, Thomas is perhaps more like a twentieth-century person than any of the other disciples. His "show me" attitude is the approach our scientific world was built on. We are more comfortable with Thomas than, say, Peter in his brashness.

But Thomas does make one right move. He is willing to be shown, and so he joins his friends to hear more. Only when he does this does Jesus appear to him. It is only in the fellowship of the disciples that Christ is finally alive to Thomas.

Perhaps we give too little attention to our fellowship. Worship and fellowship are means of grace, places where the Lord becomes present to us. We look for "self-enlightenment," yet we fail to place ourselves where the Spirit repeatedly appears—in the company of the disciples.

**Prayer:** *O God, we seek you in places you do not frequent and wonder why we see so little of you. Return us to the body of believers and come alive to us there. Amen.*

**Thursday, April 7**                    Read John 20:26-31.

It was the middle of the nineteenth century; the population of the United States was growing, and only a few sectors of the country were unexplored. Reports started coming out of the country around Yellowstone of the odd features of that area. The folks "back East" in Boston and New York and Washington could not believe them. Even when artists painted pictures, it was hard to accept. The attitude was very much "I'll have to see it to believe it!"

Thomas must have felt that way too. After his skeptical reply to his friends about seeing Jesus, he is persuaded by the Lord's appearing to him. But now he has another problem—and Jesus faces him with it boldly: how can he convince others?

What evidence is sufficient to tell the world about such a wonder? The signs Jesus did among the disciples persuaded them of his resurrection, his victory over death. But this assertion is so extraordinary that it will take more than just saying it is so.

Jesus actually gave the disciples part of the answer before Thomas returned to the group. When they were gathered on Easter night, he gave four gifts: his peace, his commission, his Spirit, and the authority to forgive. The community that used these would be persuasive.

As more and more people saw Yellowstone and agreed that the descriptions were accurate, the nation started to think that these wonders could be true.

As more and more people started living the community life of the disciples, the message of the faithful took new life and began to spread.

**Prayer:** *O God, help us find those whose lives help us to believe. Amen.*

**Friday, April 8**　　　　　　　　　Read 1 John 1:1–2:2.

My congregations have tended to be a bit startled when, on my first Easter with them, I ask them to sing "Joy to the World." In our minds, we have associated that song with Christmas; yet it has a wonderful Easter message.

It is the message John's letter tries to convey. God's Savior has come, he reigns in the world, he invites us to be friends, and to that invitation we can only respond with yes!

John is firm in saying that he and the apostles are telling this as personal witness. Jesus has showed them the eternal gift of life, and they are so excited about it that they keep telling one another what it means to them and sharing it with whomever else they meet.

Now notice: When one hears this and believes in it, he or she is joined into fellowship with the apostles and all those others who have heard this message. They have a common bond, for they are all related to Jesus, to one greater than any one of them.

When we are joined to that fellowship, one common theme is to try to imitate Jesus, to do the deeds of light that made him so beloved. These deeds of light are the fulfillment of our joy—that love is spreading from heaven to us to the world. Our relationships are enriched in the body of Christ.

One thing more: If we are not in fellowship with Jesus, who will be our advocate? Who will bring us the forgiveness necessary for loving relationships? Who will stand between us and our sins?

If, however, we are in this fellowship, "Joy to the world!"

**Prayer:** *Jesus, fill our world with joy! Amen.*

**Saturday, April 9**                    Read Acts 4:32-33.

The key to winning at tug-of-war lies not in the bulk of the team (though that helps) but in how well the team members can pull together, how well synchronized they can be. When all the members pull and brace together, they will be hard to overcome.

That is how Luke describes the early church in Jerusalem. They are all of one heart and soul, totally committed to the work of the group. They are pulling together.

Now Luke adds an evaluation here. Because of this, the company of apostles has great power and great grace. But notice that it happens only in the heart of the fellowship.

Like a nuclear reactor that needs a critical mass of fuel, the church needs to gather Christ's followers into a critical mass of fellowship—one in heart and soul and purpose—before that great power can be generated.

Once that happens—look out! We speak of the growth of the church at this stage as explosive. It spreads in all directions and nothing can hold it in. New followers join the fellowship, experience for themselves the presence of the risen Lord, and set out to share that marvelous experience with their friends.

Where this unleashed power is channeled to preaching Christ, one more effect appears. "Great grace was upon them all." Grace, the blessing of God's love and Christ's forgiveness, the renewing work of God in a multitude of lives, becomes visible to the world.

**Prayer:** *Give us that power, O God, to bring our friends into your presence today. Amen.*

**Sunday, April 10**                    Read Acts 4:32-35.

We are just beginning to understand ecology, the idea that we all live in interrelated, balanced systems. Interfering with rain forests in Brazil affects our climate in the United States; and our search for air-conditioned comfort is destroying a protective layer of atmospheric ozone. We are just now learning to look for the balances.

The early Christians of Jerusalem seem to have found, in the fellowship of the risen Lord, a way to balance their social system within the group. Indeed, evidence suggests this was their best witness to the resurrection—that those who knew Christ alive in them could also find the love to meet the needs of one another.

This was their one heart and soul, that all belonged to God, that all they had was at Christ's disposal, and that it was a joy to help out if they could. It was in this community that the Easter message was shared. Christ is alive, still catching the love of people today and changing them. But how? By the fellowship community of the believers, by the church.

Our witness today may lack the power we have read about, but the machinery is still in place. As we look for the balances of nature, we look, too, for the fellowship of the believers; for it is there that the living, resurrected Christ visits most often.

If we are to meet Jesus ourselves, we must seek out that gathering of the saints; for ever since that first Easter, Christ has been in their midst.

**Prayer:** *Lord Jesus, bring us home to your family, that we may be reunited to you in the fellowship we find there. Amen.*

## CHILDREN OF GOD

April 11–17, 1994                    **George W. Bashore**✛
**Monday, April 11**                    Read 1 John 3:1-10.

In today's scripture, the writer moves beyond a generic understanding of "children of God" to a particularized experience of being "children of God." We not only enjoy living in relationship with God as Creator, but indeed we are "born of God." We are partakers of God's very nature as children of God.

The phrase "children of God" is distinct from "sons of God." The word *sons* often denotes position, rank, and legal relationship. On the other hand, the word *children* implies birth, origin, and oneness of nature. The thought here moves beyond common creation to new creation. God grants to all who believe in Christ a new nature—one that is in tune with the harmonies of God's nature. The Holy One gives us holiness; the loving Parent gives us love; the incarnate God gives us the right to become bearers of that sacred name. "To all who did receive him [the incarnate God], to those who have yielded him their allegiance, he gave the right to become children of God, not born of any human stock . . . but the offspring of God" (John 1:12, NEB). We are not only *called* God's children; we really *are* God's children!

**Prayer:** *What wondrous love you give to us, O God, that we can be your children. Help us to bear your nature and name with faithfulness and delight, through Jesus Christ. Amen.*

✛Bishop, Western Pennsylvania Conference, The United Methodist Church, Mars, Pennsylvania.

**Tuesday, April 12**                    Read 1 John 3:1-2;
                                              Mark 1:9-11.

In the first verse of Mark's Gospel, the author announces, "Here begins the Gospel of Jesus Christ the Son of God" (NEB). Immediately there follows the appearance of John the Baptist proclaiming the arrival of One who possesses authority from God and who will baptize with the Holy Spirit. That authority for Jesus' life and ministry trumpets from the heavens, "Thou art my Son, my Beloved; on thee my favour rests" (NEB). In those words, Jesus knew divine commission as well as divine companionship.

John reminds us that in our baptism we too receive the sign that we are God's children. Just as we are given personal names by our parents upon our birth, so our baptism signifies that God gives birth to us in a very personal way. The same providential love is announced to us. At every baptism in a local church, the heavens open and the voice of God proclaims, "Thou art my son/daughter, my beloved!" With that personal naming by God there come both the divine commission to live as children in God's family and the promise of God's loving companionship.

Each child has varying gifts and different needs. God cultivates those gifts and, with love and strength, responds to those needs. Rejoice in remembering your baptism, for at that moment God announced, " *(Insert your name)* , thou art my beloved daughter/son."

**Prayer:** *O most faithful and loving Companion, thank you for naming me as your own. Beyond my own imagination you provide for my needs. Use my gifts to meet the needs of others, through Jesus Christ. Amen.*

**Wednesday, April 13**                     Read 1 John 3:1-2;
                                            2 Corinthians 4:6.

John, in looking to God's consummation of history, paints no specific picture about our nature. But as God's children we have the confidence that we shall bear the nature of the One who has given us birth. Paul gave a glimpse into that nature of God: "The same God who said, 'Out of darkness let light shine,' has caused his light to shine within us, to give the light of revelation—the revelation of the glory of God in the face of Jesus Christ" (NEB).

This is not only an encouragement for our eternal nature, but it also defines our actions and demeanor now. In Jesus Christ there is the highest form of humanity. Unfortunately in our day many persons use the phrase "We are only human" as a rationalization for failure, self-centeredness, indifference, and sin. Yet the standard for the highest form of being human is found in our brother, Jesus of Nazareth. As children of God, we have been given our human nature as a gift to be used for God's purposes, not as a detriment. In Jesus Christ we see the image of God from which we are to reflect our humanity as God's children in the world.

In the face of Jesus Christ we see the glory of God. In kneeling to serve—healing the lepers, casting out demons, calling for peace and integrity, and giving his all to defeat sin—Jesus made the image of God manifest. And it continues to be so.

**Prayer:** *O gracious Creator, make clear your image in and through me for the sake of your world. Thank you for Jesus Christ, the way. Amen.*

**Thursday, April 14**                    Read 1 John 3:3;
                                              Luke 11:24-26.

For most of us, purity of heart seems to be an elusive goal. At the same time, the scripture reminds us that it is desirable—indeed, expected. John very pointedly says that those who are God's children purify themselves, "as Christ is pure" (NEB). Years ago most of us learned Jesus' beatitude, "Blessed are the pure in heart: for they shall see God" (Matt. 5:8, KJV).

Several words in the New Testament are translated "pure," and they often refer to ritual purity. They can be translated "clean," meaning "unsoiled." They can imply "having been washed." That is why some persons use language such as "washed in the blood of the Lamb" to describe the cleansing from sin and the renewal of purity for those in Christ.

Years ago, Søren Kierkegaard wrote a book entitled *Purity of Heart* in which he said that purity of heart is to will one thing. As God's children we are called to will the highest good. Our focus is to be undiluted. The highest good is to fulfill God's purposes, so purity of heart means singleness of direction in living those purposes.

The tragedy of the Lukan story of the man whose life was possessed by unclean spirits is his failure, having been cleansed, to fill his life with good "spirits." Prayers of confession for cleansing are vital. In addition, the home of holiness welcomes wholesome guests: prayer, service of love, praise, nurture in scripture and community of faith, justice advocacy. Purity is both gift and cultivated focus.

**Prayer:** *O great Purifier, help me to fill my life with good "spirits" and singleness of purpose in Christ. Amen.*

**Friday, April 15**                                    Read 1 John 3:4-5;
                                                        Luke 24:35-48.

In that great prayer of repentance in Psalm 51, the real offense of sin is against God: "Against You, You only, have I sinned" (v. 4, NKJV). At the root of all our misdeeds, injustices, and indifference is our failure to love God. This God imparts to us as offspring the very divine nature, that radiates shalom (peace and wholeness) and love, calling all of creation to exhibit the same unifying forces. Whenever we break that harmony in our relationships within the universe, we are offending against the nature and purpose of God. John defines sin as lawlessness, for it is breaking God's laws that are designed to bring the whole universe into a unity with God. So, indeed, our sin is against God.

Only God, against whom the real offense is committed, can grant pardon. The risen Lord declared the freeing word to his friends on the road to Emmaus that through repentance in the Messiah's name, forgiveness of sins is found. Peter, after explaining the power of the risen Christ in whose name the crippled man at the Beautiful Gate was healed, turned the hearers to the Source of wholeness, "Repent then and turn to God, so that your sins may be wiped out" (Acts 3:19, NEB). Thanks be to God who birthed us and who "rebirthed" us through Christ, so that the divine nature will be manifest through us.

**Prayer:** *O great Deliverer, in my offenses against your children I have sinned against you. Make me clean again to serve you in undiluted faithfulness through Christ. Amen.*

**Saturday, April 16**                    Read Ephesians 2:11-22.

How can I feel at home in a world that is fragmented, moving in so many directions at the same time, and in which we pass one another uncaringly while all of us are searching for home? Boredom, resentment, and depression issue from a disconnectedness. A feeling of not belonging is a malady of our time. To paraphrase Augustine, our spirits will wander restlessly, longing for home, until they are at home with God.

The second chapter of Ephesians gives us hope in our search for home. No one needs to stand outside, looking longingly or resentfully for peace—for home. "Your world was a world without hope and without God. But now in union with Christ Jesus you who once were far off have been brought near through the shedding of Christ's blood. . . . Thus you are no longer aliens in a foreign land, but . . . members of God's household" (NEB).

We are members of God's household—God's children—at home with our Creator and Sustainer. In the midst of pain, sin, and disillusionment, the gracious invitation comes to dwell with our gentle Guardian. Retired United Methodist bishop Leontine Kelly, preaching at Ocean Grove, New Jersey, said that when she graduated from seminary after much struggle and sacrifice, others may have been walking to "Pomp and Circumstance," but she was marching to "Amazing Grace." Zacchaeus, the penitent thief on the cross, the woman who touched Jesus' garment—all experienced God's grace, that same amazing grace that continues to welcome us home.

**Prayer:** *O caring Spirit, you keep tenderly calling me to be at home with you. May I embrace your amazing grace with delight and faithfulness to Christ. Amen.*

**Sunday, April 17**                    Read 1 John 3:1-10;
                                        Psalm 4.

A child of God is one who is righteous, as God is righteous. The psalmist calls upon followers of Yahweh to offer "sacrifices of righteousness" (KJV). *Righteous* is more than an adjective describing God's nature; it is that action of God that moves beyond strict equality in protecting human dignity to a generous self-giving in showing mercy to the poor and in lifting the fallen.

Righteousness is the living of life for the benefit of others and the glory of God. It moves beyond calculated acts of goodness and the demands of the law. It champions the oppressed, feeds the hungry, heals the sick, creates peace, forgives when wronged, sacrifices for others, overcomes evil with good, and loves unselfishly. John states unequivocally in his epistles that you cannot shut your heart toward a brother or sister in need and claim that you are a child of God. Since such action is contrary to the very nature of God, it is lawlessness. Therefore, all who act in such fashion are, rather, children of the devil.

These are strong words. In other sections, John makes it clear that, indeed, Christians do sin and have need of continual cleansing. Here, however, he cautions that sin is not to be taken lightly. Righteousness is inherent in the nature of a child of God. The world will become convinced of the power of a righteous God when it sees convincing acts of righteousness by the children of God.

**Suggestion for prayer:** *Think of those who need to overcome evil. Pray for them. Pray for ways and strength to help. Then pray for your own life, that more and more you will overcome evil with good and live the righteousness of God..*

# THE ART OF SHEPHERDING

April 18–24, 1994                                          C. Elliott Graves✠
**Monday, April 18**                                       Read 1 John 3:16-17.

This week we will look at scriptures that describe the characteristics of a good shepherd, and we will explore how following the Good Shepherd can help us develop the art of shepherding.

John 10:11-13 tells us that the good shepherd is one who is willing to love people enough to lay down his or her life for them. A hireling is not only unwilling to lay down his or her life for another person but will even take away from other people what is theirs. In the scripture reading for today, the writer uses a question to raise a distinct difference between being a shepherd and being simply a hireling. The writer asks a pointed question, "How does God's love abide in anyone who has the world's goods and sees a brother or sister in need and yet refuses to help?"

I recently watched a panel discussion on public television in which three executives of high-tech businesses were interviewed. During the conversation someone pointed out that some new developments would expand existing technologies in the state where these businesses were located. After some discussion about what these new technologies meant, the moderator of the program asked the executives how many more jobs this new technology would mean for the state. One of the chief executive officers responded by saying, "This is not about jobs; this is about making money." Was this man a good shepherd?

**Suggestion for meditation:** *In what ways have I not shared myself with others in greater need than myself? How can I share more to show God's love?*

---

✠Pastor, Mosca United Methodist Church, Mosca, Colorado; writer and career consultant.

**Tuesday, April 19**                    Read Acts 4:5-7.

I serve on a local board that works with a big brother/big sister-type program. Young children with behavioral difficulties are paired with older youth and young adults so they can have role models who can help them change their behavior. The program has operated in this area for ten years and is very successful. This past year we decided to expand the program to include older adults in the business community. We applied for a grant from a regional agency to help start this new program. After spending a year working with the granting agency, filling all their requirements for approval and finding out that we still hadn't justified ourselves well enough, we dropped the idea.

In today's scripture, Peter and John are having to do the same thing with the authorities of their day. They had recently healed a lame beggar and preached about the power of God to heal people if they would only believe in God through Jesus Christ (3:1-26). For these acts, the two apostles were arrested and brought before the rulers, elders, and scribes in Jerusalem, including Annas, Caiaphas, John, and Alexander, who were members of the high priestly family (4:1-4).

It was in this setting and standing as prisoners in front of these authorities that Peter and John were asked, "By what power or by what name did you do this?" In other words, people who felt their positions of leadership threatened were telling Peter and John, "Justify yourselves and your actions." Shepherds do not ask that of their sheep. Instead, they support them, guide them, and rejoice in their health and healing.

**Suggestion for meditation:** *When and how often do I have to justify myself to other persons? How often do I require other people to justify themselves to me?*

**Wednesday, April 20**                    Read John 10:11-13.

As I write this meditation, the U.S. is still in the midst of a recession. The unemployment rate is still high, people continue to lose their jobs, and there are more homeless and hungry people in this country than ever before. At the same time, large corporations and their executives continue to do quite well. On the television news recently, a story mentioned that several corporations fired their chief executives because these people had not laid off enough employees for the companies to make "reasonable profits." At the same time there are stories about how laborers working for major companies are being fired while executives receive million-dollar raises.

In the Gospel of John, Jesus speaks to a similar situation, one that was common in his day. During a discourse at a feast of dedication, Jesus clearly presents the difference between one who is a good shepherd and one who is a hireling. Jesus lifts himself up as a good shepherd who "lays down his life for the sheep." Jesus continues by saying that a hired hand who does not own the sheep really is not interested in their welfare and will leave when he sees a wolf coming. Then the wolf can snatch the sheep, scatter them through the countryside, and eat them at will (AP). The reason the hired hand runs away is that he does not love the sheep.

A good shepherd, on the other hand, will stay with the sheep and protect them from the dangers of the world even if it might cost the shepherd's life. Jesus became the ultimate example of what it means to be a good shepherd. Many saints have followed Jesus and have given their own lives to serve others.

**Suggestion for meditation:** *Who do I know who exemplifies the example of Jesus as a good shepherd? What does this person do to show such an example? How can I apply this example to my life?*

**Thursday, April 21**                    Read John 10:14-18.

For the past few days we have been exploring how people are often left to fend for themselves or are actually shoved out of employment, homes, or the ability to take care of themselves because of the greed and self-serving acts of others. However, there is another way to treat people, and many people practice this other way.

Jesus speaks of this other way in today's reading when he refers to himself as the "good shepherd." He points out that he knows his own and they know him and continues, "And I lay down my life for the sheep." He also says that other sheep are not yet in the fold, and he must go out to bring them in. Jesus concludes this portion of the discourse with the idea that he does what he does of his own accord. "No one takes it [his or her life] from me, but I lay it down of my own accord. I have power to lay it down, and I have power to take it up again." These are the words of the Good Shepherd, who chose to give his life for his sheep (people) so his life would be taken up in the Spirit by those who believe and be continued throughout history.

Today when people tell me of their plans, I often hear them say, "I have to . . ." on a regular basis. This phrase indicates they are being forced into doing something they do not choose to do. In many instances, they truly feel trapped into positions of not being able to make a decision.

I have known several shepherds in my life. They tend sheep not because they "have to" but because they enjoy their work, and they love the animals with which they work. Given the life of a shepherd, one would have to love the work to stay with it very long.

**Suggestion for meditation:** *What has Jesus done for my life because he chose to? What have I chosen to do for others in response to God's love for me?*

**Friday, April 22**                                        Read Acts 4:8-12.

When we last visited Peter and John on Tuesday, the religious and secular leaders were questioning them about how they could heal a lame man and then speak of the power of Jesus Christ, through whose spirit the man was healed. Today the story picks up with Peter's bold response to the question of their authority.

Peter responded by saying that the lame man was healed by the power of Jesus Christ. Hinting at all the ways people attempt to save themselves, Peter points out that mortal human beings can be saved only through God's act of divine love: God's son, Jesus Christ, chose to give his life so all might be saved.

Because of Peter's confidence, the presence of the healed man during the leader's questioning (v. 14), and the large crowd awaiting the outcome of the hearing, the leaders backed off and let their two prisoners go (4:13-22). This story shares two points about the art of shepherding. First, we must learn to follow the Good Shepherd; second, we must be bold in our actions as we follow.

In officers' training school, we spent the first six weeks doing whatever the upperclassmen told us to do. We were told, "In order to be good leaders you must know what it is like to follow." In our Christian training, we need to follow the example of the Good Shepherd of our lives—Jesus Christ. Learning to follow Christ enables us to become good shepherds. That's what Peter and John were doing. In healing the lame man and in preaching boldly, Peter and John claimed the power of Jesus' powerful love for themselves so they could tend and heal the flock. We, too, need to claim that power in our lives.

**Prayer:** *Gracious God, help us follow you so we may become better shepherds of your people. Give us the confidence to give our lives boldly for others as Jesus gave his life for us. Amen.*

**Saturday, April 23**     Read 1 John 3:18-24.

Being a shepherd is not an easy task. It involves living alone in isolated parts of the country, working outdoors in all kinds of weather, and taking care of animals that seem to have no mind of their own. One has to love the work in order to be a shepherd. The mountain meadows near where we live, far from a major city, provide an excellent area to raise sheep. However, it is extremely hard to find anyone—even those who say they like sheep—to live and work in these conditions. So, many who raise sheep in this area have to hire Basques from Spain. These immigrants come to the United States to herd sheep. They enjoy the lifestyle.

The Christians of the first century had a very difficult time during the Roman occupation and persecutions. They often fought among themselves (1 Cor. 3:1-4) or isolated themselves from others in order to feel safe. In such a time, the author of First John wrote these words, "Little children, let us love, not in word or speech, but in truth and action." People were calling themselves Christians and saying they had the love of God in them, but they did not always live as though this were true. It is always easier to assume a name or title or to promise to do something than it is to make the sacrifice and be what we say we are or do what we say we will do. At this point, Christians often struggle in their attempts to follow Christ. To be a true shepherd, we need to claim the confidence and boldness of God's loving power and use it to live our lives in truth and action. Being a shepherd means more than just saying, "I am a shepherd"; it means living with the sheep regardless of the conditions. Being a Christian means living as a Christian in our actions, not just saying we are Christian.

**Suggestion for meditation:** *When have my words and actions been inconsistent? How can I, with God's help, make them more consistent?*

**Sunday, April 24**                                    Read Psalm 23.

This very familiar psalm is divided into two parts. The first four verses provide us with a metaphor of the Lord as a shepherd. Verses 5 and 6 seem to reflect on the Lord more as a generous host. In the first section, the psalmist is one of the sheep tended by the shepherd; in the second section of the psalm, the psalmist is a guest.

This psalm is filled with action. Just as a shepherd's life is filled with many activities in tending the sheep, so the description of the Lord as our shepherd contains many active phrases. The Lord (our shepherd) "*makes* me lie down in green pastures," "*leads* me beside the still waters," "*restores* my soul," "*leads* me in right paths." And what a comfort this is! Regardless of the valley's darkness, we need not fear any evil, for the shepherd's rod and staff with which to ward off predators are present to protect us. In the second section, God, acting as host, "*prepares* a table before me in the presence of my enemies," and "*anoint*[s] my head with oil."

The psalmist's comfort in God as the Good Shepherd derives from all the things God has done and is doing for him. When we likewise have experienced God as our shepherd, we return to this experience, knowing the security that God continues to offer.

Once we know and understand the activities involved in being a shepherd, we can begin practicing the art of shepherding in our own lives. We do this by accepting the life of the Good Shepherd; by following the Shepherd with boldness and confidence; by acting on our faith; by loving others as the Shepherd loves us; and by leading others by word, action, and example as the Good Shepherd leads us.

**Prayer:** *Our gracious and loving God, we thank you for being our good shepherd and for showing us what being a good shepherd requires. Help us, as we follow you, to practice the art of being good shepherds ourselves. Amen.*

## ABIDING IN GOD'S LOVE

April 25–May 1, 1994           **Pamela S. Henderson**✝
**Monday, April 25**           Read John 15:1-5.

Disobedience separated Adam and Eve from the will of God, from their intimate communing with God, and from their position of dominion over the earth. Through our own disobedience we too lose something. We lose communion with God, we lose sight of God's love for us, and we lose a sense of the security of God's care. In mercy and love for us, God sent Jesus, a new Adam, the last Adam. Jesus paid the cost to restore our broken relationship with God. He set the stage for all humankind to regain connection to the Source of life and love.

In this passage, Jesus used Old Testament images when he described himself as the true vine and his followers as its branches, branches that would bear good and abundant fruit as his essence flowed through them and they are pruned for maximum productivity. The pruning shears were the word of God, sharper than a two-edged sword, cutting away the flaws and cleansing our minds, thus enabling our obedience.

Jesus abides in God's love and is one with God. As we abide in Jesus as his branches, in living union, we are restored to the intimate relationship with God that Adam and Eve abused and lost. We again have access to God's love, mercy, and power.

**Prayer:** *Thank you, God, for providing us a way back to your love through the love of your Son, Jesus. Help us bear good and abundant fruit, for Jesus' sake. Amen.*

✝Associate editor, *The Upper Room* magazine, Nashville, Tennessee.

**Tuesday, April 26**                    Read John 15:9-17.

Sincere, committed friends are a treasure and a gift from God. True friends share the values, motives, and interests of one another without the coercion needed by servants. Servants do what they are told; friends do what is best for one another.

In these verses, the disciples graduate to a new level of relationship with Jesus—from servants to friends. Jesus shares knowledge of God's redemption with his friends for their understanding. He takes them into his confidence in order that they might claim this redemption as their own, be committed to it, and share his joy in its advancement. They are being asked to join their wills with Jesus' will as dear friends.

We may sometimes wonder how many real friends we have, friends that are as committed to our welfare as we are to theirs. Often people in this world receive our acts of friendship as license for abuse and self-gain. We are to portray God's love to everyone, including difficult people, but it is hard for Christians to experience true friendship with those who oppose God. Genuine Christian friendship is based on shared values, goals, and life perspective, all of which is grounded in the love of God.

Jesus expressed a high opinion of friendship. Here, he solicits our desire to share his friendship and love—love that manifests itself in practice as caretaking action toward others. As Christians, we are committed to loving one another and others, demonstrating our friendship with Jesus and our friendship with God.

**Prayer:** *God, thank you for being our faithful friend, enabling us to act on your behalf in loving relationship with others and to proclaim you as the hope of humankind. For Jesus' sake. Amen.*

**Wednesday, April 27**                    Read John 15:6-8, 16-17.

The wonderful privilege of abiding in Jesus is the experience of answered prayer, whether the answer is yes, no, or wait. We have a covenant relationship, friendship, with God; we are united to God by the finished work of Jesus. Jesus directs us to ask and teaches us how to ask in prayer for what we need. The will of God is "no" only when that is truly in our best interest and the best interest of others. The will of God is that we know and honor God and that we carry out God's intents. God's will is not hidden or secret, but we must seek to know it more clearly.

Prayer and scripture reading help join our wills with the will of God and banish the unbelief that causes us to hesitate in our praying. Whenever our faith-filled prayer requests comply with God's promises or purposes, whether we pray for health, physical needs, peace and joy, opportunity, or anything else, God is glorified in our answered prayers.

When we pray, we are not just pulling God's strings for our selfish benefit. Rather, we are taking hold of God's promises in order to carry out God's will for us, to bring us to our highest potential as Jesus' disciples, and to be better witnesses of God's love.

God grants our desire when we pray to have what is good and right and thus equips us to serve, for that is God's own will for us. We can know that God is both willing and able to perform it.

**Prayer:** *Teach us to pray, Holy Provider, and use us as your instruments in the fulfillment of your supreme purposes. Change our wills to your will in our hearts, and let your will be done on earth as in heaven. In Jesus' holy name. Amen.*

**Thursday, April 28**　　　　　　Read John 15:20-27.

We could describe the life of a disciple of Jesus in overlapping, linear stages—training days, trying-out days, and trying days. As disciples, we are in some aspect of each phase all the time. Each time we successfully pass through a cycle, we experience spiritual growth.

Training days are times when we are acquiring new learnings, particularly early in our discipleship. This stage may correspond to the times Jesus' disciples spent listening to and learning from Jesus immediately after they were chosen. Trying-out days are when we first move on to stand and then to walk in our new learning. The disciples were sent out prior to the crucifixion to heal and to teach. They reported their progress to Jesus, who continued to advise them. Testing days (which are often referred to as the wilderness, the valley, or dark night) are those times that challenge the faith we have developed. God allows such testing to bring out the best in us. Sometimes, however, we become discouraged and turn from following Jesus.

Jesus attempted to prepare the disciples for their trying times. He knew that their mutual love and support would be necessary to get them through the time until they received the Comforter and that they would emerge from the ordeal with full joy. That same Comforter is available to us.

**Prayer:** *Gracious God, help me to know your presence with me even during the most difficult times, that I might be true to your will and be a faithful disciple. Amen.*

**Friday, April 29**                    Read John 15:18-25.

Jesus had encountered hatred throughout his ministry and understood it clearly. Those persons who hate the truth and reject it are hating Jesus and God who sent him. Jesus is Truth. The world system and the hearts of those who are of the world are based on a lie: that humankind can go its own self-determined way, independent of God.

When confronted with the truth, either we begin to accept it or we become even more passionate about the way we already are and hate or work against what opposes it. The Gospels present stories of many in the world who eagerly abandoned their old lives and accepted the truth—the blind man (John 9:1-12), the woman at the well (John 4:1-29), the lepers (Luke 17:11-19). There are also stories of many who reacted passionately against Jesus and hated the truth.

Jesus was aware of those who hated him to death, those who would not even consider giving up their own self-determined way. Those of the world who were the most passionate in this were the ones who had the most invested in worldly systems, the most to lose—the money-changers, the Pharisees, the priests, Herod.

Jesus clearly knew what lay ahead for himself and his followers. The world hated them. However, Jesus reflected upon this coming crisis in an almost unchafed way. He provided comfort and assurance for his disciples to allay their fear and intimidation during the persecutions sure to come. If they would only abide in him! The lie could not conquer the truth, hate could not overcome love, and the world could not prevail against God's kingdom. The battle belonged to God.

**Prayer:** *O Sovereign God, wellspring of truth, we praise you and your righteousness. Keep us in the way of truth. In the name of Jesus, whom we exalt. Amen.*

**Saturday, April 30**
Read 1 John 4:12-13;
Acts 8:26-40.

Anticipating the cross, Jesus made a promise to the ones he loved. He would send a Comforter to them, a helper, teacher, and guide for their trying time. He would send the Holy Spirit (John 15:26-27). The Holy Spirit would be his emissary, the proxy for Jesus' presence and power.

All that any follower of Jesus would ever need, then or now, in order to accomplish God's will would be supplied and nurtured by the Spirit. The Holy Spirit infuses believers, at our invitation, and joins us to Jesus to empower our witness, bestow spiritual gifts, convict us of our sins, help our prayers, and guide us to acts of greater love.

Philip, not noted before as a spokesman, was led by the Spirit to witness with great power to the Ethiopian. Philip was empowered to open up the scripture to this man in terms that he would understand and with such convicting power that the Ethiopian accepted Christ's salvation and urgently desired baptism.

We are called to do the will of Jesus, but often we try to do it on our own power. We often study scripture without getting the message that is there for us, or we are unable to convey that message to others. We need the aid of the Spirit. Often when God calls us to do something, it is something that challenges us to face and name our own biases or greed or dishonesty or unforgiving hearts or unloving natures before we act. We cannot do that unless we first submit ourselves to rely on the Holy Spirit to empower us to carry out God's will.

**Prayer:** *O come, Holy Spirit, and fill us with the resurrection power of Jesus. Give us all your good gifts that we may express greater love and glorify God. Amen.*

**Sunday, May 1**                    Read 1 John 4:7-21;
                                     Psalm 22:25-31.

Love is a fundamental characteristic of God, and God loves humankind uniquely of all creation. We are called in these verses not only to be recipients of God's divine love but also to be channels of this love to others. We are called to be God's partners in making God's love and redemption known. God seeks to gain the hearts of sinners through our witness. Our response to God's love and our own redemption is to act toward others to express God's love for them and God's desire and provision for their salvation.

Witnessing results from a grateful heart. The psalmist came face to face with pain, humiliation, and a horrible death that was inevitable had it not been for the Lord's salvation. We share that which is most important to us with those we love, those who are close to our hearts, those we would like to see share in its benefit. Declaring this work of the Lord in the great congregation seemed only natural, giving hope to those loved by God and loved by the psalmist.

Each of us has a story of salvation and the mercy of God to offer those we love. Nevertheless, to be a witness is not so much something we do as something we are. It is not so much what we say to others about God as what we are to others because of God. Our love for all people, in response to God's love for them, moves us to make each act of our lives a praise, witness, and thank offering to God before them, that God may use our lives to multiply the Lord's kingdom on earth.

**Prayer:** *Holy Creator, let my life be a testimony of your love and deliverance. Give me the courage and wisdom to share the word of truth with others, that together we might celebrate your saving grace. In Jesus' name I pray. Amen.*

# THE COMMANDMENT TO LOVE

May 2–8, 1994        **Jung Young Lee**✠
**Monday, May 2**        Read John 15 9-17.

Jesus summarized his teachings in the commandment of love: love God and love neighbor (Luke 10:25-28). This is the commandment of commandments, the summary of divine laws. This week's passage from John represents the core of our faith and will help us understand the real meaning of this commandment.

In an ultimate sense, commandments and love are inseparable. To obey commandments is to love God and love one another. Thus, as First John 5:2-3 states, "By this we know that we love the children of God, when we love God and obey his commandments. For the love of God is this, that we obey his commandments."

As we read the John passage daily, we may discover new meaning in the familiar words and thus experience new challenges as we try to live by Jesus' commandments about love. On Tuesday we will consider the nature of God's love and on Wednesday the relationship between love and obedience. The joy found in Christian love is Thursday's topic, and Friday we consider the sacrificial nature of Christ's love for us and, thereby ideally, of our love for others. Saturday we will deal with our friendship with Christ, and finally on Sunday we will see what it means for love to bear fruit.

**Prayer:** *Help me, O God, to repeat your words again and again, so that they can live in me and enlighten my thought. Amen.*

✠Professor of Systematic Theology, Drew University Theological School, Madison, New Jersey.

**Tuesday, May 3**                           Read John 15:9-17.

As we read the passage from John today, let us focus our attention on verse 9: "As the Father has loved me, so I have loved you; abide in my love."

For me, this verse speaks of a threefold love that involves the Father, the Son, and all of us as children of God. We know more of the nature and certainty of God's love for us because we saw Jesus demonstrate that love in daily life. Jesus' love is an immanent, concrete expression of God's great transcendent love. Because the love that Jesus demonstrated resides in God, we can understand God's love for us to be both transcendent and at the same time immanent—complete, perfect love. Without its transcendent aspect—that of being unconditional, all-encompassing, and freely given—God's love would be similar to human expressions of love, expressions that are good but rarely, if ever, completely selfless and unconditional: the love between parent and child, husband and wife, siblings, and friends.

At the same time, without its immanent aspect, that is, the demonstration of love in the midst of everyday reality, God's love for us becomes only abstract theory.

Because the transcendent love is revealed in the immanent love of Christ, we experience God's love when we abide in Christ's love. As we acknowledge and experience God's love for us, we recognize ourselves as children of God.

**Prayer:** *Help us, O God, to abide in your love and to reflect your love to the people in our daily lives. Amen.*

**Wednesday, May 4**　　　　　　　　Read John 15:9-17.

After reading the entire passage, let us take up verse 10: "If you keep my commandments, you will abide in my love, just as I have kept my Father's commandments and abide in his love."

Abiding in Jesus' love means keeping the commandments of the Father, because love is the summation of all commandments. However, we are not quite sure how to relate commandments and love, for they seem to be opposite in character. Keeping commandments seems to imply obedience; while love, certainly God's love, brings unconditional acceptance. If God's love is unconditional, what role does obedience to God's commandments play? Love accepts us regardless of who we are, what we are, or how we do. How then can we suggest obedience as a condition for a love that is unconditional? Obedience to commandments and unconditional love seem to be in tension with each other.

This tension between commandments and love is overcome because of their interconnectedness. Just as immanent love is the basis for our experience of transcendent love, abiding in Jesus' love is the basis for fulfilling God's commandments. No one can truly and completely obey all the commandments. The only way for us to keep them is to abide in love, for love fulfills them. We do not obey commandments first and then love as a result. Rather, it is our experience of and response to Christ's love that helps us obey God's commandments. Love, then, contains obedience. Without obedience, love is romance; without love, obedience is punishment. Thus, love demands obedience, just as obedience is possible because of love. Loving God compels us to an intent to obey God's will to the best of our ability.

**Prayer:** *May your love abide in my obedient heart, O God. In Jesus' name. Amen.*

**Thursday, May 5**

Read John 15:9-17;
Psalm 98:1-3.

Again, read the entire passage carefully. Pay special attention to verse 11: "I have said these things to you so that my joy may be in you, and that your joy may be complete."

The joy of abiding in Christ's love is also the joy of fulfilling all commandments of God. We have many joys in our lives: the joy of having something that we have not had, the joy of seeing friends we have not seen for a long time, the joy of succeeding in our achievements, or the joy of participating in meaningful activities. However, among all of life's joys, the joy of being loved and of loving exceeds all others. All other joys are temporal and incomplete. The joy of meeting friends or the joy of possessing what we wanted never lasts too long. But the joy of love is eternal and complete.

Because our joy is complete in love, love is the ultimate goal of our lives. No matter how much money we may have, how successful we might be, or how powerful we may become, we still seek love. Food can nourish our body, ideas can stimulate our thought, and senses can add pleasure to our lives; yet none of these alone can bring lasting joy. Love alone can complete our joy of life.

The joy of Christian love includes the joy of helping, serving, and struggling with others. We experience true joy when we help the needy, when we serve the weak, and when we struggle with the oppressed for liberation. It is the joy of giving rather than of receiving.

**Prayer:** *Forgive my foolishness that seeks instant joy in material things, O God. Give me joy in your love. Amen.*

**Friday, May 6**                                    Read John 15:9-17;
                                                        Acts 10:44-48.

Read the entire passage, and then concentrate your thought on verse 12: "This is my commandment, that you love one another as I have loved you."

In this verse, we learn that Christ's love is an exemplary love for all of us. We perceive what love is only when we perceive the nature of the love of Jesus expressed by his life. Love is not just a sentiment but an expression of the whole self. How did Jesus love us? He loved us with his life, the life of service, suffering, death, and resurrection. His love is most intensely manifested in his suffering on the cross. His is the love that surrenders the whole being for the sake of those who reject him. In other words, it is the love that loves the enemy.

When Jesus said, "You love one another as I have loved you," he certainly meant that we have to love others with the kind of love Jesus gave us from the cross. In other words, our love of neighbor cannot be mere sympathy or emotional identification with them. Loving others means more than helping them when they need us. Loving with the love of Christ means bearing the cross. It means to suffer together and even to die together for the sake of justice and peace, as Jesus did for us.

Loving one another means being disciples of Christ in our daily living. We are joined together in his suffering and death. Love without suffering is a sentimental love, and suffering without love is difficult to bear. As followers of Christ, we, like Christ, are asked to suffer in love and to die in the hope of resurrection.

**Prayer:** *Give us courage, O God, to bear the cross, so that the crucified love unites us in our discipleship. Amen.*

**Saturday, May 7**                    Read John 15:9-17.

Again read the entire passage, giving special attention to verses 13-15: "No one has greater love than this, to lay down one's life for one's friends. You are my friends if you do what I command you. I do not call you servants any longer, because the servant does not know what the master is doing; but I have called you friends, because I have made known to you everything that I have heard from my Father."

There is no greater love than to die for one's friends. We often boast about our popularity and claim that we have many friends. However, the true friend who is willing to give his or her life for us is almost nonexistent in our time. (And it is unlikely that the friendship we offer others is any more self-sacrificing.)

A traditional Korean saying goes like this: "Although there are many drinking friends, there is no real friend who helps you when you are in need." Many people come for drinking, eating, and parties, but they often avoid us when we need them. Jesus Christ became the true friend who died for us, even though we are not worthy to be called his friends.

Jesus became our friend not because he needed friends. He became our friend because he loved us. His love restored us from servanthood to friendship. In his love he lowered himself so that we became equal with him. Servants do not know what the master is doing. To know what the master is doing is what makes a friend different from a servant. We became Jesus' friends because he opened himself for us. In him we find not only his will but also the will of the Father. He is, therefore, our true friend.

**Prayer:** *Loving God, in the world where the true friend is rare, you give me Jesus as my friend. Thank you for your giving love. Amen.*

**Sunday, May 8**                    Read John 15:9-17;
                                              Acts 10:44-48.

By now you have almost memorized the text. Let us finally consider verse 16: "You did not choose me but I chose you. And I appointed you to go and bear fruit that will last, so that the Father will give you whatever you ask him in my name."

This verse deals with the mission of love. True love is expressed in action. Love that does not act is not real love, because love is dynamic in nature. When we really love, we do not attempt to convey it in words only. We act in love. When love lacks action, it does not bear fruit.

When love is expressed in action, it is in fact an act of mission, the mission of all those who keep God's commandment to love. Love has been freely given to us from above. To accept God's love for us means to respond to God's desire that we love one another. Those who are loved are to love others; they are missionaries of love.

The fruit that comes from power, wealth, self-pride, and self-interest is temporary; but the fruit that the mission of love bears will last, for love is lasting. The lasting fruit, therefore, not only brings spiritual maturity to individuals, but it also re-forms society to be more nearly like the kingdom of God, where loving coexistence of all people is possible. Ultimately, the lasting fruit is the coming of God's reign on earth.

**Prayer:** *God of love, appoint us to be your missionaries, so that we may bear the lasting fruit of love. Amen.*

## STANDING UP

May 9–15, 1994                                      **Charles D. Whittle⳨**
**Monday, May 9**                                      Read Acts 1:15-17.

*Standing up among believers*

"In those days Peter stood up among the believers" (NIV).

Peter always seemed to be standing up and speaking up.

When Jesus invited Peter and Andrew to leave their nets and follow him, Peter immediately stood up and followed (Matt. 4:18-20).

When Jesus asked the disciples, "Who do you say that I am?" Peter spoke up, saying, "You are the Christ, the Son of the living God" (Matt. 16:15-16, NIV).

When Jesus told his disciples that they would all fall away because of him, "Peter replied, 'Even if all fall away on account of you, I never will. . . . Even if I have to die with you, I will never disown you'" (Matt. 26:33, 35, NIV).

Something about Jesus' presence and the company of fellow believers gave Peter courage. Like Peter, we need the strength and encouragement that come from gathering regularly with the believers so that we may go out as Christ's representatives to stand lovingly as witnesses, leaven, and catalysts.

**Prayer:** *Let me today, Lord, determine always to stand up for you. Amen.*

⳨Superintendent, Big Spring District, Northwest Texas Conference, The United Methodist Church.

**Tuesday, May 10**                          Read Acts 1:15-17.

*Standing up for the scripture*

Peter stood up for the scripture. "Peter stood up . . . and said, . . . 'The Scripture had to be fulfilled'" (Acts 1:15-16, NIV).

In the early days in the United States, church members were taught to give every person a fair hearing but to weigh what the person said against what the Bible said. When I enrolled in seminary as a young minister, an older minister friend advised me, "Check out what you hear against what the Bible says, and when they differ, go with what the Bible teaches. It will be here long after others have gone."

John Wesley taught that we should base every decision in life on what we call the quadrilateral. What does scripture say? What do we learn from tradition? What do we learn by reason? What do we learn by experience?

We need a foundation on which we can stand. Christ is the chief cornerstone of the church; we are the stones, the parts, all aligned with him. But the foundation is scripture, the written word of God.

The Bible reveals God, reveals self as we are and self as we can be, reveals our mission in life, and reveals Christ's promise of his presence with direction and power for living.

There is a great hunger today for biblical truth, for a word from God. All sorts of voices are crying, "This is the way. This is the truth." We need to respond, "What does the Bible say?"

**Prayer:** *"Your word is a lamp to my feet and a light to my path." (Psalm 119:105.) Amen.*

**Wednesday, May 11**                    Read Acts 1:21-26.

*Standing up as witnesses*

When the disciples gathered following the resurrection of Jesus, Peter declared that another should be chosen to take the place of Judas to "become a witness with us to his resurrection." Notice the word *become*.

Just before his ascension, Jesus had gathered his disciples and told them, "You will receive power when the Holy Spirit has come upon you; and you will be my witnesses" (Acts 1:8). Notice the word *be*.

I believe that witnessing is the primary task of the Christian. We witness in many ways—with our words, our attitudes, our deeds; with our lifestyle, which includes where we place our priorities. We witness not only with our actions but with our reactions.

I have asked many persons, "Who influenced you to follow Christ?" I have received many answers: "my parents," "my Sunday school teacher," "a high school teacher," "a spouse," "a child," "a friend." The answer to the question, "How did they influence you?" is almost always the same: "They cared about me."

Paul wrote to the Ephesians, "We are God's handiwork, created in Christ Jesus to devote ourselves to the good deeds for which God has designed us" (Eph. 2:10, NEB). We are his witnesses, his handiwork, his examples.

Years ago, in Montebello, California, I heard the Reverend Leslie Ross tell his congregation, "You may leave this building, but you can never leave this church; because where you are, there the church is."

**Prayer:** *Dear Jesus, may my life as well as my lips draw persons to love, trust, follow, and serve you. Amen.*

**Thursday, May 12**     Read Luke 24:44-53; Acts 1:1-11.

*Standing up with a blessing*

After Jesus had commissioned his followers to become his witnesses and promised that they would receive the power needed to become witnesses (Acts 1:8), he led them out to Bethany "and lifting up his hands, he blessed them. While he was blessing them, he withdrew from them and was carried up into heaven" (Luke 24:50-51). Luke then tells us that they worshiped him and returned to Jerusalem with great joy and were continually in the Temple blessing God.

Ask people what they want out of life, and you will get many answers: security, health, family, but the bottom line is happiness. When we ask God to bless us, we are asking God to make us happy.

Happiness comes not in personal power or possessions but in being fulfilled. Is not the knowledge and experience of being a child of God the highest fulfillment? As a child of God, we find ourselves in the center of God's will and approval along with the promise of God's continuing presence.

Happiness begins in a relationship of mutual love and trust and extends in our being a blessing to everyone we meet. God's blessing brings out the best in us. Our blessing of others brings out the best in them.

A great Christian layman, Harry Denman, used to pray, "O God, help me to love all persons redemptively." Bringing out the best is redemptive love, both God's and ours.

**Prayer:** *O God, heavenly Father, thank you for your blessing. Help me now, this day, and every day, to be a blessing. Amen.*

**Friday, May 13**                                    Read Psalm 1.

*Standing up with character*

Character begins with the heart, the motives, the attitude. Character is first being, then doing.

Today's psalm tells how we develop godly character. The psalm contrasts the godly with the ungodly person.

Persons who are blessed, or happy, who know the favor, the protection, and the joy of the Lord delight in obedience to God's word and ways.

They do not "follow the advice of the wicked, or take the path that sinners tread, or sit in the seat of scoffers." Or as we might say, they avoid listening to and following the advice of those whose intentions are dishonorable and those who are cynical and skeptical about the godly life.

Affirmatively, godly persons know the law (the ways) of God and live in the awareness of that law. Laws are intended to set free, not restrict; to protect, not harm.

To follow the advice given in Psalm 1 is to be like a tree planted by the river, which in times of drought can sink its roots deep into the soil, draw moisture, and produce fruit.

Godly character is the same under all circumstances. It is dependable. It stands up to scrutiny. It brings peace of mind and soul. It attracts confidence. And it results in happiness.

Ask persons to name someone who has had a positive, profound influence upon them and then tell why. Almost without exception, they will name persons not necessarily of wealth and power but of character and integrity.

**Prayer:** *O God, eternal God, I delight in knowing and living according to your will. "To be happy in Jesus, . . . [is] to trust and obey."* * *Amen.*

*From the hymn "Trust and Obey" by John H. Sammis.

**Saturday, May 14** Read 1 John 5:9-13.

*Standing up with assurance*

Verse 13 provides the key phrase in this passage, "To you who believe in the name of the Son of God, so that you may know that you have eternal life." What is the secret of assurance? It is believing in the name (character, person) of the Son of God.

We have the assurance of history—the facts of Jesus' life, death, and resurrection, brought to us through preaching and human testimony. We have the assurance of God's Spirit speaking affirmation to our own heart. We have the assurance of faith—believing, accepting, acting on.

Christian assurance is a result of our accepting Jesus as the Son of God, receiving him as the Lord of our lives, and living a life that acknowledges and reflects Jesus' place in our lives. All is tied to the person of Jesus and our relationship with him.

For this reason we study scripture, the written word of God, so that we might know Jesus, the living Word of God. Life is in the Son. We place our faith in a Person, not a doctrine. The more we know about Jesus, the more we know about God. And the more we know Jesus, the more we know God.

Years ago I read this statement: "The center of our faith is set, but the circumference is not. The aim of Christian living is to relate the ever-expanding edges to the center—the person of Jesus Christ." We do this with the confidence that comes from the assurance that Jesus is who God says he is and that believing in him, we can be all that Jesus says we can be.

**Prayer:** *I believe, Lord, I believe. Today I act on this faith—today and every tomorrow. Amen and amen.*

**Sunday, May 15**                    Read John 17:6-19.

*Standing up in prayer*

John 17 is often called the high priestly prayer. It is Jesus' last prayer before his betrayal, arrest, and crucifixion.

In this prayer he prays for himself (vv. 1-5); he prays for his disciples (vv. 6-19); and he prays for his church, "those who will believe in me" (vv. 20-26).

Here we focus on Jesus' prayer for his disciples. Jesus asks not for their material comfort but rather for protection for them in a hostile world. He prays that they will live in the same quality of unity that he himself experiences with God (v. 11), that they will be filled with joy in spite of the world's treatment (v. 13), that they will be kept from evil power (v. 15), and that they may be made pure and holy by the truth (v. 17).

We feel the strength and power that come from personal prayer. We feel the strength and power that come from the prayers of our loved ones and friends. We feel the strength and power that come from corporate prayer. Think of how much strength and power come from Jesus' prayers for us. Think of the comfort of knowing that Jesus the Christ prays for us and calls us God's gift to him.

We can face any temptation, any struggle, any conflict with that knowledge. His presence is within us, offering all the power we need to face the demands of each moment.

As God sent Jesus into the world, so he sends us (v. 18), and we go "standing up . . . in prayer."

**Prayer:** *Thank you, Jesus, for praying for me. Now send me forth on missions of love. In your name. Amen.*

## THE WONDER OF THE SPIRIT

May 16–22, 1994            **Joe A. Harding**✜
**Monday, May 16**           Read Psalm 104:24-34.

Suppose you could meet someone who loves you very much, someone who prayed for you before you were born and who has prayed for you and helped you every day of your life. Suppose you could meet someone who draws you much closer to Jesus Christ, who could give a continuing sense of God's presence. Would you be interested? Suppose this person was very shy and never talked about self, but spoke of Jesus and God and God's creation. Suppose you could meet someone who could give you lasting love, joy, peace, patience, and self-control. Suppose this person could transform your church and help your friends and family. Interested? Suppose this person could give you new energy and hope—even a new life! Of course you know I mean the Holy Spirit! What an adventure awaits us these next few days as we consider the Spirit's work.

We begin with the Old Testament. Psalm 104 is a magnificent psalm of gratitude and praise. In your imagination, picture someone standing on a beautiful hilltop looking in every direction and saying, "O LORD, how manifold are your works!" Take a deep breath—relax, slowly release the air. Repeat. Now place yourself on that hilltop. How did the beauty happen? The psalmist affirms, "When you send forth your spirit, they are created; and you renew the face of the ground."

**Prayer:** *"I will sing praise to the LORD as long as I live; I will sing praise to my God while I have being." Amen. (Psalm 104:33.) Affirm this text many times today.*

---

✜Director of VISION 2000, General Board of Discipleship, The United Methodist Church; Distinguished Evangelist (UMC); clergy member of the Pacific Northwest Conference, Richland, Washington.

**Tuesday, May 17**                    Read Romans 8:1-27.

Romans 8 is one of the most inspiring and helpful sections of the New Testament. In particular, it enlightens our meditations upon the Holy Spirit.

Paul makes it clear that it is hard to draw sharp lines among the persons of the Trinity. Paul uses the words *Spirit* (Holy Spirit), *Spirit of God*, and *Spirit of Christ* interchangeably. The Spirit's identity and work is mysterious and wondrous. The Spirit of God raised Jesus from the dead. That same Spirit gives life to our mortal bodies. The Spirit has resurrection power!

The Spirit is the inner witness to our identity as children of God and fellow heirs with God (8:16-17). As new creations in Christ we manifest the first fruits of the Spirit (8:23).

Most amazing of all, Paul affirms the Spirit's assistance in our spiritual formation. The Spirit is our prayer partner! "Likewise the Spirit helps us in our weakness; for we do not know how to pray as we ought, but that very Spirit intercedes with sighs too deep for words. And God, who searches the heart, knows what is the mind of the Spirit, because the Spirit intercedes for the saints according to the will of God." What a wonderful affirmation of the wonder of God's grace. For the next seven days, as part of your prayer time, simply relax and invite the Holy Spirit to search your mind and to pray for needs in ways that you may not even recognize.

**Prayer:** *Holy Spirit, thank you for making Jesus real to me, for guiding my life and creating concern for God's purpose and plan. Thank you for your prayers and love. Amen.*

**Wednesday, May 18**                    Read John 15:26-27.

In the Gospel of John, Jesus speaks of the Spirit as counselor (RSV). The Greek word is *parakletos*. The word has been translated "advocate," "comforter," "helper," "counselor." The word suggests one who stands beside a person in need, perhaps in a legal setting for strength, comfort, direction, and reassurance. In a sense, *parakletos* brings *paraklesis*. *Paraklesis* is translated twelve times into English as "comfort," twice translated as "consolation," six times translated as "encouragement," five times translated as "exhortation." The theme of personal help is consistent.

It is clear that God, through the Spirit, seeks to build up and encourage the receptive disciple for ministry in the world.

The Spirit gives confidence to the believer as the Spirit is a witness to Jesus Christ. Paul expresses a parallel thought when he writes to the Corinthians. God has given us the Spirit in our hearts as a guarantee (2 Cor. 1:22). Ephesians also speaks of the Spirit as the guarantee of our inheritance (Eph. 1:13-14).

The Spirit brings assurance, which overcomes all the uncertainties of life. Wesley demonstrates the power of this assurance to change life. "I felt my heart strangely warmed. And an assurance was given me, that he had taken away *my* sins, even *mine*" (John Wesley's *Journal*, May 14, 1738).

**Prayer:** *May my heart be open to your Spirit, O God, to receive the assurance that builds strength for service. Amen.*

**Thursday, May 19**                    Read John 16:4*b*-15.

This text from the Gospel of John has its setting in the Upper Room in Jerusalem. It is the night before Jesus' crucifixion. Feet have been washed, bread has been broken, the cup has been shared. Jesus now speaks words to prepare the disciples for the shattering loss they will experience. Jesus tells puzzled followers it is to their advantage that he go away. Only then will *parakletos,* the Counselor, come.

The Spirit will continue the disturbing ministry of Jesus. The Spirit will convince the world of sin, of righteousness, and of judgment. These themes are unpleasant for most of us. It is clear the Spirit has not come to make us feel good but to make us good. We must face the realities of human sin and the certainty of God's righteousness and judgment. Without this work of the Spirit mortals could be pleasant, smiling destroyers of human life and creation itself. The work of the Spirit brings repentance and changed lives.

It is reported that a Pentecostal grandmother said to her grandchildren, "It is not how high you jump or how loud you shout. It is what you do when you come down that really matters!" The Spirit's guidance is not just for theological truth but also for the hard realities of daily living.

Above all else, the Spirit glorifies Jesus—not gifts or experience. Finally, Jesus gives assurance that we can face anything with good courage, because we know the victory has been won already (John 16:33).

**Prayer:** *O God, let me live today expecting to receive your guidance in every area of my life. Amen.*

**Friday, May 20**                                    Read Acts 2:1-13.

Acts 2 is one of the most important and inspiring chapters of the Bible. It is our birthday story. Read the words with anticipation and joy.

*Pentecost* is a Greek term for the Jewish Feast of Weeks, which fell on the fiftieth day after the festival of the barley sheaf in Passover.

Pentecost was one of the great days of the Jewish liturgical calendar. People from all over the ancient world filled Jerusalem. The followers of Jesus were all together in one place—obeying Jesus' word to wait in Jerusalem for the Spirit.

A series of powerful word clues begins with Acts 2:2. The word *suddenly* bothers many people. We prefer words like *gradually*, *slowly*, *annually*, and *quadrennially*. *Suddenly* suggests something not in the bulletin. *Suddenly* suggests the action of God acting in God's time. This idea is reinforced by "the rush of a violent wind." This sound must have made the disciples think of Ezekiel 37 and the vision of the moving of God's *ruach* (breath) to give life to a defeated army. Perhaps the disciples recalled the great words of Ezekiel 37:14: "I will put my spirit within you, and you shall live."

"Tongues, as of fire, appeared among them, and a tongue rested on each of them." God's spirit broke the barriers of distance and privilege. The fire symbol of God's presence had always been remote and distant. Through the Spirit, the fire was present over each disciple's head! What a candlelight service!

"All of them were filled with the Holy Spirit and began to speak in other languages, as the Spirit gave them ability." The Spirit reverses the separation of languages brought about at the Tower of Babel (Gen. 11:1-9). A new community is created and empowered to continue the presence and ministry of Jesus.

**Prayer:** *Breathe on me, breath of God. Amen.*

**Saturday, May 21**                    Read Acts 2:14-21.

We must hear Peter's message on the Day of Pentecost against the discounting laughter brought by the mocking statement, "They are filled with new wine" (v. 13). That was the cynical explanation of the amazing joy and enthusiasm of the people. Peter immediately set the Day of Pentecost in its proper place as the fulfillment of God's promises.

Notice the inclusiveness of Joel's language. God's Spirit is poured out not upon some but upon *all* flesh. The word *flesh*, "sarx," is a very earthy term.

Notice that "daughters shall prophesy." Not only is sexism inappropriate in the age of the Spirit, so is ageism. No one is to be put down because he or she is too old or too young. Some dreams and visions are given to both young and old.

Class and racial barriers are now broken as we are reminded that we should hear the clear word of God from "slaves, both men and women." We must listen for God's word to the poor and oppressed.

The purpose of the Spirit's outpouring is not to create "goose bumps" in Christians or to create a separate elitist group but to enable the preaching of Jesus Christ with such power that salvation (*soteria*, "healing") is made available to every person. In Jesus Christ a new creation appears! (2 Cor. 5:17).

**Prayer:** *Into our hearts, come into our hearts, Lord Jesus. Come in today, come in to stay. Come into our hearts, Lord Jesus.\* Amen.*

---

\*Based on the song "Into My Heart," by Harry D. Clarke. Copyright © 1924. Renewed 1952 by Hope Publishing Co., Carol Stream, IL. All rights reserved.

**Sunday, May 22**                          Read Acts 2:41-47.

What happened on the Day of Pentecost when Peter finished preaching? Some opportunity for response must have been given. Luke does not say, "So those who received his [Peter's] word went home and continued life as usual." No! Luke says, "Those who welcomed his message were baptized, and that day about three thousand souls were added." Is it too shocking to suggest that Peter gave some kind of invitation? The response of three thousand persons reveals a powerful and positive response!

The response continued, "And day by day the Lord added to their number those who were being saved."

Is it embarrassing to observe that the early church grew? Growth was expected. Acts 3 tells of the healing of a lame man who begged by the "Beautiful Gate" of the Temple. His "walking and leaping and praising God" (3:8) attracted a large crowd in the Temple. Peter again preached the message of salvation in Jesus Christ. Now the number of persons responding surpassed Pentecost by 2,000! Before long, "The number of the disciples increased greatly in Jerusalem" (6:7).

Growth in numbers was accompanied by faithfulness in study, worship, prayer, and fellowship (see Acts 2:42). The atmosphere of joyous, expectant praise was present with the people. Can you picture your congregation as a modern, dynamic, caring, outreaching fellowship? Visualize joyous growth.

**Prayer:** *Loving God, create in our hearts a desire to be faithful disciples. Amen.*

## LOVED, FORGIVEN, AND FREED

May 23–29, 1994                    **Michael J. O'Donnell✚**
**Monday, May 23**                    Read Isaiah 6:1-8.

When we compare ourselves to the power and majesty of God, we pale in comparison. We are overwhelmed by God's power. We are even more easily overwhelmed by the scope of the problems in the world today.

This is the scene that opened before Isaiah. He beheld the glory of the Lord and his own unworthiness in the light of that glory. Isaiah knew his limitations. He knew that he had sinned and fallen short of God's expectations. He felt lost.

And yet he was open to the intervention of the Lord. God used divine power to remove Isaiah's sin from him. Having been cleansed of his "spirit dirt," Isaiah then answered the summons to do the Lord's work.

Too often we want to be relieved of our sins. We want a clean record. But having received that, we fall back into our old ways. God wants us to use our spiritual cleanliness as a beginning point of service. What good is it to be freed from our sins if we fail to let go of them?

Forgiveness is not only freedom from our past; it is also freedom for our future. When we entrust ourselves to God for that future, we will never be disappointed.

**Suggestion for meditation:** *What sins, hurts, or behaviors do you hold on to that impede your growth as a servant of God?*

✚Senior pastor, Christ United Methodist Church, Akron, Ohio; Abbot of the Order of St. Luke; editor, *Sacramental Life*.

**Tuesday, May 24**                    Read Psalm 29.

We do not use the word *ascribe* much these days. In the context of this psalm, it simply means, "Give the Lord what the Lord is due." All that the human eye can see is of God. God's divinity permeates all of creation—the mountains, the seas, the trees, the deserts, the inhabitants of the earth.

The human mind tries to conjure up images of God that allow us to understand the personal relationship God has with us. A common image is God as a white-bearded old man with either gentle or fierce eyes (depending on how one feels about the state of one's soul). While we freely admit that we know this is not how God looks, many refuse to give up on the image, because it works for them.

When I sit in my cabin in the woods overlooking the mountains, God becomes quite real to me. I find myself "ascribing to the Lord." Usually it comes out more like, "God, you do good work!" for I am overwhelmed by the majesty, the beauty, and the vastness of God's creative love.

But the thing that really overwhelms me is that the God who created all this beauty not only created me but loves me. It is more than I can comprehend. That is when the old images come back to my mind's eye, for how else can I understand it? Then I remember Jesus. "If you know me, you will know my Father also" (John 14:7).

Yes, God, who built mountains and trees out of nothing, has also created me and raised me out of nothingness into something loved.

**Prayer:** *O God of majesty and beauty, you have formed the world to your liking and have given it life. Thank you for your many gifts to us. Amen.*

**Wednesday, May 25**                    Read John 3:1-18.

Jesus had a knack for seeing into the soul of individuals and telling them what they needed to do in order to be faithful. Nicodemus had been raised as a religious leader. His primary source of wisdom and knowledge of God was through the Torah. He came inquiring of this vagabond rabbi who seemed to be teaching from a different perspective. Nicodemus was probably as confused as parents were several years ago when the new math was introduced. It seemed to make sense, but it went against all they had learned.

When Nicodemus spoke, Jesus saw past his words and into his soul. He saw not only Nicodemus but the whole religious community locked in a mind-set that couldn't comprehend the truths that Jesus knew. Since Nicodemus had grown up in this tradition, Jesus told him that in order to understand and receive the benefits that God has to offer, he must undergo such a radical change that it could be likened to being born all over again.

At birth, Nicodemus was born into the temporal world with its understandings, its traditions, its viewpoint. But if Nicodemus was to be part of the reign of God that Jesus was teaching, he must forsake all that he carried to this evening meeting.

When we come before the Lord, we bring with us all that we are. In order to receive the multitude of blessings that is offered to us, we must be willing to relinquish all that is detrimental to us. God fills the empty spaces with grace, love, and power.

**Suggestion for meditation:** *What is it that I refuse to give up but know I must in order to make room in my heart for the Lord?*

**Thursday, May 26**                    Read John 3:9-17.

What great secret did Jesus know that transformed the Torah's understanding of God to this new radical thinking? For hundreds of years, the Law had been their way of life, their connecting point with God. When they were faithful to the covenant through obedience to the Law, God looked kindly upon them. When they became unfaithful, God used justice, and finally, mercy.

The mercy that always followed harsh judgments is a key to understanding God. It explains why God would not just give up on the people. The Gospel writer John sees the heart of God and describes it, "For God so loved the world that he gave his only Son, so that everyone who believes in him may not perish but may have eternal life."

God's love for the whole world, and humanity in particular, is the reason behind God's mercy. God cannot give up on us because God loves us so much. No matter how badly we mess up, no matter how often we let God and ourselves down, no matter how miserable we make ourselves and others, God still loves us. We may have to suffer the consequences of our sins, but one consequence that will never happen is God's ceasing to love us.

This is not license to do whatever we want. It is a path past our guilt and into the realm of feeling God's presence with us again.

**Prayer:** *O God, who loves me even when I don't deserve it, enter my heart anew today that I might become all you are calling me to be. Amen.*

**Friday, May 27**                    Read Romans 8:12-15*a*.

For Paul, the beginning of the Christian life was putting behind the worldly life, which he called "life according to the flesh." When our thoughts and actions are governed by the things of this world, we condemn ourselves to failure. It is only when we put on the Spirit that we truly come alive.

We do not leave this world; we simply view the world through God's eyes as empowered by the Holy Spirit. The world is still very much present with us. It still overflows with anxieties and problems. But it no longer overwhelms us. Now we see beyond the everyday pettiness around which so much revolves. We see the freedom that Christ offers us.

This freedom is not tied down by our past. It is freedom to receive the power of God, freedom to face the future in hope. Hope is not merely wishful thinking. Rather, it is confidence that God, who created the heavens and the earth, has a handle on how it will finally work out.

God chooses us to help work out that future. When we live "according to the flesh," we stymie the plan. When we live according to the Spirit, we help expedite that future. When we live in the Spirit, we can boldly say, as Isaiah did, "Here am I; send me!"(Is. 6:8)

When we live in the Spirit, we have nothing to fear.

**Prayer:** *Grant me courage, O God, to put aside my pride and personal desires that I might live in your Spirit through Jesus Christ. Amen.*

**Saturday, May 28**                    Read Romans 8:15*b*-17.

God depends on all of us to do our part to make God's plan come true. It will happen with or without us. To live as Spirit people means that our foremost desire is to do God's will. But to do God's will means that we must mold our will to God's. Usually we try it the other way around. When we do that, we lose every time.

The key is to remember that we are in a relationship with God. We are God's children. We have been promised a God-filled future. This is God's will for us. It is also what we ultimately want from God. So what's the problem?

The problem is that we still cling to what we can see. We want instant gratification, instant answers, instant results. The vagueness of God's promises fills us with hesitation—not that it won't happen—just that this other thing is happening right now, and we find it easier to respond to the immediate situation.

The trick is that we *do* need to respond to the immediate situation, but we need to respond through the eyes of the Spirit, rather than the eyes of human expectation. Only then can we see how we are to respond in a manner that is faithful to God. And sometimes that response seems foolish by human standards.

If it seems foolish, so what? Jesus set a good example of foolishness and suffered for it. The result? He has been glorified by God. And when we respond in the same spirit, that is our inheritance as well.

**Prayer:** *Teach me your ways, O Lord, that all I say and do today might bring my earthly world closer to your kingdom, by the power of your Holy Spirit. Amen.*

**Sunday, May 29**                    Read Romans 8:12-17.

We have seen the God of the Law, the God of freedom, the God of mercy and grace, the God who offers us new life and the power to live it. We have God the creator, who formed the earth, its mountains and streams. Our God is the one who sits on the throne of heaven while angels stand singing, "Holy, holy, holy, Lord God of hosts." Yet this is the same God who came to us through Jesus to be among us.

God did this because God loves the world, God's own creation, so much. This is a good day to get lost in the wonderful mystery of God. As you reflect on God's love for you and all the world, pause and give thanks for God's concern for you.

**Prayer:** *Help us, O God, to see beyond our limited words and images to the fullness of your glory, through Jesus Christ our Lord. Amen.*

# GOD'S WAYS ARE NOT OUR WAYS

May 30–June 5, 1994 **D. S. Dharmapalan✢**
**Monday, May 30** Read 1 Samuel 8:4-9.

Today's passage suggests that the establishment of a monarchy in Israel was an act of rebellion against God. Until that time, a theocratic form of rule under such charismatic judges as Samuel was an established norm. Certain judges, however, such as the sons of Samuel, were beginning to corrupt this form of rule (v. 3) by perverting justice for their own benefit.

The elders' demand for a king seemed rather legitimate— except that, according to the passage, it would leave God out. However, later in First Samuel 9:16, we read that God commands Samuel to "anoint" Saul as ruler over Israel. Perhaps this may seem a contradiction. We'll realize later that it is not so.

It is easy for those of us in positions of power, when confronted by opposition, to be tempted to abuse God's words to Samuel by quoting verse 7. We have to remember that we are conditioned by our own backgrounds and lacking proper information and experience. Further, we may have certain personal ambitions, along with hidden agendas of our own, that often confuse the purposes of God for us.

Our prayers should be for humility to allow the ways of God to take place in our lives. When we do that, we may be pleasantly surprised at the results; we will know that God's ways are not our ways and that our thoughts are not God's thoughts.

**Prayer:** *Dear Lord, free us from the pride of position, and give us a spirit of humility that will enable you to work out your purposes in our lives. Through Jesus Christ our Lord. Amen.*

✢Pastor, Wesley United Methodist Church, Dorchester, Massachusetts.

**Tuesday, May 31** Read 1 Samuel 8:10-22.

Here God is not trying to say to Samuel, "Let the people have their way." Instead, God is forewarning the people of Israel through Samuel about the consequences of having a king rule over them in place of the judges. Even though the people were being granted their request, God still wanted to provide a last chance for them to change their minds (vv. 11-18).

Sometimes our attempts to override the ways of God do not leave us necessarily to our own devices. More often, God seems to intervene to help us understand the mistakes of our ways, just as God was doing with the Israelites.

Our tendency to view decisions related to certain human situations purely in terms of personal benefits is nothing new. It happened then. The Israelites were naively convinced of the benefits of having a king. They failed to see the downside. There is always pain involved in having God intervene to let us know the long-term implications of our actions. However, when God does that, it is always done with a deep love and sincere concern for our well-being.

Like the Israelites, many times we want to live and act as others do, to make the compromises others make (v. 5). But God seems not to give up on us in spite of the compromises we make with the world. God seems always to turn our compromises with the world to the realization of God's purposes in our lives.

What we need to do here is to find out what God's will is and consider how we may reconcile our will with those purposes. That certainly is not going to be easy. Samuel struggled to do so, many saints of yore have struggled to do so, and so must we if we are to realize our spiritual destiny.

**Prayer:** *We thank you, dear Lord, that when we heed your bidding, you help us to make your will our own. Grant this grace, we pray, that we may fulfill your purpose in our lives. Through Jesus Christ our Lord. Amen.*

**Wednesday, June 1**                    Read Psalm 138:1-8.

One way to reconcile our wills with God's will is through worship. Worship connects us to God and God to us in a very special way.

Psalm 138 sums this up in the most fascinating way. The psalmist moves from a personal confession of praise (vv. 1-3) to a vision of a universal praise (vv. 4-6), and then ends with a sense of confidence in the divine protection (vv. 7-8). The progression of this psalm helps us understand worship that can lead to a "connection" between God and us.

Seeking to reconcile our wills with God's will requires great humility on our part. Why do our prayers often fail to receive an immediate answer from God? Perhaps we do not pray with humility as much as we should.

Let us be honest. Often we hesitate to "ask" because the answer may not be what we expected. Therefore, our prayers become generic in nature. Our prayers do not invite or demand answers. We need to pray expecting answers.

Another aspect we see in this psalm is the greatness of the God whom we worship; "though the LORD is high, he regards the lowly" (v. 6). This gives us confidence, the psalmist implies, to draw near to God just as we are; to understand the will of God, and to do God's will to our utmost.

The act of worship also helps to renew our spirits, that we may experience God's utmost in keeping covenant with us. It is this that ultimately reflects God's profound kindness and enduring love toward us (v. 8).

**Prayer:** *Give us a heart to praise you, O God, that we may be set free from the bondage of sin and death, so that with humility and obedience we may fulfill your perfect will. Through Jesus Christ our Lord. Amen.*

**Thursday, June 2**          Read 2 Corinthians 4:13-15.

To allow God's ways to become our very own, we must be willing to have the courage and the faithfulness of our Lord. Paul acknowledges this as he quotes Psalm 116:10. He seems also to accept the inexorable law of Christian living: "No cross, no crown!"

The great Hoover (Boulder) Dam in Nevada, when completed, brought in the much-needed irrigation and fertility to an area that was virtually a desert. At the time of its construction, accidents took the lives of many workers. On completion of the dam, a plaque was placed at the site with the names of those who had died. The inscription reads, "These died that the desert might rejoice and blossom as the rose."

Just consider this. Through the years of your life, you have faced many calamities and much sorrow. You have also endured illnesses and losses. You may have even experienced death in the family. Will you not agree that through it all, just as Paul says, you too have come to know the Lord better? And will you not agree that by the grace of God, your spirit has been renewed? One of the places God meets us is in the difficulties we experience in life. God knows how to turn those "crosses" into "crowns" of glory.

Moreover, when we make God's ways our own, then we, like Paul, become ambitious, in the best sense of the word, in wishing that God's grace may abound "to more and more people" (v. 15). Thereby, we not only learn to bear the trials of life ourselves, but we also learn to share the grace to help others bear their burdens.

**Prayer:** *Give us your spirit, O Lord, that our ambitions may be worthy of your grace. Help us to share our experience of your grace with others. Through the same Jesus Christ our Lord. Amen.*

**Friday, June 3**　　　　Read 2 Corinthians 4:16-18; 5:1.

Robert Louis Stevenson tells the story of an old garbage collector who lived and worked in the town dump. One day, someone who saw him at the dump expressed great concern about the man's working conditions. He replied, "Sir, he that has something ayont (beyond) needs never weary."

When we allow God's ways to take precedence in our lives, "we do not lose heart," because "our inner nature is being renewed everyday" (v. 16). Therefore, we do not grow weary. On the other hand, when we do not have faith in God or in a future life, when we know nothing about Jesus, when our world view is that of a mechanical process without any spiritual values, then the difficulties of daily living will influence our whole outlook. Then trouble will seem to be disaster; pain, calamity; and sorrow, tragedy.

For Paul, the experience with the living Christ transforms his entire being. This transformation brings meaning to Paul's statement in 4:18 and 5:1, a statement that immediately changes our whole understanding of this passage. Previously, Paul has been trying to place the "moment" in the context of "eternity" and the "visible" in the context of the "invisible." "We look not at what can be seen," he writes, "but at what cannot be seen." In other words, we no longer look forward to an "earthly house" but to "a house not made with hands, eternal in the heavens."

Because we look for that "ayont"—that beyond—we do not "grow weary in well-doing." That certainly is what gives us the confidence to follow the ways of our God.

**Prayer:** *Dear Lord, in this world of changes and chances, help us focus our lives on that which is eternal. Through Jesus Christ our Lord. Amen.*

**Saturday, June 4**                    Read Mark 3:20-30.

We can understand best the reason the Jewish scribes called Jesus names by reading Mark 1:23-27. They were convinced that Jesus' power came from the chief of demons. Belief in the power of demons was common in Jesus' time. Even to this day some Eastern religions advocate the beliefs that the only way anyone can vanquish the power of demons is by invoking the power of a greater demon and that illness is the result of demon possession.

In such a context, Jesus was trying to make the people understand that evil cannot destroy evil. "If Satan has risen up against himself and is divided," Jesus said, "he cannot stand." He would only come to naught.

In today's Western society, the reality of the power of evil has diminished greatly in our thinking. Often we are not even conscious of the evil because it hides behind the facades of modern lifestyle. As a result, we spend a lot of our time discussing the origin of evil and hardly any time dealing with the problem of evil. However, Jesus believed in vanquishing the powers of evil.

To do that which is pleasing in God's sight is to do that which works against evil. Invoking some other power or something else in this world to combat our temptations will not defeat evil. Jesus is saying to us that only God can help us face evil and combat it.

Jesus demonstrates to us that the struggle between good and evil is at the heart of the human life. He pleads with us to accept his ways for a life of joy and peace, here and now.

**Prayer:** *Lord Jesus, come now and bind all that is evil and undesirable in us that we may be set free to do your perfect will. Through Jesus Christ our Lord. Amen.*

**Sunday, June 5**                    Read Mark 3:31-35.

Jesus' purpose on earth was to do the will of his heavenly Father. Likewise, the ultimate goal for Christians is to do the will of God—in our day-to-day life, in the context of our family, in our work place, and in our church life. Especially, in the life of the church, where often doing the will of God is taken for granted, we need to ask ourselves whether we are really doing God's will. Are we following the ways of God by seeking to understand the purpose of God for us, being compassionate to all people, and leading persons to a deeper knowledge of Jesus Christ?

After all, the church is you and I. When we are doing these things, no other agendas will take precedence over the primary reason why we are the church.

If ultimately, in all the things we do, we do not seek to make the kingdom of God real here and now, our faith certainly is in vain. We may be called "crazy" for doing what we do, as they did with Jesus. We must remember that the call to Christian discipleship is also the call to experience spiritual tension. The supreme claim of the will of God transcends the restraining claim of those who are near and dear to us. We need the absolute conviction that, rather than being "crazy," we are the followers of Jesus Christ, who is the Way, the Truth, and the Life. No other foundation for an enduring world has been laid.

**Prayer:** *Dear Lord, help us be faithful to you in the face of ridicule from those we love. Through Jesus Christ our Lord. Amen.*

## To Be Led by God

June 6–12, 1994                                          Sally Dyck✢
Monday, June 6                          Read 1 Samuel 15:34–16:13.

God continually surprises us by choosing the unlikely ones. In a culture where the oldest son would be expected to be chosen king, God chose the youngest. Samuel almost chose Eliab for his comely appearance but listened to God who looks not on the outward appearance but on the heart.

We judge people by how they look and where they stand in our social scale. How often have I felt the sting of prejudice against women as ministers? How many times have I wished I were tall and weighed more than 105 pounds so I would not have to *begin* with a deficit of respect?

Can you imagine the comfort this scriptural precedent brings to anyone who does not measure up to outward standards of worthiness? Many can imagine all too well. Many know far better than I the limitations and the physical dangers of being judged by their race, color, social class, or other factors—many of them determined by birth.

God's chosen are many and diverse. While tempted at times to look upon society's favorites, let us be like Samuel, who trusted in God's pattern of choosing the unlikely ones whose hearts are turned toward God.

**Prayer:** *O God, help us to see others as you see them. Help us to do the things that make our hearts attractive to you. Amen.*

✢Pastor, Church of the Redeemer, Cleveland, Ohio.

**Tuesday, June 7**                                    Read Psalm 20.

Psalm 20 is like a letter interrupted in the midst of being written. Something big happens between verses 5 and 6. An enemy army surrounded the city of Jerusalem. How long would the people of Jerusalem be under siege, and what would be the outcome? The psalmist gives words of hope in verses 1-5.

A woman only twenty-eight weeks into her pregnancy with twins was crying in her hospital bed. She had been on bed rest for several weeks already with early contractions, but now her water had broken. She was fearful for her babies.

Well-wishers called and said, "Everything will be all right!" She nodded, but the words only made her feel worse. She knew that everything might not be all right. She knew too much; she was an ob-gyn doctor. As her pastor, I knew that she and the babies needed hope. How do you walk the fine line between "everything will be all right" and trusting God while you wait? Maybe that is hope: the narrow way in the midst of despair.

We prayed, and it could easily have been a reinterpretation of Psalm 20:1-5. "God, be with her and the babies in this time of distress. Send your help through the doctors and nurses. Surround her and the babies with your protecting care. Hear our prayer and prayers from around the world (her family was praying from Europe; his from the Caribbean). *Please* (we begged as the Israelites must have begged for victory) *let them be born strong and healthy.*"

What would happen now? When I left the room, she was trying to walk that fine line of hope.

**Prayer:** *O God, we live our lives between the times of waiting and seeking to "walk by faith and not by sight." Strengthen us for those times and help us to know your presence. Amen.*

**Wednesday, June 8**                    Read Psalm 20.

So much of life, too much for some, is lived between verses 5 and 6 of Psalm 20. For the woman who was pregnant with twins, the time between waiting in hope and finding out what would happen was almost four weeks. Through the miracles of medical science and faith, her babies had almost a month to gain weight and develop. Then she delivered two healthy babies.

Just as the Israelites could have boasted in chariots and horses—their modern technology—this new mother could have given all the credit to modern medicine. She gave it ample due, but she also gave credit to God. Once again her tears flowed, but this time they were in thanksgiving and praise to God.

God had granted her heart's desire. It is not her way to "shout for joy," as did the Israelites, but finally she laughed again after almost two years of battling infertility, the pain of a miscarriage, and a high-risk pregnancy.

Everything does not always turn out all right. In a similar situation a year before, I had buried a baby. Then as now, we called upon God to answer our prayer. Then as now, we felt God's presence with us. The outcomes were drastically different but God's presence was sure.

Through it all, all I know—but of this I am persuaded—God is with us in the fearful, tearful waiting. God is with us in the joyful or sad outcome. In the silent interruption between verses 5 and 6, where most of us live our lives, God is with us.

**Prayer:** *O God, thank you for your abiding presence in our lives. When our waiting turns into mourning, be ever near. When our waiting turns into a joyful morning, may praise spring from our hearts. Amen.*

**Thursday, June 9**                    Read 2 Corinthians 5:6-10.

The central theme along my journey of faith has been "to be of good courage." Courage is more than bravery in battle; courage is a virtue essential to Christian living. The English word *courage* stems from a word meaning "heart." The heart was considered to be the source of all emotional, intellectual, and spiritual energies in ancient thought. Courage is the mobilization of one's whole self to strive for good in the face of opposition, to be of "good heart."

My early Christian education was filled with the stories of the martyrs who courageously faced death for their faith. In order to fulfill one's calling, courage is necessary. We may not face the danger of death in our daily living, but we do face a multitude of threats in society that can kill our spirits and that threaten the good we seek in Christ Jesus.

Sexism, racism, and classism pervade our society. We need courage to resist their sin. We need courageous people of the faith who stand in opposition to society's systems—and sometimes even to the church—when violent blows are dealt against human equality.

Paul makes it very clear in verse 10 that we all stand in judgment according to the measure of courage that we show in living out our faith. As we live courageously, other Christian virtues blossom and grow. It requires hope to "walk by faith, not by sight." One can be courageous only if one is hopeful.

In a world that "just doesn't care," love is a courageous act. Loving those involved in sexism, racism, and classism, as well as loving the victims, necessitates the mobilization of one's self to do the good.

**Prayer:** *O God of grace and courage, who strengthens our heart for the good: encourage us, make us hopeful and loving in a world broken by sin. Amen.*

**Friday, June 10**                    Read Mark 4:30-34.

Speaking in parables may seem strange to us. Would it not have been better if Jesus had simply stated all his knowledge clearly and straightforwardly to his confused disciples? Our problem begins with what a parable is. A parable is a story that describes a truth or a comparison of two things, one of which is well-known in order to give insight into what is less familiar to the listener. Therefore, a parable is not in mysteriously coded language but in everyday language using ordinary experiences.

Parables were the primary way Jesus talked to his disciples because the stories and comparisons helped them to unlearn and relearn concepts about God. They saw with new eyes and heard with new ears. New images of the ways of God and the kingdom of God broke apart old ways of thinking, and their hearts and minds were challenged. It was through the parables that "he explained everything."

Many congregations enjoy good children's sermons because they are a form of the parable, or an object lesson. A good children's sermon describes something of God in light of a familiar object. A too lengthy or moralistic explanation of the comparison can be its downfall, but the simple comparison can provide new insight into the spiritual life.

Jesus seems to be encouraging his disciples to develop their own object lessons and parables from their own experiences. In this way, we learn to "theologize," that is, gain new understandings about God through what we know and see around us.

**Prayer:** *O God, creator of all that we see and know, help us to use our imaginations in such a way that we can come to understand what it is we do not readily see and know otherwise. Amen.*

173

**Saturday, June 11**                    Read Mark 4:26-32.

Gardening provides a needed experience for me each year: a reaffirmation of the Creator God. The garden in my backyard is an object lesson of faith, a "faith garden," if you will. Jesus compares the kingdom of God with the scattering of seeds on the ground and their stages of growth into maturity.

Planting seeds brings out the doubt in me. When I look at those dry, dead-looking seeds, I can hardly believe that much will come of them. The fact that a handful of seeds can produce more vegetables than a refrigerator, a freezer, and a storage shelf can hold is truly amazing! Perhaps it is not so much disbelief as a sense of awe at the abundance of God, the abundance that comes from sowing seeds.

Much of what we do in the church is akin to planting seeds. *How can this routine, mundane task possibly have anything to do with the kingdom of God?* we wonder. Our disbelief emerges when we forget the miracles and abundance of God. What seems like a small, insignificant act can become vital and essential in our own lives or in the lives of others.

It is through the faithful nurturing of small things that the great can happen. A phone call to a sick friend, a card to a shut-in, a few minutes to listen to a troubled teenager are all the small seeds that when sown produce an abundance of spiritual wealth in the recipients' hearts—and in our own. The mustard seed is very small, but it grows rapidly into a large bush. When we are doing small acts of kindness, we need to keep the vision of God's abundance in our minds.

**Prayer:** *Creator God, thank you for making me who I am because of small seeds sown in my life. Help me to believe in your abundance and thereby sow seeds of kindness and love every day. Amen.*

**Sunday, June 12**  Read 2 Corinthians 5:14-17.

If we slithered out of our skins periodically like a snake or walked out of our shells like a crustacean or burst forth from our cocoons like a butterfly, we might better understand what it means to be "in Christ" and a "new creation." Changing and growing are expected stages in the lives of God's creatures. These other creatures shed their outer coverings because the body inside has grown too big and is being restricted and confined. It is probably similar to wearing shoes that are too small for the feet.

When we open ourselves to the power, love, and grace of Christ, we also are expected to be growing inside in our spiritual lives. Like God's creatures, we grow in stages until periodically we emerge as new creations.

As we are growing in Christ, we shed our restricting, confining behaviors, attitudes, and habits. These are our shells, and they are what keep us from being all that God calls us to be. Slowly, often painfully, we must break out of them, leaving them behind.

When we leave our old shells and skins behind, we feel vulnerable and uncertain until we form new behaviors, attitudes, and habits to replace them. It takes time to learn the ways of a new creation. Bitterness, anger, guilt, and resentment are hard to shed. We get discouraged easily in our effort to live in Christ. We must remember that we will *always* be growing, that growth is a process we strive for until all "the old has passed away, [and] behold, the new has come."

**Prayer:** *O God, who is the same throughout the ages, give us the courage to change and grow throughout the various stages of our life and faith. Amen.*

June 13–19, 1994                        **Ron James**⁜
**Monday, June 13**              Read 1 Samuel 17:1*a*, 4-11.

*Giant Despair*

The theme of despair and deliverance connects the four scripture passages and seven meditations for this week. I use seven titles from *Pilgrim's Progress* to illustrate the theme.

The giant Despair imprisoned Pilgrim and kept him from his journey to the Celestial City. And the giant Goliath threatened the existence of Israel. The Philistines and Israelites were deadly enemies. What a picture the text paints: This huge man striding back and forth before Saul's army, sun blazing from his bronze armor, the shaft of his spear like a weaver's beam! He taunts Israel, his voice booming across the valley, "Who dares fight me?" No one responds, so invincible does he seem.

There are giants too in our lives, that paralyze us with fear and bring us to the point of despair. To despair, of course, is to lose hope. Criticism is one of the giants in our lives, undermining our confidence in self and in God's purpose for us. Failure is another, telling us we are nobody. Worry, sapping our vitality; grief, eroding our spirits; the depletion of the heart that comes in a broken relationship. Ah! There are enough giants who shout their taunt, "Where is your God?"

In Romans 7, Paul vividly describes the human struggle and asks what we all ask in a time of despair, "Who will rescue me?" (v. 24) Scripture provides an answer: God will raise up a deliverer—David, in our text, and a son of David for the world.

**Suggestion for meditation:** *What giants do I face in my life?*

⁜Retired Presbyterian pastor; free-lance writer, preacher, and retreat leader, Carbondale, Colorado.

**Tuesday, June 14**                    Read 1 Samuel 17:19-23, 32-49.

*The Slough of Despond*

Christian, determined to make his way from the City of Destruction to the Celestial City, falls into the Slough of Despond. It is a bog, a swamp; and loaded with his sins as he is, Christian begins to sink.

The army of Israel stood in despondent fear before the might of Goliath. The saying goes that it is darkest before the dawn. That is often the time when, at the end of our rope, God's deliverance surprises us. And what an unlikely source provided God's deliverance for Israel—a lad, a keeper of sheep. Young David faced Goliath with fuzz still on his cheeks and an innocent trust in God in his heart. Hearing the taunting of Goliath, he offers himself as Israel's champion. At first Saul rejects the offer as ridiculous. Then he listens and finally agrees. Perhaps something in the lad's passion, in his confidence in God, won Saul's consent.

So David goes to face the giant. He has no heavy armor, no great spear—only a sling and five smooth stones from the brook. The giant roars in disbelieving laughter, as David's sling begins to circle. Then the Philistine champion falls and the rest is history. David, a man after God's own heart, delivered his nation from defeat and despair.

No one escapes a sense of loss. Our own folly, hidden faults, a friend's betrayal, the loss of someone deeply loved, the failure of a dream, some seemingly senseless accident can cause us to sink in despair. In this time of loss, when we are at the end of our human resources, God will send deliverance. Wait for it. It will surely come. We are a resurrection people.

**Prayer:** *God of the darkness and the light, I rest in your sustaining grace. Amen.*

**Wednesday, June 15**                    Read Psalm 9:9-20.

*Apollyon*

Dragon-winged and fish-scaled, Apollyon is Christian's deadly adversary. Putting fear aside, Christian must strive against him, for in his resistance is the secret of his deliverance.

Our text sets a similar scene. Those who are beset by evil seek a place of security and deliverance. Verses 9-10 make a ringing affirmation: "The LORD is a stronghold for the oppressed." The psalms are the poetry of human experience. They are so intense in their personal appeal that we often fail to give them a broader reference. This psalm gives such a reference, for it speaks of the afflicted, the needy, and the poor, and faults "all the nations that forget God" in their oppression of others. It is this sense of God's solidarity with all the despairing on which our own solidarity with the oppressed rests. It is woven into the fabric of our faith, both in the Old Testament laws of mercy favoring the poor and the stranger, and in the compassion of Jesus who says, "Come to me, all you that are weary and are carrying heavy burdens, and I will give you rest" (Matt. 11:28).

Then the text makes an affirmation: God "is a stronghold for the oppressed." The affirmation rings true because it is written by one who feels the hand of oppression. The truth here is obvious: out of one's own anguish comes an identification with those who suffer. Because I feel my pain, I can feel yours as well. My anguish makes me a brother to you in your pain. My experience of God's deliverance in the midst of my pain gives my word weight and allows my help to reflect God's care for you and God's delivering mercy. The Christian calling rises out of God's deliverance, for it is always a call to work for the relief of the oppressed and despairing.

**Suggestion for meditation:** *Where is God leading me to help someone in trouble?*

**Thursday, June 16**                    Read Psalm 9:9-20.

*The Valley of the Shadow*

Bunyan, in *Pilgrim's Progress*, describes this valley as "a place also most strangely haunted with evil things."* "See what I suffer from those who hate me," says our text.

Many things in this text belong to the kingdom of death, things that tear life down. We feel the anguish as the psalmist speaks of the cry of the afflicted, the nations who forget God, the needy who are forgotten, the poor whose hope is perishing. Reading this text is like reading the newspaper; the suffering of the world is so deep and constant that it numbs our senses, and we must turn aside to save our sanity and faith. No wonder the writer appeals to God, "Be gracious to me . . . you are the one who lifts me up from the gates of death."

The remarkable thing about the text is not that evil prospers—nothing new there—but that the psalmist has such hope in God. Though pain and injustice abound, there is a moral order, there is a final court of justice, a compassionate God whose purposes shall prevail. But why is God so slow?

This wrestling with God is a hallmark of the psalms. "What are you doing?" the psalmist seems to say. And how can it not be so with the Christian as well? "When are you going to set things right?" is as genuine a prayer as I know. It is not an affront to God, since it is spoken by one who knows God's name and trusts God (v. 10). On the basis of that relationship, and with a compassionate longing for peace and justice, we plead for life and light in the valley of the shadow.

**Prayer:** *Help us, O God, for this is your world before it is ours. Stir up in us a passion to build and not destroy, to love and not harm. Amen.*

---

*John Bunyan, *The Pilgrim's Progress* (London: J.B. Lippincott Co., 1902), p. 345.

**Friday, June 17**                    Read 2 Corinthians 6:1-3.

*The Delectable Mountains*

Early in his journey, while far from the Celestial City, Christian is taken to the top of the Palace Beautiful and sees at a great distance the Delectable Mountains. They are beautiful with vineyards, fruit, fountains, and woods. That, he is told, is Immanuel's Land.

Today's classic scripture text points toward Immanuel's Land as well. The context is a warning to the Corinthian Christians lest they fail to pursue the journey of faith and discipleship, working together with Christ. Paul exhorts his beloved church with words that have been preached in ten thousand sermons: "See, now is the acceptable time; see, now is the day of salvation!"

Much of Christendom today has lost its sense of urgency. Light for our darkness, forgiveness for our erring behavior, a road marked "home" in the midst of all our wandering, a center of meaning, the embrace of God, "the inheritance of the saints in the light" (Col. 1:12)—all of this is gospel, news too good to keep. Christian preaching and teaching is more than information; it is urgent proclamation. Such urgency lies at the heart of the Christian gospel. "See, now is the acceptable time; see, now is the day of salvation." Don't delay!

Paul saw himself as the chief of sinners (1 Tim. 1:15). Most people in our culture do not. They obey the laws, give to charity, pay their taxes, love their children. On balance they are not bad people. Is there, then, a despair from which they need to be delivered? In the sense that every human heart is restless until it rests in God, yes. In the sense that our human years are prelude to that which is to come, yes!

**Suggestion for meditation:** *In what sense does my life mirror the gospel's urgency?*

**Saturday, June 18**                    Read 2 Corinthians 6:4-10.

*The Valley of Humiliation*

This passage is particularly relevant for all of us who, as Christ's followers, are also ministers to one another. Here Paul spells out the characteristics and conditions of faithful ministry. Few would find fault with his catalog of spiritual graces: purity, knowledge, patience, kindness, holiness of spirit, genuine love, truthful speech, and the power of God. Some might want to add one thing or another, but that's an impressive list! It indicates a spiritual maturity all could crave, a heart united to do God's will.

But nobody said it would be easy. Part of Paul's commending himself "in every way" to the Corinthian Christians is his endurance in suffering. The genuineness of his love for Jesus Christ and his commitment to the church of Christ is plain in the things he has suffered: afflictions, calamities, beatings, sleeplessness, hunger, to name a few. He bears in and on his body the scars of his discipleship. Such evidence is not easily discounted.

The literary quality of this passage is outstanding. Balanced antitheses and rhythmic cadence mark these verses as eloquent and beautiful. Paul's catalog of seven unforgettable truths beginning in verse 8 is classic: "We are treated as impostors and yet are true; as unknown, and yet are well known; as dying, and see we are alive; as punished, and yet not killed; as sorrowful, yet always rejoicing; as poor, yet making many rich; as having nothing, and yet possessing everything."

If one is given to emotional expression at all, that's a place to shout, "Hallelujah!" It rings clear as a silver bell with its truth. Though it can be a valley of humiliation and hardship, what a privilege to be in ministry! What a message to proclaim!

**Prayer:** *Calling and empowering God, I am grateful for the privilege of serving you. Amen.*

**Sunday, June 19**                    Read Mark 4:35-41.

*The River of Death*

If I were preaching a sermon on this remarkable text, I would alliterate it like this: storm, stress, stillness. I might even add "serenity" for the Christ who sleeps while the storm rages. Who could read such a text and not love it? What drama! What contrasts! What commentary on this man, Jesus!

Biblical scholars talk about the quick storms that rise on Galilee, something about the winds that spill down the slopes on either side, whipping the water into whitecaps. Being there once in a small boat, I was surprised at the expanse of water and remembered "the calming of the tempest."

As in most gospel narratives, the basic story is unadorned by detail. Jesus was in the boat, asleep. A great storm arose. The disciples awoke him and cried out their fear. He calmed the storm and rebuked their lack of faith. They were dumb with awe and murmured, "Who then is this, that even the wind and the sea obey him?"

With the waves mounting in intensity and the boat's beginning to take on water, the disciples are at the point of despair and cry out for deliverance. Incredulous that Jesus sleeps, in panic they wake him. They do not want to die. If anything is characteristic of a Christian view of mortality, it is an appeal to the calming presence of Christ when we are close to the river of death. We want to hear his word, "Peace! Be still!" and to know his presence leading us through that mystery to the Celestial City. That is how we commit our dead to eternity, always in the hope of the resurrection to eternal life made possible by Jesus Christ.

**Prayer:** *Lord Jesus Christ, resurrection and life, speak your calm to all my troubled seas. Amen.*

## BLESSED INTERRUPTIONS

June 20–26, 1994                Carolyn E. Johnson☩
**Monday, June 20**               Read Psalm 133.

*Interruptions that renew*

Rush! Rush! Rush! I had planned my daily activities down to the last second, and somehow each activity was taking far longer than I had expected. A meeting at work was full of the conflicts and turf battles that create negative energy. It was not shaping up to be the best day I had ever had. On leaving, I dashed to the bank, hoping for a quick stop with no lines. I was in a hurry! But the bank was full, and it seemed that others were as impatient as I.

Then it happened. A young woman, who I later learned was an employee on leave, came into the lobby with her infant daughter, only four days old. Several people left their desks to ooh and ah; and before long, we all had to look at the baby.

What a wonderful interruption! Strangers, who only a moment before had been isolated and impatient, were in common accord about this child. The coldness was replaced with a warmth and spirit that brought smiles. Perhaps this infant evoked memories of newborns in our own families, or perhaps she just brought the refreshing joy and hope that comes with seeing the opportunity afforded to new life. How soothing it was, this pleasant and blessed interruption! The day appeared a lot better. I was renewed.

God has a way of penetrating our being, interrupting our routine, and providing us with new insights that refresh, renew, restore, teach, and test our faith.

For these blessings, we are forevermore grateful.

**Prayer:** *Gracious God, may we slow down and look forward to your interruptions and greet them as blessings. Amen.*

☩President, Women's Division, General Board of Global Ministries of The United Methodist Church; researcher, Purdue University, West Lafayette, Indiana.

**Tuesday, June 21**                     Read 2 Samuel 1:1.

*Interruptions that bring peace*

How sweet their faces looked, these young teens who were taking our luncheon orders. Yet the life menus they had known were far different than the sweetness of their faces would have you believe: incest, molestation, rape—all manner of sexual abuse. These children, housed now in a residential child-care facility, were victims of dysfunctional, turbulent families. They were the victims of the worst of adult behavior, the victims of a war being waged in their very homes, victims of a destruction not of personal property but of spirit and personhood. This mission project was a resting stop, a needed interruption in the war that was being waged in their lives.

The scripture records David's return to Ziklag. This becomes interesting, because it was to Ziklag that he restored both property and people following its destruction (1 Sam. 30:1-31). Perhaps after the weariness of war and the long string of battles, David realized that peace is not when the fighting stops but when the restoration, the bringing back to life and wholeness, begins. Given that, it was important to rest in a place where restoration was more than a hope; it was a reality. As a community of faith, we watch too many children ravaged by war, drugs, abuse, neglect, poverty, hunger, and illness. For this hurting world, we have an opportunity to be a "stopping" place, an interruption that can bring peace and begin to restore wholeness to shattered lives. We have an opportunity through our individual mission projects to be faithful to the pledges we have made to care for children.

**Suggestion for meditation:** *Close your eyes and imagine a peaceful setting. Think of yourself as that setting—a place offering peace, security, restoration, and wholeness. Whom would you invite to your place? Who needs you?*

**Wednesday, June 22**                    Read Mark 5:25-34.

*Interruptions that teach*

Jigsaw puzzles can be great fun. Often you think you know exactly where a piece goes only to find that as the pieces come together you misunderstood that piece's position in the total picture. This woman thinks the robe of Jesus is the final answer; touching it will solve her problem. It seemed to work. The bleeding stopped; her body felt better. But was this the true lesson?

A friend was only twenty-four when the doctors told her a hysterectomy was necessary to relieve the pain she endured because of tumors. She was devastated. This young teacher loved children, and the dream of having her own was soon to be lost. She sought another opinion. The final advice was the same, but the process was different. Since it was not emergency surgery, the doctor told her to wait, to seek counseling, and to become mentally and spiritually ready to face the surgery, not with fear of dreams lost but with possibility. She did and was ready for the surgery. To her amazement, the surgery was no longer necessary. The tumors had gotten smaller, and the pain ceased.

Miracles do happen. For my friend, the miracle was not the physical healing but her strengthened faith that had allowed mind and spirit to accept new fulfillment. Her renewed faith brought peace and hope.

The woman in today's scripture learned the same lesson. Jesus did not let her slip away; she had reached out and now she must encounter his true message and lesson. Had she gone away, she might have assumed her healing was due only to his garment and thus put this miraculous event in the realm of magic. Instead, he made sure she understood that it was faith that healed her. The faith that caused her to come to Jesus was the first step; faith would bring the true healing, in mind and spirit as well as in the body. We have a role to play in the miraculous—it is our faith that both brings us to Jesus and helps to heal us.

**Prayer:** *God, help us to know the Christ who interrupted this world with a lesson of faith and salvation. Amen.*

185

**Thursday, June 23**                   Read Mark 5:21-24, 35-43.

*Interruptions that teach trust*

Jesus was constantly healing and performing miracles. Surely that is what prompted Jairus to ask for his help in the healing of his daughter. Yet before they could get there, Jesus was interrupted by the woman who needed healing from her bleeding. He was interrupted, yet that interruption was only another example of his power to heal. Nevertheless, some members of Jairus's household found death final. They did not want Jairus to trouble the teacher any longer. After all, death had come.

The entire account of this story is interrupted by a teaching lesson, yet that lesson did not seem to take hold. Christians often are challenged to use information gained in one aspect of our experience and bring it to new situations. This is what it means to trust in the power of God's word, to believe that God's miracles are not time-locked in history but are possible today.

It must have been very frustrating for Jesus to teach the same lesson again and again. Each healing brought a new lesson, a lesson that taught faith, and yet persons still distrusted the power of his word to heal. Do we trust God's word to heal and be there for us? We often ask for God's intervention when we pray, but do we think some final possibility exists beyond God's capability? That thinking lessens trust.

Because of their own disbelief, the people around Jesus continued to be amazed. We must learn to trust so that when blessed interruptions come, we recognize and accept them as God's wonderful power working in our midst.

**Prayer:** *Loving God, help us to place our trust in you and the power of your word. Amen.*

**Friday, June 24**                    Read 2 Corinthians 8:7-15.

*Interruptions that test sincerity*

"We interrupt this program for a special bulletin." How many times has such a bulletin interrupted our television viewing—the announcement of some aspect of news so important or a warning so vital that it requires an interruption of the regularly scheduled program? Occasionally, it is even good news. Christians have a special message for the world, one pronouncing "good news" and a living out of that message by sharing it with the world.

I often wonder about products that are recalled. A special announcement warns users that some flaw has been detected. For most consumers, the product is working perfectly well; the flaw has yet to create a problem, but the potential for trouble is there. The industry discovered the flaw through its quality control—testing and retesting products, making sure they maintain a standard of excellence, recalling them when they do not.

Christians sometimes think of giving as our product, yet this thinking can prove to have a hidden flaw if we consider giving our end point. Instead, giving is a way of being, a way of sharing. Its quality control test is that of sincerity and eagerness, of being willing to stay with a project or activity until it is finished and done well, and of maintaining a sense of eagerness throughout. No easy task! We must constantly remind ourselves that the focus is not the amount but the accompanying sincerity.

Quality control checks are blessed interruptions for the Christian. We stop to take stock, to evaluate, to test that we are what we hope. We monitor not just our end point but our journey.

**Devotional exercise:** *Devise a "quality control" test for yourself. Are you eager in your giving? Do you excel in sincerity? Write down ideas for an "improvement" plan.*

187

**Saturday, June 25**                    Read 2 Samuel 1:17-27.

*Interruptions that test love*

The melancholy words from the spiritual "Nobody knows the trouble I've seen. Nobody knows but Jesus" are a good example of the depth of pain and sorrow we experience while grieving. It is difficult to find words adequate enough to express one's loss. It seems impossible that anyone can really understand the emptiness, despair, even anger that we may be suffering. We often want the world to stop and be as sad as we are. We want some indication that the world does not just go on as if nothing had happened. Intellectually we know our experience may not be unique; but for the moment, grief becomes a self-centered, albeit necessary, state in handling the realization of death.

The death of Jonathan saddens David immensely. They were like brothers, secure in their love and respect for each other. Yet surely he is tested in love by the loss of Saul—Saul, the one who had loved him, mentored him, and who finally turned against him. David was in and out of Saul's favor. Thinking David had betrayed him, Saul chased David in war and tried to destroy him. Could David still love Saul despite all of this? Was he genuinely sorry that Saul was gone?

People who love each other may experience tension and changes in their relationship. These become tests of love. David still loved Saul despite all that had happened.

**Devotional exercise:** *Think of those persons with whom you may have had a breach in your relationship, either temporary or permanent. How did this test your love? Offer a prayer for their well-being and the well-being of all who may be experiencing relationship tensions.*

**Sunday, June 26**                    Read Psalm 133.

*Interruptions that refresh and soothe*

We are often news obsessed, saturated with dose after dose of bad news. Yet from time to time, a glimpse of the good breaks through—a special act of generosity or a coming together in adversity despite and across racial and social lines, for example. These special acts of unity often cannot be expressed in words alone; rather, they require a special kind of imagery. Understanding this need, the psalmist describes the unity of brothers and sisters, the unity of the human family as refreshing and soothing.

As an only child I often watched the neighborhood children fight with their brothers and sisters. Yet there was no stronger bond than when those same brothers and sisters came together.

Sometimes we are parched, dry, longing for refreshment—a condition so ingrained we do not know how thirsty we really are until we take that first drink and understand the quenching ability of water to refresh. Christ's spirit refreshes and soothes us, making us new and better people.

Watching the news, we see a world whose hunger and thirst for goodness is subsumed in a desire for war and devastation. If we could just interrupt. Then there are those moments of pure goodness—an act of generosity, a coming together across racial, class, or social lines—when hope of bonding becomes real. These interruptions refresh us, giving us hope.

**Prayer:** *Gracious God, help us interrupt and proclaim your wondrous word as a source of refreshment for parched spirits in a thirsty world. Amen.*

## STRENGTH THROUGH WEAKNESS

June 27–July 3, 1994                    **Willis H. Moore✛**
**Monday, June 27**              Read 2 Corinthians 12:2-10.

Perched atop a mighty ocean freighter, the pilot guides his vessel through swift currents and the narrow towers of the Sidney Lanier Bridge. Mighty engines throb against the surging currents as the vessel plows toward port. Yet, the pilot only needs to move the wheel gently to guide the massive ship. Cooperating with technology, human weakness unleashes immense power. Similarly, in submitting to God, human weakness becomes a conduit to release God's power.

The Lord assured the apostle Paul, "My grace is all you need, for my *power* is greatest when you are weak" (TEV). Is there a more graphic example of God's strength being magnified through human weakness than that of the apostle Paul?

We who live in the United States tend to be greatly impressed by power and put off by weakness. Yet all power comes from God. We are but a vessel of God, a conduit. Most of the history of Western civilization has associated power with human physical strength, the might of the elements, machine strength, monetary strength. The scripture alerts us to a new view: weakness is power in God's hands; mighty power made or used by human beings pales before the mighty hand of God.

**Suggestion for meditation:** *Today be aware of mighty machines you are accustomed to seeing: ships, large earth-moving machines, giant aircraft, trains, ships, buses, or trucks. Consider the contrast of mighty power being released through the comparative weakness of the human operator. Imagine your weakness becoming the conduit of God's mighty power to those who need strength.*

---

✛Willis H. Moore. United Methodist minister; Associate Director, South Georgia Conference Council on Ministries, St. Simons Island, Georgia.

**Tuesday, June 28**          Read 2 Corinthians 12:1-10.

The apostle Paul reports three acts of God upon his life that are difficult to explain. First he is given a vision in which he is taken "up into" Paradise. Next he is committed to silence about the paradise experience. Finally he is afflicted with a "thorn . . . in the flesh." For Paul, it is a physical and emotional roller coaster ride. With no initiative on his part, Paul receives an out-of-body experience. (Because the experience was not of Paul's own doing, he speaks of it in the third person.) He is speechless (now there is one for you—Paul speechless!). It was all Paul could do to keep from boasting about his vision—in fact, he did not refrain entirely. When he did boast, he managed to do so that the experience may "show how weak I am" (TEV).

But something else kept Paul from boasting: his "thorn . . . in the flesh." Paul does not tell us what the condition to which he referred was. It might have been a painful physical condition or a shortcoming that affected his ability in some area. Whatever it was, Paul came to accept it as a clear reminder of his utter dependence upon God. He did not blame God; instead, he saw his thorn in the flesh as the work of Satan: "Satan's messenger to beat me and keep me from being proud" (TEV). Paul sees the pain as a chance to draw closer to and more dependent on God.

Life can be painful. We do not have to live long or venture far to feel life's pain. But the pain of our human condition does not have to defeat us. There is one who loves us and upon whose strength we can rely.

**Suggestion for meditation:** *About three hundred years ago, Brother Lawrence, a cook in a monastery, learned he could be aware of God's presence in even the most mundane of his daily tasks. He called this awareness "practicing the presence of God." Today, open yourself to God's strength by practicing God's presence during every waking moment.*

**Wednesday, June 29**                    Read Psalm 48:1-8.

The powerful imagery of the psalmist reminds me of times of turmoil and triumph in my life. In my dark, painful times, almost always I have seen the face of God in the faces of others: strong teachers, great writers, faithful church members, and family members, whose steadfast love of God demonstrates strength and feeds my spirit.

In times of great vulnerability, we reach out for strength—the strength that lifts, holds, and comforts. From the sacred hill of Zion, the community of faith reaches across the centuries, extending just such strength. Human frailty notwithstanding, God, mighty in strength, lives in and redeems the community of faith.

Unlike the psalmist, we do not see many of God's enemies on the run, "seized with fear and anguish" (TEV). But our view tends to be limited. The psalmist knew that our strength is in God. Like the psalmist, we have power to overcome all things if we act out of the strength God gives us. "We have heard what God has done, and now we have seen it in the city of our God, the LORD Almighty; he will keep the city safe forever" (TEV). This is as much a statement of the psalmist's faith as it is reality for the faith community. For those who have only heard but have not yet seen, it is a call to hope—hope in God who will never, never forsake.

In moments of great despair, the psalmist's word of hope lifts us and gives us power. Just as a low-voltage surge can ignite dynamite, such a nudge can turn our life toward dramatic transformation.

**Suggestion for meditation:** *Thank God for your mentors in the faith, by name. If possible, write several of them a thank-you note for the strength they gave you.*

**Thursday, June 30**                          Read Psalm 48:9-14.

When the city of my birth was taken to court for having God's name in its official seal, I felt directly assaulted. As a North American, I write from the perspective of a rapidly changing scene. The church no longer has the primary influence in its community. Christians in the United States live in an almost alien world today. We live in a mission field rather than a churched culture. But this is no time for the church to roll over and die. In the midst of the alien assaults, there is hope and help. The psalmist invites us to take stock, to find the real strength of our faith. I can almost see the psalmist gesturing magnificently as he exults, "Inside your Temple, O God, we think of your constant love. . . . People of God, walk around Zion and count the towers; take notice of the walls and examine the fortresses so that you may tell the next generation: 'This God is our God forever and ever'" (TEV).

The psalmist's call is a call of hope. Let us not forget, the psalmist reminds us, that at the heart of all is God's steadfast love. "Take a tour," "wake up," "get off your couch," the psalmist challenges. God is power and strength—and that is worth telling to future generations. Eternity is a long time. God will be there. There is hope.

**Suggestion for meditation:** *Close your eyes and reflect upon your first faith experiences. What feeds you yet? In your mind's eye see the faces of your mentors. What weaknesses/strengths of your mentors have magnified God's power for you? What abiding hope does the church offer you? Think about and plan for the next time you take Holy Communion. Feel Christ's vulnerability at his sacrificial death and the* power *of his resurrection!*

**Prayer:** *O God, your steadfast love sustained the psalmist, and it sustains me. In thanksgiving, I will tell others the good news of your love. Amen.*

**Friday, July 1**                    Read 2 Samuel 5:1-8.

Today's scripture reading assures us that David's anointing as king was the will of God. You and I have a problem with this. God does guide and provide, but the blood-spattered boulevard that leads to the throne gives us pause. Can this gruesome story be a true account of God's activity with the chosen people? Strength assaulting strength, power assaulting power; we wonder, *Why doesn't God stop it all?*

Looking back from the vantage point of thousands of years and a different culture, we view David's ascent to the throne through the lens of the new covenant Jesus Christ offered us. Still, we wonder how God accomplishes God's will in the midst of such violence. Even as I write this, the debris from the World Trade Center bombing in New York City is being examined and cleaned up. It is apparently the work of zealot terrorists. Near Waco, Texas, this morning, a standoff between an armed religious cult and federal agents has resulted in deaths on both sides.

In trying to do God's will, we, like David, become power hungry. We seek our own self-serving purposes and our values become twisted.

We all stand under the sovereign lordship of the God of Abraham, Isaac, Jacob, and David. We too need God's grace and power to deliver and redeem us. We take courage from David's story. From shepherd boy to mighty king is quite a leap. Yet even the mighty king was too weak to maintain a life of integrity. Thus, David's transformation demonstrates God's power most dramatically. And the covenant continues.

**Prayer:** *Eternal God, my story has its share of stumblings and willful disobedience. By your mighty power, deliver and redeem me. Amen.*

**Saturday, July 2**                    Read Mark 6:1-6.

A strange scenario develops in today's reading. Jesus returned home. When he began to teach in the synagogue, people had two reactions: awe and anxiety. Jesus' friends and relatives could not believe what they saw and heard. They asked, "Where did he get all this?" (TEV) Jesus' teaching commanded attention but not adherents.

Whatever their reason, the homefolks rejected Jesus. They tried to figure him out, classify him, trim him down to their image of him ("Isn't he the carpenter, son of Mary?" [TEV]). Strange, isn't it? When we face challenges beyond our comfort zone, we try to cushion the blow of reality to protect the sanctity of the familiar.

My home region has those who are called "good ole boys." It is a term that denotes acceptance and privilege but also exclusion of those who do not fit the pattern. Certain behaviors are not only expected but are required if one is to remain in good standing as a "good ole boy." Jesus' hometown had its "good ole boys," and Jesus did not fit. Their low expectations chilled his opportunity. He could not do for his own what he had done for others. Their refusal to accept deprived them of abundant blessings.

The scene is repeated over and over again today by Jesus' own people, the church. We try to deny God's mighty acts. We come to worship and enter into service for God with low or no expectations. As graphically displayed in today's reading, expectations tend to shape results.

**Suggestion for meditation:** *How do my low expectations limit God?*

**Prayer:** *O God of miracles, let me always be open to the possibility of one of your miracles in my life. Amen.*

**Sunday, July 3**                          Read Mark 6:7-13.

Unlike yesterday's episode, this episode does not end on a low note. This passage contains preaching and healing and liberation—and a lot of personal touch. Do you see it? Jesus sent out those whom he had called. They were his intimate friends; most of them were untrained, ill-equipped, and rough around the edges. Maybe he felt a little apprehensive; perhaps he had second thoughts. Nevertheless he sent them, knowing that they went not under their own strength but God's.

The sent ones go out two by two, carrying faith power. (The pairs of disciples became a paradigm of the church. As an extension of that model, we do not go alone.)

An annoying goad in this episode is that the sent ones are to travel light. The urgency of their mission requires traveling light. This directive raises the issue of simpler living for each Christian. It also raises the issue for the church. How much baggage do we need to accomplish the church's mission?

What do our locks, bars, security cameras, and alarms say about the business the church is in? Has the church encumbered itself with baggage, or is it packed for the journey on which it is sent? Have we packed things we want, or have we packed only the necessities for serving those to whom we are called? The answers are neither easy nor final. The prior question must be, "Do we trust in and give our life in obedience to the One who has called us?" Left to our own devices, we cannot accomplish the mission to which Jesus calls us; but with God's power we will be victorious.

**Suggestion for meditation:** *How would simpler living free you for ministry for Christ? List nonessentials you might need to rid yourself of. Ask God's guidance as you proceed.*

## SOLIDARITY WITH GOD

July 4–10, 1994            **John D. Copenhaver, Jr.✝**
**Monday, July 4**            Read 2 Samuel 6:1-5.

God is on the move! Theologically, that sounds a bit ridiculous. According to Aristotle and Aquinas, God is the *Unmoved* Mover. Nevertheless, God *is* on the move in this passage; God is moving in history.

For preexilic Israel, the ark of the covenant was the symbol of God's presence and power. For twenty years following its short capture by the Philistines, the ark had languished in an obscure town. Rather than returning the ark to Shiloh, its original home, David boldly decides to move it to Jerusalem. Jerusalem had already become Israel's military and political center, but now it becomes Israel's heart. David wanted God to be central, not peripheral, to Israel's life.

We determine our destiny by our response to God's movement. We can seek to obstruct God's movement in history as Pharaoh did, or we can help prepare the way as David does. David joins his destiny to the God of Israel by bringing the ark to Jerusalem. His decision demonstrates his solidarity with God.

The issue of solidarity with God reminds me of a story about President Abraham Lincoln. On one occasion, he was asked by a reporter whether God was on the side of the North. Lincoln answered that he was more concerned with whether the North was on God's side. Are we on God's side?

**Suggestion for meditation:** *God continues to move in the world: liberating, healing, caring, and reconciling enemies. Let us ask ourselves, "How am I preparing the way for God?"*

---

✝Chair of the Department of Religion and Philosophy at Shenandoah University, Winchester, Virginia.

**Tuesday, July 5**                    Read 2 Samuel 6:6-15.

This passage from Samuel provides us with two examples of how character determines the way a person responds to God.

In verses 6-11 we read the frightening story of Uzzah. Many lectionaries omit this passage because it presents us with a punitive image of God. Uzzah, with apparently good intentions, reaches out to steady the ark and, according to the writer, God angrily strikes him dead. We can interpret the cause of Uzzah's death in other ways (perhaps his terror at touching the ark), but we can learn something from Uzzah's action.

God was on the move, and apparently Uzzah felt that God needed his protection. Uzzah saw God's movement in history as a fragile undertaking that required his assistance. Uzzah's error lay in his exaggerated sense of self-importance.

Although no one of us is essential for God's purpose in history, we are instrumental in extending God's reign. The ark itself was designed so that priests could carry it on poles passed through rings in the ark. Thus, they carried it without touching it, and God's purpose in history is realized through consecrated people. But like Uzzah, we are tempted to exaggerate our importance, which often leads to foolish actions. Uzzah's character is revealed in a foolish action that determines his destiny.

In contrast, David's self-forgetful joy demonstrates his utter confidence in God. God advances on the praises of those who forget themselves in the service of God. David's joy in God's presence demonstrates his solidarity with God and enables him to be God's instrument in Israel's history.

**Prayer:** *Holy God, we rejoice that you are at work in our world. Free us from anxiety about your progress and give us such confidence in you and love for you that we forget ourselves in your service. Amen.*

**Wednesday, July 6**                    Read 2 Samuel 6:16-19.

This passage offers us another insight into how our character affects our relationship to God's movement in history. The writer provides us with a glimpse into Michal's character and its effect on her attitude toward what God was doing in her time.

As the ark entered Jerusalem, Michal watched from her window in the royal palace. From this perch she could see David leaping and dancing. The author observes that as she watched "she despised him in her heart." The writer could not have expressed Michal's revulsion more forcefully. The use of the word *heart* here is significant because it indicates that she despised David with all her being, to her very core.

There is some speculation about what factors predisposed Michal to feel this way. Perhaps as Saul's daughter she resented the waning fortunes of her family or resented being taken from her husband Palti (1 Sam. 25:44), or resented the other wives of David (1 Sam. 25:42-43). But it seems to me that Michal's revulsion at David's display may have been an expression of her solidarity with royalty, with pomp and privilege. David's action offended her sense of royal decorum.

In contrast to David, Michal had little or no interest in the ark, in God's movement in history. Appearance was all-important to her. Her response to her husband's shameless display was concern for the way that she was shamed by association. David demonstrated his solidarity with the fortunes of God while Michal revealed her solidarity with the fortunes of the royalty. Like Paul and the other apostles, who became "fools for the sake of Christ," David became a fool for the Lord, but Michal could not understand. Are we willing to become fools for Christ?

**Prayer:** *All-wise God, may the awareness of your holiness and love so fill my heart with joy that I forget myself and become a fool for Christ. Amen.*

199

**Thursday, July 7**                                    Read Psalm 24.

As the people of God entered the sanctuary, they sang this beautiful psalm. Some scholars suggest that it was also sung during a procession of the ark. We may speculate here that David and the people of God joyously sang it as they ushered the ark into Jerusalem.

The psalm begins with a confession of faith, an acknowledgment of God's sovereignty. The earth is the Lord's, and it exists according to God's purpose. The psalmist then asks who it is that can stand with God. Who is it that lives in solidarity with God?

Those who live in solidarity with God "have clean hands and pure hearts." Clean hands are hands unpolluted by disobeying the law of God, hands not defiled by doing violence, receiving bribes, taking what belongs to others, or making idols. Clean hands may symbolize the outward purity of the person who rejects every evil act.

The clean heart represents a higher standard of righteousness, a purity that reaches to the springs of our desires and will. Søren Kierkegaard, the great Danish philosopher, in his devotional classic *Purity of Heart* wrote that purity of heart is to will one thing. The person living in solidarity with God wills one thing— the will of God! Genuine purity of heart requires a death—death to our self-serving disposition. We cannot serve God and narrow self-interest. The pure in heart are so enamored of God that they love all creatures in and for God. Like Jesus, their will is to do the will of God.

**Prayer:** *Like incense, O God, our prayers rise to you. We offer to you the sweet savor of our own willfulness being burned in the furnace of prayer. Purge our hearts with the fire of your love that we may joyfully serve you. We pray in the name of him who unfailingly willed your will, our Lord Jesus. Amen.*

**Friday, July 8**                    Read Mark 6:14-20.

Perplexity can be mighty convenient!

Herod enjoyed listening to John the Baptist, but our text says that "When [Herod] heard him, he was greatly perplexed." From what we read in the Gospels, John the Baptist does not seem to be the type of speaker to cause confusion. He impresses us as a passionate, plain-speaking prophet. If anyone told it like it was, it was John. When people questioned him, John gave them straightforward answers. When tax collectors asked him what they should do, he simply replied, "Collect no more than the amount prescribed for you" (Luke 3:13). I could understand Paul's perplexing Herod, but not John.

John's message was not perplexing. Herod was perplexed because it suited his purposes to be perplexed. As long as he was confused about John's message, then he did not have to deal with its obvious implications. If he had taken John seriously, as he apparently did, then he would have had to terminate his illicit relationship with Herodias. Therefore, it was convenient to be perplexed.

How many of us are perplexed when we read the Gospels, not because they are hard to understand but because the simple message runs counter to our own interests! Like Herod, it suits us to be perplexed. As long as we are perplexed, we can enjoy the appearance of piety while avoiding the challenging demands of Jesus. Let us be honest with ourselves and recognize when our perplexity is a subterfuge for not accepting the yoke of Jesus.

**Prayer:** *O God of truth, help me to be honest with myself. Deliver me from covering my disobedience with the cloak of perplexity. Give me grace to confront my failures and to seek amendment of life. I pray in the name of the One who is the way, the truth, and the life. Amen.*

**Saturday, July 9**                    Read Mark 6:17-29.

This grisly account of John's execution reveals Herod's deeply flawed character. On his birthday, he played the great man and then chose to protect his prestige rather than to protect the innocent.

Herod invited the glitterati of Galilee to a banquet on his birthday. When Herodias's daughter danced and pleased his guests, Herod, his ego apparently inflated by alcohol, made an incredibly foolish promise to grant her whatever she wished. The crafty Herodias, previously frustrated in her attempts to have John executed, saw her opportunity for revenge and urged her daughter to ask for John's head on a platter.

Herod faced a dilemma. He could admit his foolishness and dismiss her request as impertinent, or he could keep his foolish promise. The former option would humiliate him before his guests but would protect John, a man Herod viewed as righteous and holy. The latter option would cause the execution of an innocent man but protect Herod's prestige. This time Herod displayed no perplexity or confusion—the text says that *immediately* Herod sent the soldiers to behead John. Herod could decide quickly when his prestige was at stake. He was a man whose solidarity was not with God or even with justice but with his own self-serving pride.

How often we imitate Herod by our stubborn refusal to admit our wrong or by seeking to embellish our reputation while ignoring Christ's call to serve the needy and seek justice for the oppressed! May Herod's lethal foolishness remind us of the vanity of pride, and may our Lord's foot-washing example (John 13:1-20) remind us of the sanctity of humility.

**Prayer:** *Lord Jesus, whose humble service stands as constant challenge to my ego-enhancing drives, give me grace to serve you in humble gratitude. Amen.*

**Sunday, July 10**                    Read Ephesians 1:3-14.

Most of us who are Christians today had pagan ancestors. The words of Peter express well what has happened. "Once you were not a people, but now you are God's people; once you had not received mercy, but now you have received mercy" (1 Pet. 2:10). Through Christ we have been made a part of the covenant people of God. But our covenant with God is not some impersonal legal obligation; rather we are adopted members of the family of God. Jesus, our brother, has opened up unprecedented possibilities for solidarity with God.

We have been made part of the family of God, not because of any merit on our part but because of the lavish grace of God bestowed in Christ. This grace is profuse, but it is not cheap. "We have redemption through his blood." Expanding upon this theme, Dietrich Bonhoeffer wrote that God's grace "is costly because it cost God the life of his son: 'ye were bought at a price,' and what has cost God much cannot be cheap for us."*

This grace is costly to the disciple of Jesus "because it costs [us] our life, and it is grace because it gives [us] the only true life."* Life in Christ cannot continue as it was outside of this costly grace. In Christ, we die to our willful self-interest and are raised in newness of life to do God's will. Like the apostle Paul, we have been crucified with Christ, and it is no longer we who live but Christ who lives in us. In Christ our solidarity with God is complete—God lives in us.

**Prayer:** *O God, we thank you for adopting us into your family. So fill us with gratitude for your kindness that we will joyfully offer our lives in your service. We pray in the name of our brother Jesus. Amen.*

*Dietrich Bonhoeffer, *The Cost of Discipleship* (New York: Macmillan Publishing Company, 1963).

## JESUS CHRIST IS OUR PEACE

July 11–17, 1994                                    **Bruce C. Birch**✢
**Monday, July 11**                             Read Ephesians 2:13-14.

In this last decade of the twentieth century, we desperately hope that real peace is drawing closer, and we see many hopeful signs. Yet, we are also aware that conflict, injustice, oppression, and poverty are all too real in our world, and they stand in the way of lasting peace.

In Jesus Christ we see a peace that goes beyond the uneasy quiet between conflicts. In him we see the dividing wall of hostility broken down, and we are made one. If we are to follow Christ, we cannot settle for tolerance or mutual self-interest with those we have considered our enemies. We must seek those paths that end hostility and move us to unity.

Behind this text is the Hebrew concept of *shalom*. This word can be translated as "peace," but its basic meaning is "wholeness." It encompasses all of those things that make for wholeness: justice, compassion, health, righteousness, and love. To seek *shalom* is to work actively for wholeness rather than settling for the absence of conflict. As long as any of our neighbors in the global community of humankind live in brokenness of body, mind, or spirit, then we ourselves cannot experience true peace.

Jesus Christ, in his openness to all persons and his concern for all who were broken in body or spirit, showed us the path of seeking *shalom*. In this week of readings we shall try to discover more of what it means to follow his path to peace.

**Prayer:** *O Lord of all the earth, who desires our wholeness in all things, make us instruments of your peace. Amen.*

---

✢Professor of Old Testament, Wesley Theological Seminary, Washington, D.C.

**Tuesday, July 12**                                    Read Psalm 53.

There is no shortage in our time of "those who work evil" (RSV). I work in a city where drug-related violence is a constant source of concern. We all live in a world where poverty and injustice create brokenness and deny us the peace for which we hope.

The temptation in the face of evil is to think that if we can just find the right program or the right security system or the right political initiative, we can neutralize evil in the world by our own efforts. This psalm teaches us that this is a false hope.

God is the true source of opposition to evil in the world. Those whose actions and words fail to acknowledge this are no better than fools. Yet, we continue to mount program after program as if our crises had no spiritual dimension.

In our own lives we often compartmentalize God into "church" activities and live the rest of our lives by the values of our workplace or our politics or our cultural setting. We live as if God were not the source of true peace in all our doings.

Of course we are to use our own resources to oppose evil in the world. But if we do not understand God as the source of power for wholeness standing behind and beneath our efforts, then we too are lacking in understanding and fail to call upon God (v. 4). Despite our best efforts and intentions, we may then be numbered among "those who work evil."

**Prayer:** *O God, the source of genuine understanding, cleanse our hearts and minds of the foolish belief that our power alone can save us. Amen.*

**Wednesday, July 13**                    Read 2 Samuel 11:1-15.

No other story in the Old Testament better illustrates the abuses of power that make for brokenness than this tragic tale of David, Bathsheba, and Uriah. David is at the height of his power and is pacing idly on the roof of the palace when he sees a beautiful woman bathing on her roof. There is no hesitation. He sent. He took. He lay with her—even though he was told that Bathsheba was the wife of Uriah, one of his own military commanders.

Unfortunately, this story demonstrates the way in which our intentional breaking of *shalom* compounds itself. A child is conceived, and what follows is an attempt to bring Uriah home and deceive him into believing the child is his. When this does not work, due ironically to Uriah's faithfulness to David, the king resorts to murder. David, the greatest of Israel's kings, the royal line from which the Messiah will come, is now reduced to acts of violence in order to cover his own acts of greed, power, and lust. What has gone wrong?

A small clue may lie in this observation. All through David's story it has been clear that God was at work. Even in his victory over Goliath when David was a young man, it was to God that David gave the credit. But this story does not mention God. It is as if David had grown so powerful and successful that he left God behind. He believes that he is the source of his own power; therefore he acts in his own interest. He casually tells the messenger who brings news of Uriah's death, "Do not let this thing be evil in your eyes" (v. 25, AP). But the last line of this story says, "This thing was evil in the eyes of the Lord" (AP).

**Prayer:** *O Lord, forgive us when our own sense of power blinds us to the source of wholeness that lies in you alone. Amen.*

**Thursday, July 14**                    Read Mark 6:30-36.

From yesterday's story of broken *shalom* we now come to a story of need for *shalom* and those who minister to that need. The disciples have returned from a mission of preaching and healing, and Jesus hears their report. Still people throng to them so that they "had no leisure even to eat." They decide to seek some quiet time away so "they went away in the boat to a deserted place by themselves." But the crowd ran around the shore of the lake and got there ahead of them. Seeing them, Jesus had compassion and taught them. As the hour grew late the disciples worried about how the crowd would be fed. Jesus and the disciples, seeking their own peace (*shalom*), found themselves in the presence of human need, both spiritual and physical.

How common it is to think of true peace as a pulling apart from the world. Yet God constantly reminds us that wholeness is most needed where there is brokenness. Elijah flees in discouragement into the desert to Mt. Horeb seeking God's still small voice, only to have that voice send him back into the turbulent world of Ahab and Jezebel (see 1 Kings 19). At the Mount of Transfiguration, the disciples want to build booths and remain there, but Jesus calls them back to their ministry of teaching and healing among the people (see Luke 9:28-36).

We find the peace (*shalom*) of Jesus Christ in the presence of need and in our willingness to serve that need.

**Prayer:** *O gracious God, amidst our desire to be alone, empower us anew for the task of service to a broken world. Amen.*

**Friday, July 15**                    Read Mark 6:37-44.

"Feed all of these people?" The disciples are amazed. They did not object to Jesus' teaching of the crowd, even though they had hoped for some time alone. But they assumed they were responsible for the people's spiritual needs, not their physical needs.

What follows, of course, is that well-known story of the feeding of the five thousand from only five loaves of bread and two fish. When the disciples take responsibility for the people's need, there is enough—even twelve baskets over!

Often the church has tended to limit its ministry to the spiritual realm. But God's concern for our salvation has to do with God's desire for our wholeness in every respect. In a broken world we, as God's people, are to be present to the needs of all who are denied wholeness in any way. We are to feed those hungry in body as well as hungry in spirit.

When Jesus took the five small loaves "he looked up to heaven, and blessed and broke the loaves, and gave them to his disciples." This language reflects the breaking of the bread at the Last Supper and reminds us of our breaking of bread at the Lord's table. We as the church make a connection between life's bread and the bread of life. Out of brokenness we are made whole.

In the feeding of the multitude, Jesus calls the disciples and us to a new awareness of our ministry to bring wholeness (*shalom*) wherever we find human need and in whatever form that need takes.

**Prayer:** *O God, the giver of bread and of the bread of life, feed us by your word, that we may feed the needs of a troubled world. Amen.*

**Saturday, July 16**                    Read Ephesians 2:11-15.

"He is our peace." In Jesus Christ the brokenness of the world is restored to wholeness. It is not accidental that the early church chose to refer to Jesus by the title found in Isaiah 9:6, the "Prince of Peace" [*shalom*].

If we are to seek peace in our world as followers of Jesus Christ, then we must attend carefully to the model of peacemaking here.

The peace of Jesus Christ breaks down the dividing walls of hostility. What remarkable times we have been through in recent years. Political and social barriers we thought impregnable have begun to come down in Eastern Europe and South Africa and the former Soviet Union. But it is remarkable how often the walls of our hostility stay in place. We do not easily give up our enemies. And it is remarkable how tenacious the walls of hostility created by racism, nationalism, economic injustice, and ignorance can be erected in new places even as they come down in others.

The peace of Jesus Christ is incarnational. God in Jesus Christ took flesh in our midst to show us a new humanity of oneness in the midst of our divisions. So too we must take flesh in the midst of the world's division. To bring peace, wholeness, to a divided world we must dare to be physically present as the church wherever hostility still divides us. As the church, we must constantly and prayerfully seek to face the issues that divide us in our congregations, in our communities, and in our world. To avoid them is to remove ourselves from the peace of Jesus Christ.

**Prayer:** *O God, give us the courage to seek wholeness of life in all of those places where hostility yet divides us. Amen.*

**Sunday, July 17**                    Read Ephesians 2:16-22.

The peace of Jesus Christ is not without cost. It comes through the cross. Jesus faced the hostility of a broken world and brought wholeness (*shalom*) by his willingness to suffer and die for the sake of that broken world.

This is not the way in which the world seeks peace. We speak in our political forums of peace through strength or peace as the prize of victory over enemies. The peace of Jesus Christ is the peace that comes from an ability to love our enemies, to seek out the outcast, to give ourselves for the needs of the world rather than our own needs.

The church too often imagines that it can serve Jesus Christ in the world without paying any price. We want the new life of resurrection without the pain of the cross. But it cannot be.

When we gather at the Lord's table we break the bread and remember Christ's broken body, but then we take that brokenness into ourselves as a reminder of the broken world for which Christ died and to which we are sent.

We are called in the preaching of the peace of Jesus Christ to bring the far-off near, to make their pain ours, to seek wholeness not as the result of our own success but at the cost of our sacrifice and commitment to the way of the cross. Who are the far-off in our lives and in our communities who must be brought near? Can we sacrifice our own comfort and success for the sake of true peace in Jesus Christ?

**Prayer:** *O God, strengthen us to take up the cross in our world as followers of Jesus Christ, who alone is our peace. Amen.*

## THE FAR-REACHING LOVE OF GOD

July 18–24, 1994       **Marcia M. Thompson✠**
**Monday, July 18**       Read 2 Samuel 11:1-15.

How far does God's love reach? Does God forgive me even when I have committed a most grievous wrongdoing?

Several years ago, a friend came to me to tell me that he had developed a physical relationship with a married woman. Clergy and laity alike have been involved in sexual transgressions since men and women discovered each other.

Sometimes the church has tended to view sexual misbehavior as the unforgivable sin. Despite the fact that the Bible sees certain behaviors as wrong, it always has allowed room for forgiveness when a child of God has strayed.

The story of David and Bathsheba is a classic example. David's sin not only included sexual misbehavior, it also included murder. Despite all of this, God still was able to forgive David and to use him for God's purpose.

This story says more about the power of God's love to reach out to us when we are far from God than it says about human repentance. God came to David before David was even willing to acknowledge his sin. Through Nathan, God convicted David of his sin, then moved him to a place of grace. God's love was able to reach out as far as David had strayed. In the same way, God can reach into our human predicament to wherever we have gone and bring us back to a place of grace.

**Suggestion for meditation:** *Are there sins in our lives that we wonder if God can forgive? Think on David!*

---

✠Pastor, St. Andrew's Evangelical Lutheran Church; freelance writer; Baltimore, Maryland.

**Tuesday, July 19**                              Read Psalm 14:1-3.

There is a dance that each of us must participate in as human beings. It is the dance of faith. It is not like some would have us believe, a once-in-a-lifetime decision. Faith is a lifelong process, a lifelong dance. Even those who opt not to believe participate in the dance. They must dance the dance of disbelief.

The psalmist calls the one who discounts God a fool, the one who dances the dance of disbelief unwise. Yet when God searches all humankind, there are not any who seek after God. All have gone astray. All dance the dance of disbelief at some point in their lives.

The word *faith* means to believe and trust. To believe in the existence of God is actually quite easy. To trust one's life to God is another matter.

About a year ago, I danced the dance of disbelief in my own life. It was not that I doubted the existence of God. I doubted whether or not God had a future for me. My period of disbelief came after a stream of outside traumas which led me into a darkness where I felt only hopelessness. I learned something of God's love in that darkness. I learned that God can reach us even in the darkness. Even when we are foolish, when we say that there is no God or that God has abandoned us, God's mysterious love can reach out to us.

God came to me in rather simple, ordinary ways: a book given by a friend, the counsel of a professional colleague, a new and unexpected relationship. During my dance of disbelief, God continued to be my companion. God continued to dance with me, despite my inability to see God.

**Prayer:** *In the moments of faithlessness and darkness Lord, grant us enough light to see you holding onto us. Open our eyes to see you in all the simple and ordinary ways you touch us. Amen.*

**Wednesday, July 20**                    Read Psalm 14:4-7.

The remaining verses of Psalm 14 have two major themes. The first theme is that of the evildoers who hurt others. The second theme is that of God's deliverance. The psalmist's mood turns from despair into hope with the final verse. In order to appreciate the hope, one must first linger for a moment in the despair.

The verses leading up to God's rescue are ones that make us acutely aware of the evil in this world. There are those who would "eat up my people." There are those who "confound the plans of the poor." Before we point the finger at others, we must be aware that the beginning of this psalm made it clear that *all* have gone astray. We all stand guilty of these wrongs.

It has always been a basic belief of mine that God gives us the abilities and resources to solve many of the problems that exist in the world. Take the poor, for example. So many dire situations in this world could be changed if human beings were not so greedy. After spending some time in Nigeria, I learned that the ruler of the land was one of the wealthiest men in the world. In the midst of desperate hunger, an elite few boasted great wealth.

In the United States, I once talked to a woman who was bemoaning her poverty. She lived in a two-hundred-thousand-dollar home and vacationed in an equally nice summer home.

Despite our neglect of the poor, God still promises us deliverance. How can this be? It is because of the far-reaching love of God that can touch even the most resistant heart.

**Prayer:** *Change me, Lord, not only that I might realize my own greed but that I might become willing to turn my life and my possessions over to you. Amen.*

**Thursday, July 21**                    Read Ephesians 3:14-19.

What a wonderful prayer! The prayer is that the readers of this letter might comprehend the breadth and length and height and depth and love of Christ, a love that surpasses knowledge. Oh to experience and soak up the love of Christ!

There have been times in my life when the love of Christ has been that evident. While some of those moments have been monumental and marked by significant events, at other times God has surprised me in simplicity. For example, the time of prayer when suddenly the Spirit makes itself known by a gentle sensation of peace like a warm summer breeze. Or the time when another person suddenly connects with you in communication, and for a brief time you experience a kindred spirit. These are the moments when we realize we are standing on holy ground.

The prayer that we might comprehend the breadth, length, height, and depth of the love of Christ is a prayer that we might begin to see God in all of the ordinary and simple ways that God exists in our life. We experience God in so many and various ways each day—in quiet moments when the soul has a chance to breathe, in the tender minutes when two friends awaken enough courage to say, "I love you," in the funny times when laughter dresses the heart.

The gift the writer of Ephesians asks for us is that we be granted enough grace to realize that so many moments in our lives are already God's being wrapped around us, like ribbons wrapped around a package to be given to someone special.

**Prayer:** *Grant us grace enough, Lord, to see you today in the ordinary and simple moments of our lives. Grant us an awareness of the magnitude of your love. Amen.*

**Friday, July 22**                    Read Ephesians 3:18-21.

I have always been intrigued by the expression *fullness of God*. During the sixties, the charismatic movement used this expression to describe an encounter with the Holy Spirit which often included speaking in tongues.

In the Greek, the word *pléres* means full or complete. Fullness, *pléroma*, means that which fills us, that which makes us complete. The Hebrew word *shalom* has a similar meaning: a kind of total harmony for the individual and the community, completeness or wholeness. I am inclined to believe that these two expressions are very close in meaning. To experience the fullness of God is to experience completeness or wholeness in our lives, completeness or wholeness which can come only in relationship to the Almighty. In that relationship we become totally that which God has created us to be.

As a pastor, I am constantly amazed at how many people are living their lives without this fullness or wholeness. Major problems aside, this lack of wholeness is evident in the petty jealousies that exist in congregations when one member receives recognition and another does not, in families where a child hungers for parental affirmation and receives only criticism, in negative attitudes and power plays among people in general.

Where does one begin to find God's fullness? Where does one begin to heal in order to experience a wholeness in Christ? Obviously, prayer is where the journey to wholeness begins. Over the years, I have also become a firm believer in counseling as I discovered that the word *therapy* comes from the Greek word *therapeuo*, to heal. The safe places where we can heal and become whole are the places where we can taste the "fullness of God."

**Prayer:** *Lead me to your fullness, God. Amen.*

**Saturday, July 23**                    Read John 6:1-15.

The last two passages for this week deal with miracles. In these passages, Jesus turns love into concrete deeds. Once again, God's far-reaching love cuts into our lives with a statement on how much God truly seeks us.

The scene is a large crowd. They have come to see Jesus. They have come because they have heard of his miracles. Jesus complies and multiplies the loaves and fishes. He does so not to impress them but to invite them into love.

This passage calls us to two significant actions. First, the miracle calls us to have faith. Faith is that which makes us whole. It is that which makes us complete. Christ knows that without it our lives are incomplete. Second, this story shows us how to love. Spiritual lives are ones concerned with the daily needs of others. Jesus concerned himself with practical issues in people's lives, like whether or not they had enough to eat.

When we are touched by love and faith occurs, we cannot help but be compelled by the stories of Christ which show us how to extend this love into a world which desperately needs to be loved.

Theresa of Avila was a simple saint who lived in the sixteenth century. She was deeply rooted in prayer. Her experiences of God led her to become a Carmelite nun. Despite her awesome encounters with God, her spirituality never allowed her to dismiss the needs of those around her. Like Jesus, she gave us an example of how our faith can be translated into life in the most practical ways.

**Prayer:** *Gracious God, for all those who have showed me your love, who have taken seriously the practicality of their spirituality, I give you thanks. Amen.*

**Sunday, July 24**                          Read John 6:16-21.

In the final story this week the disciples find themselves in a storm, and Jesus comes to them across the water to calm their fear. His immediate presence is that which gives them both the peace and the courage to finish their task.

I have reflected on this text especially during the times in my own life when storms have prevailed, not weather's storms but the storms of the heart. During those storms it becomes difficult to see God. Darkness comes upon us; and in darkness, one *cannot* see God. It is not that we don't want to, it is that sight is impossible. In our spiritual turmoil, we are blind to God's guidance.

I remember one particular time when storms raged in my heart. One evening during that time, I could not sleep. My restlessness sent me into my basement, where I rooted through old boxes filled with items now deemed useless. As my empty heart flipped through dusty memories of days gone by, I came across an old bent-up poster. The caption read, "When I have gone as far as I can, Christ takes me the rest of the way." The poster showed a tiny kitten being carried in a jacket pocket. All I could think of was my own situation. I began to weep as those words spoke to me. I recognized the voice of my God in that poster. God opened my heart and Jesus quieted the storm within.

**Prayer:** *For all those who have been your presence, God, and for all the holy moments that have broken through the darkness, to you be the glory. Amen.*

217

## SPEAKING THE TRUTH IN LOVE

July 25–31, 1994                         **Gerrit S. Dawson**✝
**Monday, July 25**                      Read Ephesians 4:1-16.

The ordination vows for officers in our church include this question: "Do you promise to further the peace, unity and purity of the church?" This query seems to contain a contradiction.

In the name of unity (a great mask for my fear of conflict!), I may refrain from responding to someone's comment that for me is not faithful to Christ's teaching. For the sake of peace, I may never summon the courage to broach the subject of the affair or to unmask the deception. Why stir up trouble when everyone seems content?

At the same time, we can do serious damage to the unity of a church by a neurotic insistence on its purity. A church may be split while we wonder why so few people can understand true doctrine as we do. Or legalistic adherence to our pet understandings of Christian behavior can cause us to overlook Christ's rule of love. My righteous anger at her language or his leadership style can drive a wedge between Christians who are called above all to love one another.

The writer of Ephesians understood this tension between purity and unity as he wrote to the church in Ephesus. He urged them to continue "bearing with one another in love." At the same time, he was adamant that Christians not be "blown about by every wind of doctrine." The strong middle ground seemed to be "speaking the truth in love," our theme for the week.

**Suggestion for meditation:** *Consider the tension in your life between peace and purity. When do you stress the right thing so much that you become unloving? When do you suppress a concern for truth in favor of a path of least resistance? What correctives may God be suggesting?*

✝Minister, First Presbyterian Church, Lenoir, North Carolina.

**Tuesday, July 26**     Read 2 Samuel 11: (14-15), 16-27.

In his fall, David submerged his conscience. The spiritual part of him had to be rendered unconscious. The saddest expression of what this great soulful man had become was not in his heinous deeds involving Bathsheba and Uriah as much as in his world-weary lie to the messenger who brought the news of Uriah's death. David said, "Do not let this matter trouble you, for the sword devours now one and now another" (v. 25). It is as if he had said, "That's war for you. Your number can be up at any time; the next arrow may have your name on it."

Some years, all the pieces of our lives fit harmoniously. Relationships, work, finances, and faith may balance one another in a satisfying life. We may be ruling the realm wisely. But if we are not vigilant, such contentment can lead to a neglect of some critical area. We lose connection with the truth. That is, we no longer deal honestly and straightforwardly with who we are in the presence of God. We lose touch with our mission. We become spiritually unconscious.

When that happens, other people and their needs may become expendable. We take them for granted. Before we know it, our days of abundance slip into days of despondency. We have committed acts of neglect or unkindness unimaginable earlier on. And still, if our usual comforts are pacifying us, we may chalk up the losses as simply the way life is. The sword devours now one and now another.

How long can we go on that way? Unless someone intervenes, the slide can continue indefinitely.

**Prayer:** *Dear God, I pretend that parts of my life don't exist. I easily slide into an unconscious life. Wake me up. Let me see who I am, and what I am called to be that I may return to you. Amen.*

**Wednesday, July 27**                    Read 2 Samuel 12:1-13*a*.

Thankfully, God intervened in David's life. The Lord sent the prophet Nathan to him, a trusted confidant of the king. Nathan, knowing what David had done, told him a parable. In it, a man rich with many sheep and cattle snatched away the one beloved lamb of a poor man. Greedy and pitiless, the rich man used the lamb merely as an evening's meal for a guest.

The story burned David's heart. He was furious. "As the Lord lives, the man who has done this deserves to die." Nathan replied simply, "You are the man!" David was cut to the quick. Nathan's parable had opened him up to experience the feelings of the powerless when they are trampled upon by the powerful. David felt the injustice. And then Nathan turned the story to David as if it were a mirror. He said, in effect, "See yourself; see the truth of what you have done to Uriah by taking Bathsheba."

There are times in our lives when the most loving words a person can say to us contain the truth, "You are that one." Nathan saved David from sinking deeper into denial. He risked the truth in order to wake up David so David could return to his relationship with God and his duties as king. Many people today recall that their lives turned around when someone opened their eyes by a loving but piercing observation. The path to healing often begins with the realization that we are far from whole.

Sometimes we are called to perform Nathan's task for our loved ones—not in judgment but in love. We stop turning a blind eye and speak the truth. Sometimes we must hear from another the truth about ourselves, even though we blush with shame. Our future health may depend on our receptivity.

**Suggestion for meditation:** *Who are the people that will tell you the truth in love? When have they helped you most? To whom have you been called to speak such a loving, true word? What happened? What situations today will require the truth?*

220

**Thursday, July 28**                          Read Psalm 51:1-9.

After Nathan confronted David, the king made no excuses. He said bluntly, "I have sinned against the LORD" (2 Sam. 12:13). Psalm 51 is the confession ascribed to David following Nathan's speaking the truth in love.

Reading this prayer, we can see David flat on his face with arms outstretched. He held nothing back. David's guilt had driven him to the depths of verse 5, "Behold, I was brought forth in iniquity, and in sin did my mother conceive me" (RSV). The issue was not his parentage but his understanding of himself as being tainted from conception with a propensity to sin. David realized that he was hopelessly mired in his own evil.

And yet, the paradox of our faith is that the only way to learn to feel better about ourselves involves first feeling worse. God knows us through and through, knows that we are far more sinful than we can even imagine. No harmful thought, no cutting word, no spiteful act is wholly foreign to us. We are capable of almost anything. God already knows that. Confession is for our benefit, not God's. Once we own the depths of our sinfulness consciously before the Lord, we can start down the road toward forgiveness.

I am certainly not talking about embracing the false guilt and low self-images imposed upon us by a perverse society or a dysfunctional family. Such voices whisper that we are not worth forgiving and so goad us to hide all unworthiness. Our faith, however, encourages us to admit all precisely because God has declared us worth redeeming. We are loved enough to be forgiven, so we are free to value our lives enough to admit the truth.

**Prayer:** *O God, I tremble to admit my sin because I fear your rejection. Yet, you already know everything and still receive me in love. So here I am without one plea except your grace. Amen.*

**Friday, July 29**                    Read Psalm 51:10-19.

After admitting his sin, David pleaded, "Create in me a clean heart, O God, and put a new and right spirit within me." He asked for nothing less than to be remade from the inside out. David understood that his problems with Bathsheba and Uriah were only symptoms of his problems with God. By nature and habit, he had chosen against God. Something in his heart was not right, and David knew he could not change it by himself.

Today, Twelve-Step groups have brought to light the mystery of relying on a higher power to transform us when we are in the grip of destructive behavior. David went even further when he prayed, "Uphold me with a willing spirit" (RSV). He knew that he needed God just to be willing to live in a different way.

God alone can create in us the desire for new life. And only God can wash clean what seems to be the indelible ink of our transgressions. After the damage we have done to ourselves and others, we may have no hope of recovering gladness in living. But God can restore to us the joy of salvation (v. 12). It all depends on God.

David's "broken and contrite heart" opened him to the renewing graces of the Spirit. Our wounds cause us to come before God in openhearted prayer. There, our weaknesses become our strengths. Our broken pasts become the foundation for future wholeness. Our shattered self-reliance gives way to a faith in God that abandons our dependence on self and our attempts to secure for ourselves the world's rewards. It is a scary place to be until we discover that when we are beyond hope, God's grace is wholly reliable.

**Prayer:** *O God, I cannot come to you unless you draw me. I do not even desire you unless you place the desire within me. You alone can create my heart anew; you alone can breathe into me the breath of life; you alone can save me, Lord Christ. Amen.*

**Saturday, July 30**                    Read John 6:24-35.

David longed for reconciliation with God. From reading David's other psalms, we know he received at least some sense of forgiveness. I wonder, though, if the deepest restoration was unavailable to humanity until God came to us in Christ.

Jesus knew that we are afflicted with an ancient wound. As he taught, he recognized the eternal hunger within us. In our passage today, we hear Jesus offering to satisfy that spiritual hunger. Twice he used the words, "I tell you the truth" (vv. 26, 32, NIV). Each time he was speaking the truth in love as he unmasked misperceptions and redirected understanding. The people sought him after the miracle of the loaves and fishes in order to get more bread. They longed for literal manna like that given to Moses, but Jesus offered a more lasting spiritual food. Jesus offered the bread that was himself.

Again, we are faced with mystery. In the midst of our hunger to get what we need to live in the world, Jesus offers something that seemingly does us little good in the short run. "I am the bread of life. Whoever comes to me will never be hungry, and whoever believes in me will never be thirsty" (v. 35). To receive this soul-sustaining bread, we are simply to "believe in him whom [God] has sent" (v. 29). There for the taking is Jesus himself, the bread of heaven.

Jesus tells us the truth. We work hard for the rewards of the world and always come up hungry. We try to interpret our religion to suit our lifestyle; we would like to keep genuine transformation at bay. But Jesus offers us a greater gift. He exposes our longings and assures us that he has what we most deeply want.

**Suggestion for meditation:** *What kinds of perishable food do I pursue? What kind of spiritual hunger do I experience? How does Jesus satisfy these longings?*

**Sunday, July 31**                     Read Ephesians 4:1-16.

Now we may return to these words in light of David's experience of sin, conviction, confession, and restoration. For the Ephesians, the writer envisioned a community aware of its unity in Christ, each one bearing with others in love and humility. They were knit together as a body.

Today we realize that every member of our particular expression of the body of Christ is important. Each child, each adult in a community of faith has an indispensable role. We simply cannot let some leave in anger and pretend that our unity is still complete. We cannot overlook the gifts of some who are difficult or abrasive and still assert that we are functioning properly. This passage calls us to a love that embraces each one. Of course, the wonder is that God calls people together whom we might never choose on our own but who become gifts to us.

This body with many parts works best when individually we take responsibility for our spiritual health. I need to be, like David, acknowledging my sin and embracing God's forgiveness, not just for my own satisfaction but for the good of the body. I need to receive the truth spoken to me in love so that I may grow. And sometimes I am called to speak the truth to others, with humility, so they may grow.

Such a commitment to honesty is fraught with perils. We may wrap our venom inside constructive criticism. We may "lovingly" crush people with our observations. But the risk of the truth is needed for the health of the body. None of us will be all God calls us to be without some Nathans around to hold up the mirror for us. We belong to one another. So we are called to dare to speak the truth in love.

**Prayer:** *Lord, grant us courage to uphold your truth and humility to do so with words seasoned by grace. Help us hold to love above all. Amen.*

## DEPENDING ON GOD

August 1–7, 1994                           **Roberto L. Gómez**✢
**Monday, August 1**                  Read 2 Samuel 18:5-9, 15.

Absalom is an ambitious and impatient prince. Through a series of sibling fights, he secures first claim on David's crown. Yet, Absalom cannot wait to be king. After seeking support from the royal court and the general public, Absalom revolts against his father David.

Absalom differs greatly from David. The prophet Samuel anointed David as the future king of Israel while King Saul was still alive. Yet, David did not rebel against Saul. David was patient and depended on God to make him king. Unlike David, Absalom depends on his political savvy, his popularity, and his prowess. He does not depend on God. Absalom's forces gain a quick military victory over David's army. David flees from Jerusalem. Absalom's kingship seems assured.

David's army counterattacks and wins an overwhelming victory over Absalom's forces. Absalom loses his supporters and flees for his life on a mule. The escape route is undependable. As Absalom rides through the forest, his long hair becomes entangled in a tree. David's soldiers find Absalom hanging from a tree, his head caught in a branch. They beat him to death.

Absalom's misguided endeavor is unsuccessful. He dies a terrible death, never learning to depend on God. Meanwhile, David is faithful to God and remains king.

**Prayer:** *Too often I forget to depend on you, God. I really like to rely on myself. Be patient with me. Remind me to turn to you and to depend on your gracious love. Amen.*

---

✢Conference Council Director, Rio Grande Conference, The United Methodist Church.

**Tuesday, August 2**                    Read 2 Samuel 18:31-33.

Sometimes depending on God is not easy. David depends on God for his kingship, but David suffers greatly when his son Absalom rebels against him. Like any loving father, David hopes for the best and wishes that Absalom will escape injury and death. David thinks he can help Absalom survive. However, some of David's generals consider it best to kill Absalom for the good of the kingdom.

As king, David is faithful to God; yet David suffers greatly. When word comes to David that Absalom is dead, David grieves profoundly. David is angry at the soldiers who killed Absalom. He is angry at God for allowing Absalom to die. For a while David does not resume his kingly duties. Finally, Joab admonishes him to speak to the troops as their king. David complies with Joab's admonishment. Thus, in his grief, David remains faithful to God.

There may be times when we suffer as we depend on God. Unfortunately, we often emphasize our relationship with God as one of no suffering. The truth is that we cannot escape suffering. Suffering is part of the human condition.

The question for us is whether we will remain faithful to God in the midst of our suffering. Emotionally, we strike out at God when we hurt deep inside. God, with loving patience, comforts us and heals us. David hurts deeply but deals with his grief by depending on God. As a result, David continues serving as king. We deal with our suffering by depending on God for comfort, healing, grace, and peace. In turn, we continue in our discipleship.

**Prayer:** *When I suffer, God, console me, strengthen me, and bless me with your grace and peace so I may remain faithful to you and continue to serve you. Amen.*

**Wednesday, August 3**                    Read Psalm 130.

The psalmist knows that in life there are moments when the bottom falls out. Everything that can go wrong goes wrong, or at least it feels that way.

Despair occurs when there is a significant death in the family, one receives a diagnosis of having an incurable or chronic illness, a family falls apart, a business restructures and eliminates jobs, part of the family income is lost, a young family lacks medical insurance, a student fails to get a scholarship, a medical school denies an applicant entrance, a factory closes and workers lose their jobs, a company pension fund disappears, or one does not reach a life goal. As a result, one feels confused, angry, alone, hurt, and hopeless. Depression becomes the dominant mood in one's life.

The psalmist suggests that in this type of condition we cry out to God. In such a moment, we grasp desperately for help. It is then that we become utterly dependent on God. We are at a point where no one but God can help. Faith helps us to depend on God at this moment in life.

It is true that before God our weaknesses and sinfulness reveal our true nature. Yet God through grace, forgives, redeems, heals, gives new life, and gives new hope. We then know that God sees us through and out of the depths of despair. The psalmist celebrates that we can call on God, and God responds! So, we cry out to God, trusting that God's grace overcomes life's despair and restores us to a life of love, joy, and peace.

**Prayer:** *God, when I come to a moment in life when the bottom falls out and I cry out to you, remember me. Remind me of your love for me. Remind me of your faithfulness to me that I may respond in kind. Amen.*

**Thursday, August 4**                    Read Ephesians 4:25-32.

The writer of Ephesians concentrates on relationships among Christians. The writer exhorts those persons within the Christian community to be honest, forgiving, edifying in speech, and kind to one another because "God in Christ has forgiven you."

Sometimes families and, in turn, churches, suffer greatly because of dishonesty, unforgiveness, bad communication, and a lack of love for one another. In my ministry as district superintendent, I see persons, families, and churches crippled in their ministry because of dishonesty, lack of forgiveness, poor communication, and no love. Such persons, families, and churches waste precious energy and time fighting among themselves instead of doing effective ministry. Such actions "grieve the Holy Spirit of God" and inevitably lead a church to a slow death.

The writer of Ephesians invites us to move beyond these spiritual obstacles and depend on God in Jesus Christ to forgive us and mold us into persons, families, and churches of integrity. The grace of Jesus Christ works in us to this end.

When we do not depend on God, we fall short in our relationships as individuals, families, and churches. The more we depend on God, the healthier and more vital our relationships become within our faith community. I know of persons, families, and churches who constantly depend on God by repenting of their hurtful words and deeds. The grace of Jesus Christ helps them overcome their spiritual obstacles. On the whole, these persons, families, and churches are healthier, full of vitality, and serve our Lord Jesus with unbounded enthusiasm.

**Prayer:** *God, bless me with your presence so my will becomes conformed to your will. Amen.*

**Friday, August 5**                    Read Ephesians 5:1-2.

Depending on God does not mean passivity. Rather, depending on God means appropriate activity. The writer of Ephesians challenges his readers to be "imitators of God as beloved children."

Children are full of energy and always active during their waking hours. Children depend on their parents for sustenance, for energy, and for direction in their activity. Good parents provide food and shelter for their children and offer them appropriate orientation in life.

A parallel exists in God's relationship with us. Through Jesus Christ, God gives us spiritual food to live. Through Jesus Christ, God also gives us the direction we need for our participation in God's kingdom. In Jesus Christ, God makes us part of the family. In Jesus Christ, God invites us to the banquet to celebrate life. In Jesus Christ, God sends us to work in the kingdom.

This particular passage ends with the invitation to "live in love." This love is not just any love, but the love of Jesus Christ. Jesus Christ reveals this love in his sacrifice on the cross. The message is clear—the love we have comes to us from God through Jesus Christ, not from the world. We receive this love of Jesus Christ and incorporate it into our life. Christ's love transforms us. The love of Christ helps us live a life of honesty, integrity, edifying speech, productivity, and most important of all, a life of love in Christ.

This kind of life in Christ for us as individuals and for our faith community depends to a large degree on our active dependence on God.

**Prayer:** *Enable me, O God, to actively depend on you so I may fully participate in your kingdom. Amen.*

**Saturday, August 6**                    Read John 6:35.

We hunger and thirst for a significant relationship in life. We hunger and thirst for a significant community in life. The incident occurring at this moment near Waco, Texas, involves scores of persons who have sought a significant personal relationship and a significant community relationship. Tragically, the search for a significant relationship by the persons belonging to this particular sect has taken a wrong turn to violence and death.

Sadly, persons look for a significant relationship in the law, in tradition, in reason, in almost everything but in Jesus Christ. Jesus Christ provides a corrective measure for our often confused search. Jesus Christ points to God as the true source of a significant relationship at an individual level and at a community level.

Jesus Christ does more than point the way to God. Jesus Christ becomes the way, the means of God's grace to us. Medieval Latin theologians write that Jesus Christ is the bridge to God. There is an additional blessing. Because Jesus is God incarnate, Jesus invites us to a significant relationship with him. As our relationship with Jesus grows and matures, the bread from heaven and the living water Jesus offers to us fully and amply satisfy us.

The wholesome and renewing presence of Jesus Christ satisfies our hunger and thirst. Truly, in Jesus Christ there is no hunger or thirst. Truly, in Jesus Christ we find the bread of heaven.

**Prayer:** *God, when I hunger and thirst for a significant other, help me to open myself to Jesus Christ that my hunger and thirst may cease for your honor and glory. Amen.*

**Sunday, August 7**                    Read John 6:41-51.

Many Jews could not see or would not see that God uses Jesus as the means of grace. Consequently, when Jesus says, "I am the bread of life," his contemporaries reject his offer of himself as the means of grace.

God continually reaches toward us in many ways. To help us understand that God reaches toward us in love, God chooses an historical moment (first century), a certain place (Israel), and an individual (Jesus of Nazareth) to be specifically that definitive means of grace for us. God becomes flesh for our sake, that we may believe that God loves us.

Today some persons cannot see or will not see that a young man, the son of Joseph and Mary of Nazareth, is the bread of life. Those persons who are not receptive to this Jesus of Nazareth as the means of grace fail to receive God's love pouring through his Son Jesus.

The Incarnation points to a concrete expression of God's reality and of God's love for us. The incarnation of God in Jesus of Nazareth also is a way God helps us depend on God. In Jesus, God touches us and embraces us. In Jesus, God invites us to depend on God for our sake. In Jesus, God invites us to a significant relationship that withstands time and trial. In Jesus, God establishes a relationship with us that in due time will be glorified forever.

**Prayer:** *Dear God, often I eat food that does not nourish and drink water that does not quench my thirst. Open my eyes and spirit that I may receive your Son Jesus who even now offers me the bread of heaven and the living water so I may live instead of perish. Amen.*

## GOD ENTERS OUR LIVING

August 8–14, 1994

**Thomas R. Albin✛**
**Duane M. Gebhard✛**

**Monday, August 8**

Read 2 Samuel 23:1-3.

The God of Israel has spoken *to* men and women of faith in every age and *through* women and men of faith in every age.

The Bible clearly documents the fact that God can and does speak through men and women. David presents an example in the second and third verses of our passage today: "The Spirit of the Lord speaks by me. . . . The God of Israel has spoken" (RSV). From the beginning God interacted with Adam and Eve, then the patriarchs and matriarchs (Abraham and Sarah, Jacob, Moses and Miriam) and the prophets (Isaiah, Jeremiah, and so on). Therefore, the people of Israel never seriously questioned the authority or inspiration of holy scripture. The same is true for Jesus and the writers of the New Testament. (See Luke 4:16-21; 2 Tim. 3:14-17.) The consistent witness of the Bible is that the God of Israel does speak to people and through people.

In a few moments of silence, meditate on these questions: What do I honestly believe about the inspiration and authority of the Bible? Do I believe that God speaks through the inspired writers of scripture? Has the God of Israel spoken to me? What is God saying now? Does the spirit of the Lord want to speak through me today?

**Prayer:** *O God, help me to hear and to heed your voice. By the power and presence of the Holy Spirit, speak to me and through me today. Amen.*
*T.A.*

✛United Methodist minister; Director of Contextual Education, University of Dubuque, Dubuque, Iowa.
✛District superintendent, Northwest District, Minnesota Annual Conference, Alexandria, Minnesota.

**Tuesday, August 9**                    Read 2 Samuel 23:1-5.

The God of Israel has spoken of justice.

The opening phrase of the reading today states that "these are the last words of David," thus giving added importance to what follows. Therefore, we should be careful to observe precisely what it is that "the God of Israel has spoken."

Read verses 3-5 again. In these few rather plain lines, David touches one of the major themes of the Bible: Those who rule with justice and in accord with the will of God bring blessing, peace, prosperity, and joy to everyone around them.

Take a moment to reflect on the settings where you are a leader: at home within your family, at church, on the job, in various other groups and organizations. Do you act justly and "in the fear of God"? How might God be speaking to you in this scripture passage about your leadership within your spheres of influence?

Perhaps the greatest need of our century is the need for just and godly leaders—men and women who respect God and value every child of God, regardless of race, sex, age, creed, or social status. What a different world it might be if Christians everywhere paid attention to the word of God spoken through the last words of David, and if we began to pray seriously for all those in positions of leadership.

**Prayer:** *O God, help me to hear and to heed your voice. By the power and presence of the Holy Spirit, speak to me and through me today. In particular, I pray for all political leaders and religious leaders. By your grace, enable them to rule with wisdom, justice, and mercy. Bring peace to our troubled planet, O Lord. Amen.*
*T.A.*

**Wednesday, August 10**                    Read John 6:51;
                                             Psalm 111:1-5.

A group of senior high youth met in the church kitchen late one Saturday afternoon. Using flour, yeast, milk, sugar, and margarine, the youth worked into the evening and on through the night mixing, kneading, and baking to produce hundreds of loaves of bread. The "overnight breadbake" had become a traditional fund-raiser for a youth mission trip the following summer. At midnight, when a few loaves of bread were finished, the youth gathered together. They talked about the meaning of bread as sustenance for life, both physical and spiritual. They closed by sharing the Lord's Supper.

What does bread mean to the people of the world? How does bread represent the gift of nourishment supplied by God day by day? What responsibilities do we have to share our abundance of food with those who would otherwise go hungry? How is the output of our daily labors influenced by the concept of sharing our gifts and talents with those who could benefit by our help?

Jesus as the Bread of Life is a powerful image. He entered our world, shared our humanity, and suffered our brokenness in order that our lives could be whole. As we avail ourselves of the presence of the spirit of Christ, we are sustained for the next steps along the journey of life. We also become part of the living Bread that is offered to others. We become part of the body of Christ shared in service for others.

**Prayer:** *O God, as we eat our bread, let us also be filled with the spirit of Christ and strengthened for service in his name. Amen.*
*D.G.*

**Thursday, August 11**  Read John 6:52-55;
Psalm 111:6-10.

The Jewish leaders were not prepared to accept the strong images of eating Jesus' body and drinking his blood. We are often inclined to reject them as well.

In Jesus Christ, the creative, loving Word of God became human and dwelt among us. Jesus felt our brokenness, knew our temptations, and experienced our pain and suffering. He also shared our joys and called attention to God's Spirit present in every aspect of our life. In so doing, Jesus showed us that we become fully human not by avoiding the intensities of life but by seeking communion with God *in the midst of them.*

Jesus said we cannot be fully alive unless we take his life into ourselves. We must remember his temptations and how he reacted to them, his style of serving those in need, his ability to bring healing through centeredness in God's Spirit, his way of loving and forgiving, and his teachings about our relationship with God.

Furthermore, he suffered and died in order to make God's redeeming, forgiving love perfectly clear to us. We must let the reality of Christ's death for us soak into our being and influence who we are. Then, said Jesus, we will begin to taste eternal life.

**Prayer:** *Today, O God, help me to experience who Jesus is and to know what it means that he died for me. Amen.*
*D.G.*

**Friday, August 12**                    Read John 6:56-57.

The two key words for today are *abide* and *live*. To abide with someone means more than a fleeting hello, good-bye a few times a day; it means a continuing, lasting relationship. Abiding requires a level of trust, respect, and love that is not possible among mere acquaintances or casual friends. In John's understanding, Jesus wants—in fact, longs for—the deepest level of relationship with us, the level where close friends abide in one another.

In Jewish thought, blood contained the essence of life. Thus, as blood flowed from a wound, life ebbed away. When we are wounded physically or emotionally, it often seems as though life is trickling away. Jesus offers the gift of new life. It comes in the form of reassurance (like being surrounded by arms of love), acceptance, and forgiveness.

It is interesting that the writer of John's Gospel does not give an account of the Last Supper. Rather, the writer emphasizes our partaking of the elements of Holy Communion whenever we eat a meal. If we become aware of the body of Christ broken for us and of the life-giving energies of Jesus' love shared for us as easily and as often as we eat physical food, then we will find life in Christ—life in all its fullness.

**Prayer:** *Loving Christ, come into our lives and renew us with your life-giving energies. Amen.*
*D.G.*

**Saturday, August 13**          Read Ephesians 5:15-16.

The advice is so simple it almost escapes us: "Look carefully then how you walk" (RSV). In the same category as the admonition "Drive carefully," these words of caution suggest the common risks of living and the need to pay attention as we move about. But the writer's purpose is much deeper. The writer is emphasizing the need to pay attention at all times to God's way of life so as not to slide into the evil ways of the world without thinking. The preceding verses refer to the light of Christ that illumines our way, freeing us from having to walk in darkness.

While analyzing some of the complex issues of international relations before the National Press Club, a government leader used this phrase: "Heaven only knows what could happen under these circumstances." Often we are driven to the same acknowledgment: heaven alone *does* know. How much better if we would turn to God freely for guidance rather than walking on blindly in the dark.

The expression "making the most of" the time (or literally "buying up" the time) echoes from Colossians 4:5, where it refers to not missing any opportunity to bear witness to those outside the church. In Ephesians, however, the reference is general and applies to all of life.

**Suggestion for meditation:** *In what ways can Christ become part of my life today?*
*D.G.*

**Sunday, August 14**               Read Ephesians 5:17-20.

The implication of these words in Ephesians is that if one does not make an effort to understand God's will, one is living foolishly. Such judgment seems harsh, and we usually prefer to ignore it. Perhaps the advice to "be filled with the Spirit" is easier to swallow and to live by. But we certainly should make every effort to understand God's will for our lives.

The writer of Ephesians knew that the Christian way of life requires daily effort, and it is necessary to get down to the raw basics. The matter of not getting drunk with wine is important for everyone, although some find it much harder to follow than others. Certainly living in a loving and caring way toward others is a challenge for all of us. But would it not seem as though we are going overboard to have *all* communication be in the form of "psalms and hymns and songs"? Indeed it would!

While that might carry his advice to an extreme, the writer probably would like to see a little more happiness and praise become part of our way of dealing with one another. This passage also suggests that each of us make "melody to the Lord with all [our] heart" (RSV). How much happier would we become if we could let our hearts continue in songs of thanks and praise while we are going about our daily lives? We would probably notice a great deal of difference.

**Prayer:** *O Lord, throughout this day, help us consciously communicate love to others. Amen.*
*D.G.*

## BEING WILLING TO ACT

August 15–21, 1994
**Monday, August 15**

**Bruce A. Mitchell✚**
Read John 6:59-69.

"I Never Promised You a Rose Garden" was the title of a popular song several years ago and has probably become the title of innumerable sermons.

Jesus never promised his disciples—or any of us, for that matter—that life would always reflect the beauty and peace of a rose garden. Instead, he reminds us that human life brings unpleasant decisions, sacrifices to be made, and commitments that are hard to meet.

In some ways, to understand Christ and to fully accept our calling as Christians, we sometimes must be in conflict with situations, lifestyles, and human conditions that challenge our faith. Christians proclaiming peace find themselves having to engage in combat against the ills of humanity. That may seem inconsistent with a calling to be peacemakers; however, if we really want to understand Jesus, we must accept the fact that every Christian is called to go forth as a warrior equipped not with weapons of death but with arms of hope and eternal life. We will meet opponents, those who are centered only on personal gain and self-satisfaction. However, if we continually feed upon Christ with faith, finding inner strength and power from him, we will find the strength to meet and overcome every negative situation we might face.

**Prayer:** *Give me strength, dear Lord, to face every daily challenge with faith in Christ's power. Amen.*

✚Retired United Methodist clergy from the Florida Annual Conference; active in Christian education and biblical tour programs, Mulberry, Florida.

**Tuesday, August 16**                    Read Ephesians 6:10-13.

*Christian conflict*

"Be strong in the Lord and in his mighty power. Put on the full armor of God" (NIV).

In a very real way, we continue to experience struggle worldwide between different concepts of life. We find this struggle between cultures, between races, and even between members of the same family. Such tensions have existed since the beginning of time and no doubt will continue until the end of time.

What the passage from Ephesians challenges us to understand is that we simply cannot turn our backs on a world where power and evil are, more often than not, one. It challenges us to engage in a form of spiritual warfare that is part and parcel of the Christian faith.

In a sense, the passage is speaking of God's waging war on the enemies of God—and calling Christians to take up arms against the sins and wrongs of the world. The war we are called to wage in the name of Christ is not one of vindictiveness and oppression. Instead, the challenge we face is to carry forth a message of hope and love in a world that seems centered on disinterest, deprivation, and destruction. We see disinterest manifested in declining moral values. Deprivation shows itself through our insensitivity to the homeless and disenfranchised. Failing governments and the rise of tyranny reflect destruction.

One of the marvels of God's power is the availability of the Holy Spirit to enable even the meekest of us to do the will of God. The challenge we face is to be willing to let that power move us into action when action is called for.

**Prayer:** *Give power, God, that we might serve Christ with courage and compassion. Amen.*

**Wednesday, August 17**          Read Ephesians 6:14-20.

This passage makes a point of calling for humankind to put on the *full* armor of God. One piece of armor or weaponry is not enough.

At times, it is easy to be satisfied with a shield or a sword. However, today's reading tells us that we must be fully equipped from head to toe. We are called to wear the helmet of salvation, the breastplate of righteousness, the belt of truth, the shield of faith—even the proper footwear.

When we think of ancient footwear, we probably think of sandals. This passage calls us to choose shoes for our feet that will make us "ready to proclaim the gospel of peace," shoes that will enable us to leap into action when the call comes.

This readiness to heed the call to proclaim the gospel of peace is reflected in today's world by the Christian who is not content to be a spectator of the faith but dares to become a servant. Perhaps it is best reflected in the person who is willing to go into the world to serve. It may be the person who prepared food and serves it at a food kitchen for the homeless. It may be the person who does not wait to help the homebound but goes to where the need is. It may be the person who is willing to share Christ in personal testimony with the person who needs a message of hope.

Footwear, as a part of the armor of God, signifies a Christian who is willing and eager to share the gospel in word and deed with others who may not have heard or experienced it in their own lives. Perhaps it represents the difference between wishful thinking and the willingness to act.

**Prayer:** *Servant Christ, give me the courage this day not only to think of needs but to meet the needs of others. Amen.*

**Thursday, August 18**                    Read Psalm 84.

The family members of one of the Iran hostages belonged to a small rural church that I served several years ago. Week after week we prayed for their loved one's safe return. As months of imprisonment and uncertainty dragged on, we wondered when he would be released and what condition he would be in.

Finally, after a long period of deprivation and abuse he and his comrades were allowed to return home. How did they survive the ordeal? What gave them the strength to go on?

God, with great mercy, equips people to face persecution with courage. God provides a "shield" that gives strength to go on and inner knowledge that the future holds a measure of hope for those who believe in God's eternal power.

A U.S. soldier who was a prisoner of war in Vietnam recalled Bible verses from his childhood to sustain him during his imprisonment. Another prisoner has spoken of the power of prayer and his inner assurance that God's Spirit was always there to provide strength in the most difficult times of need.

Perhaps it takes the direst of circumstances for us to fully realize the presence and power of God. Perhaps the greatest tragedy of humanity is that we often turn our backs on God when situations become more positive.

**Prayer:** *Forgive us, God, when we come to you only in times of need. Remind us that your real desire is to be part of our continual life, in bad times and good. Amen.*

**Friday, August 19**                    Read 1 Kings 8:28-30.

One of the crucial spiritual building blocks of Methodism was the weekly class meeting—the gathering together of a dozen people to pray and seek God's renewing power. The class leader would approach each member of the class, one by one, and ask the question, "Brother (or sister), how has it been this week with your soul?" Each person, in turn, would respond with the victories or sins of the week.

Thus each member of the class would bare his or her soul in a spirit of truth, seeking forgiveness and a new indwelling of God's righteousness for the week ahead.

The class meeting, as historically structured, may play a lesser role today. Yet this passage challenges each of us to build a strong defense against the temptations and sins of the world and to be ready to acknowledge our weaknesses to God. In today's intricate and permissive society, it is all too easy to fall victim to temptation. This week's reading from Ephesians reminds us that inside each of us is the "armor" to resist that which is wrong.

If you (or I) were invited to a traditional class meeting, would we go willingly? If we were to go, could we testify to having lived a fully righteous life? How would we answer the leader's question, "How has it been this week with your soul?"

**Prayer:** *O Lord, forgive our willingness to justify things not fully Christlike. Give us the strength to resist evil and to serve Christ with courage and faith. Amen.*

**Saturday, August 20**                    Read Ephesians 6:17.

Jesus said, "Blessed are the peacemakers" (Matt. 5:9). But what is a peacemaker? What does it take to be a peacemaker?

Today's scripture passage seems, on the surface, to urge aggressiveness. Our minds immediately conjure up pictures of dueling cavaliers or ancient armies, swinging massive blades and flinging spears until one side or the other has been decimated. How can one equate this admonition to don armor and swing the sword with Jesus' call to be a peacemaker?

A decade-old country music song shared the story of "The Coward of the County." For years, as a product of his father's teaching, a gentle man had backed off from every conflict and confrontation. Ultimately the person nearest and dearest to him was terribly abused and the "coward of the county" faced up to the roughest and most evil men in the county. Despite all admonitions to back off, the "coward" found that there are times when one must be aggressive, not vindictively so, but out of the certain knowledge of what is right.

This verse reminds us that sometimes we can attain justice only by facing up to the persecutor with courage.

"The helmet of salvation" is a symbolic allusion to the mind processes that allow us to recognize injustice and express personal compassion and sensitivity. By the same token, we also are given the wisdom to know when it is right and Christlike to stand up and take action in defense of the right.

**Prayer:** *Lord Christ, give us the wisdom to know when to back off and courage enough to act in your name. Amen.*

**Sunday, August 21**                    Read Ephesians 6:13.

A number of years ago, a hymnal revision committee of a major denomination slated two hymns for deletion. One of the hymns was "Onward, Christian Soldiers."

When news of this possible deletion reached the local churches, the members sent an avalanche of letters and petitions to the hymnal revision committee, asking that it retain this traditional hymn. The revised hymnal, published in 1989, included "Onward, Christian Soldiers."

In a sense, an "army" of committed church people rose up to defend a meaningful part of their faith. In another sense, the hymn continues to remind us: "like a mighty army moves the church of God . . . one in hope and doctrine, one in charity."*

God calls us to engage in Christian combat against insensitivity, injustice, and inhumanity. God calls us to unite in righting wrongs, establishing freedom and human dignity, and restoring and retaining values that build rather than destroy.

Jesus, in the Beatitudes, teaches, "Blessed are the peacemakers" (Matt. 5:9). It takes an army—an army of God's people—to do just that. And it takes people willing to put on the full armor of God to do that. "Onward, Christian soldiers!"

**Prayer:** *Equip us, O Lord, that we might move forward joyfully in the service of Christ, using every power within us to do his will. Amen.*

---

*From "Onward, Christian Soldiers" by Sabine Baring-Gould.

## WELCOMING GOD

August 22–28, 1994      **Catherine Gunsalus González**✝
**Monday, August 22**      Read James 1:17-21.

We human beings are to do what is good. It is unlikely we would find much argument with that statement. But how are we to do it? Or more to the point, why is it so hard for us to do good? to be good? If we look around us, we do not need to look far to see that wasted lives, inhumanity, corruption and evil are very much a part of our society, from the small family unit and the neighborhood to the national and global levels.

Perhaps we have misinterpreted our role in this task. James tells us that all good deeds have their origin in God. Even as God created the universe by a word: "God said . . . and it was," so now in our midst the word of truth from God causes a fallen world to be good. If our hearts are hospitable to that word of truth, then God's own goodness begins to recreate us.

We are to rid ourselves of all that opposes the good word, to pull out the weeds of anger and sinfulness like a good gardener who wishes to make room for the good seed. The good seed is God's word. We cannot create it for ourselves but only make room and welcome it. That is task enough.

**Prayer:** *Give us hearts open to you, O God, so that your word may find a home within us. Amen.*

✝Professor of church history, Columbia Theological Seminary, Decatur, Georgia.

**Tuesday, August 23**                    Read James 1:22-27.

How do we know that we have truly welcomed God into our lives? For James, the test is clear. Those who have been with God begin to imitate God in their lives. The seed of God's word flourishes. Such people act the way God acts; they love those upon whom God showers particular affection: the helpless and needy. When the faithful turn from a study of God's word, from a time of prayer and devotion in God's presence, they do not forget who they are as God's people.

Those who truly study God's law will be led away from being judgmental and unloving. If this is not our experience of God's law, perhaps we have misunderstood its character.

James speaks of "the perfect law, the law of liberty." The study of this law makes us free and loving. It calls us to the perfection of the Author of the law, the One whose freedom and love we are to carry out into the world by loving those whom the world does not love.

James says that we are to keep ourselves "unstained by the world." It is the world that tells us to care only for those who can return the favor, to love only those who love us, to ignore those who might cost us something in money or reputation. God's law would make us free. We are invited—and commanded—to go beyond the boundaries of the "common sense" of the world. This is precisely what God did in the incarnation.

**Prayer:** *Let us so study your word, O God, that we may be imitators of your own actions toward us in our dealings with others. Amen.*

**Wednesday, August 24**                    Read Mark 7:1-8.

We encounter a serious—and frequent—problem when we substitute our ideas of what is good for God's perspective on the matter. Often our human rules cut us off from others, whereas God's law leads us into costly involvement. Indeed, God had wanted purity in the life of the people, and the washing of hands and food could be an appropriate sign. But when people view adherence to all of the minute actions about washing as making us "good," then we have perverted the whole purpose of God's law. Jesus' words are harsh: in keeping all of these external details, the people have lost sight of God's commandment.

In the midst of a fallen world, often we must choose. Do we wish to be considered "good" by others in the society whose opinion of us seems quite important, or do we wish to be considered "good" by God, who demands that we live out of a heartfelt love for others? God's goodness requires a different set of criteria than the external signs that others value. Jesus opted for God's goodness. He ate with tax-collectors and prostitutes, and healed the sick even on the Sabbath, not keeping a "proper" distance from those who were not good. Jesus called his disciples in the first century, and now he calls us to make the same choices.

Beyond personal choice, we need to consider how we as a church can support those who choose God's goodness rather than human tradition.

**Prayer:** *O God, keep our hearts and minds open to your word, and let us not honor you only with our lips. Amen.*

**Thursday, August 25**                    Read Mark 7:14-15, 21-23.

The goodness God calls us to live reflects God's own goodness toward us. God requires a good heart, not simply external actions. In our goodness of heart we imitate God, whose actions in creation and redemption stem from the overwhelming love for the world, a love so deep and so committed that it led to the cross.

What we eat and the persons with whom we eat cannot defile us. Living in a poor section of town or being unemployed does not defile us. Yet even within the church, persons often judge our worthiness based on these criteria. It is the heart that matters. We can hide our hatred and envy of others and appear to live an upright life and still be filled with all the evil things of which Jesus speaks in this passage. Truly loving hearts evidence their character in loving actions.

God deals with the heart. God's life in us, God's word in our hearts, is the transforming power that changes our actions, that eliminates avarice, deceit, envy, pride, folly, and all the other vices Jesus mentions here. These evil forces bring defilement despite our external righteousness.

**Prayer:** *O God, come into our hearts and transform our lives. Keep us from judging ourselves falsely. Give us your Holy Spirit, so that we may aspire to holiness in ourselves and support it in others. Amen.*

**Friday, August 26**                    Read Psalm 45:6-9.

This psalm was intended to be sung at a royal wedding. The note is joyful and celebrative. Yet it speaks to us even when we live in a republic, without a wedding on the horizon. The psalm gives us a glimpse of the quality of good government. Good government models God's own governing.

These verses speak of two kings: God, the ruler of the universe, and the earthly king whose wedding the psalm celebrates. The psalmist praises the earthly king because his rules is parallel to the rule of God. He loves righteousness and hates wickedness. For this reason, the people can rejoice and be glad.

Earthly kings do not rule us, but if human governments and their leadership love righteousness and hate wickedness, the people will rejoice. Perhaps living in a democracy makes our situation more difficult. Who is responsible for the government? Is it not all of the citizens? Do we really want public officials who love righteousness and hate wickedness? Would we not prefer officials who lean toward *our* interests rather than the interests of others? God's royal scepter is one of equity. If we or our special interests have more than their share of influence, do we want such equity?

The truth remains: Where righteousness is the goal of government, where wickedness has no hearing in the halls of power, then the people are glad and God blesses the rulers. They hold their power under the authority of One who seeks righteousness through or in spite of human governments.

**Prayer:** *O God, we acknowledge the power of ordinary people to influence the happiness and well-being of many others. Give us the grace to fulfill wisely and well our civic responsibilities. Amen.*

**Saturday, August 27**                    Read Psalm 45:1-2;
                                          Song of Solomon 2:8-9.

Psalm 45 is a wedding song, and the opening verses praise the beauty and grace of the king at his marriage feast. The words are appropriate for a love song. All of the Song of Solomon is a love song, and today's verses praise the beauty of the beloved, the bridegroom.

Why should love songs find their way into the canon of scripture? Why should scripture celebrate human love in marriage? For Israel and for the church, the human marriage covenant is analogous to the covenant between God and God's people. The covenant demands faithfulness and mutuality; and where that exists, there is great joy. We often break the covenant by our faithlessness, but God is the faithful spouse who seeks a renewed commitment, a second honeymoon. The prophets frequently use this imagery. Ephesians uses the analogy of marriage to speak of the relationship of Christ to the church. The Book of Revelation points to the wedding feast as the culmination of the long betrothal of the Lamb and the church.

Human love in marriage is a covenant. Unrelated people form a bond that creates a new family. In our present world, the marriage bond is imperfect. It may break. Great injustice may occur in the midst of the relationship. But the ideal of such a bond remains. Scripture celebrates such human love in ways that parallel God's covenant with us. Parents may love children and children their parents, brothers and sisters may love one another. These are blood ties. But marriage requires love that goes beyond the common natural bond. God loves us as our Creator, and God chooses us as the beloved.

**Prayer:** *O God, you have loved us with an unexpected love. Grant that we may always be faithful to you. Amen.*

**Sunday, August 28**               Read Song of Solomon 2:10-13.

Today's verses explain why the scriptural analogy of marriage goes beyond the need for faithfulness to the way God relates to us. Scripture pictures God as the Creator, the Ruler, the Judge, the Parent. Certainly we sense the inequality between God and us. It is God's role to command, ours to obey. Obviously there is truth in this that we must not forget. But it is not the whole truth.

God is also our lover. God woos us, invites us into a loving relationship. The bridegroom woos the bride, the bride yearns for the bridegroom, and the two seek an ever closer union. So God and humanity seek out and yearn for each other. The relationship is not all command; it is also love on God's part. It is not only obedience; it is also love on our part. In this passage, the lover calls to the beloved and invites her into a new life because the spring has come. God invites us into a new life also. The winter of sin is past; the springtime of renewed creation is here.

Love between parent and child exists, but until the child matures, it is an unequal relation. Even in human marriage, the legal structures may create an unequal situation. But between lovers in courtship there is a mutuality. God as lover emphasizes this side of God's relationship to us. God's continuing love makes faithfulness possible.

**Prayer:** *Open us, O God, to your love, so that our response may be willing and joyful. Amen.*

## CHRISTIAN INTEGRITY

August 29–September 4, 1994 **Joe Dunagan**✠
**Monday, August 29** Read Proverbs 22:1-2, 8-9, 22-23.

Some people seem to have it all together. They are calm in a crisis, decisive in conflict, and patient with the rest of us! The key to having it together is learning to integrate one's values— religion, education, experience, resources, and common sense.

Words have definitions that are common to everyone, but they also have histories for individuals. For my generation, the word *integrate* brings to mind the combining of public schools that previously had been racially segregated. *Integration* was a bad word. It was heavy and threatening. Most of all, it was scary. Even though the words *integrate* and *integrity* obviously are related, it was a long time before I could see the connection.

Up the road a few miles from my childhood home in South Georgia are many farms. One is unique. It has a Greek name, Koinonia. Clarence Jordan, a scholar in New Testament Greek, founded Koinonia Farm. Dr. Jordan read the words, "In Christ there is neither Jew nor Greek" and decided that the same must be true for Black and White. On his farm, he started a community based on the example of the church described in the Book of Acts. He welcomed all persons without regard to race.

His farm was integrated because his belief system and practices were integrated. He is a hero of mine because he was a man of integrity. His is a good name because of his integrity.

**For reflection and prayer:** *Recall the names of some significant persons in your life whose integrity you respect, and consider what "having it all together" implies for you.*

---

✠Clinical chaplain with Vitas Health Care Corporation; clergy member of the South Georgia Annual Conference.

**Tuesday, August 30**                      Read Proverbs 22:2;
                                            James 2:1-10.

Death is a great equalizer. As a Navy chaplain, I helped organize a reunion for a group of sailors who were stationed together early in World War II. They asked me to conduct a memorial service for members of the command. I was given a list of names of the men who were killed in the war or who had died since. One of the names was John F. Kennedy. The unit was proud of its distinction of having had a future president, but the planning committee decided that at the memorial service all the names should be listed alphabetically, without rank or other title. President Kennedy's name was read with the same respect as all the others, no more or less.

My ministry now is in a hospice. We provide care for persons whose diseases limit their life expectancy to six months or less. Physicians have told our patients that there is no cure for them, and the patients have decided they would rather die at home than in a hospital. I have been privileged to visit our patients in their homes as they live with the threat of imminent death.

The homes I visit are large and small, new and old, in some of the most expensive neighborhoods and in some of the most run-down. None of that matters. What does matter is whether one can face death with a sense of completeness for having invested his or her life well. Our patients want to tell their stories. They tell about their families of origin, their adventures, and the loves of their lives.

In a world where position and titles and wealth are so important, it is good to hear the wisdom of the scripture that reminds us that the Lord is maker of all, rich or poor.

**For reflection and prayer:** *Consider your own mortality and how that can influence your goals and relationships.*

**Wednesday, August 31**                    Read Psalm 29:3-8.

Wilma Rudolph was the youngest of twenty children. With that many siblings, hers was not a childhood of privilege. Add to that the facts that she is Black and was born in the segregated South and that she contracted polio at an early age. It would be easy to dismiss her with sympathy as a victim of circumstances. That would not take into account the faith her parents had in her, or the tremendous effort and dedication she had. Her journey began when she, in faith, threw away her braces. She did not stop working to overcome her disability until she had won three gold medals in track at the 1960 Olympics.

What began in faith matured because of tremendous work. If that is true of a great athlete, it is also true of persons in physical rehabilitation after a stroke or injury. It is true of persons struggling one day at a time with addiction. And it is true of believers as we struggle with our sinfulness.

The integration of faith and works is the essential task of developing what we might call Christian character. This character finds expression in discipline. A disciplined Christian life will not remain a victim.

**For reflection and prayer:** *List your limitations and your possibilities. Which will you choose as your focus?*

**Thursday, September 1**                    Read Proverbs 22:22-23;
                                                        Psalm 125.

This week's lessons imply a place in the community of faith for everyone. Proverbs affirms that we are created equal whether rich or poor. Later we read of the rights of the poor and the afflicted. In the epistle, the writer may cause a chuckle as he points out that it is not the poor who cause our problems but the rich! The Gospel includes references to ethnic issues with the dialogue between Jesus and a Syrophoenician. That she was a woman is also significant. The point of the exchange was the well-being of a child. Finally, a man with a handicapping condition was healed.

Our differences and diversity make life interesting. The children and infirm give us our mission. It literally takes everyone to make community complete.

Even with these realities, too often we exclude those who are poor or different. We discriminate based on fear and ignorance. For this reason, we also find issues of justice in the lessons. Psalm 125 actually calls for divine justice.

When the church excludes the poor, the sick, children, minorities, or the disenfranchised, it ceases to be the church because the body of Christ cannot lack integrity.

The story is told that Jesus sees a man sitting on the steps of a church. "Why don't you go in?" he asks. The man replies, "Because I'm gay, they won't let me in." "That's okay," says Jesus, "I've been trying to get in for years too."

**For reflection and prayer:** *Who do you exclude from your friendship circles, your church family, your work relationships? What blessings do you miss as a result of your exclusiveness?*

**Friday, September 2**                    Read Mark 7:24-30;
                                                James 2:1-5.

Pets play an important role in many households. Our family pet when I was a teenager was a miniature poodle named Andre. Early one morning before my mother knew I was awake, I heard her tell the dog, "I didn't tolerate it from the other children, and I won't tolerate it from you."

This sort of affection for pets is not uncommon. Still, the relative place in our homes of pets and children is clear. If there were a food shortage, for example, the children would certainly eat first.

The exchange of wit between Jesus and the Syrophoenician woman is difficult for us to hear because of Christ's harsh response to her request. I wish we could actually hear the conversation and witness this mother's integrity, a mother desperate enough to address Jesus at all. Maybe something in the tone of their voices indicated Jesus' compassion and the woman's determination.

At any rate, the demon was cast out of the girl, and the church itself exists as a witness to the fact that God's love, like so much bread, is enough for those at the table and those under it.

**For reflection and prayer:** *Who do you regard as acceptable to sit at the Lord's table today?*

**Saturday, September 3**                    Read Mark 7:31-37.

Through integrity of the senses, we are able to "hear" body language. I witnessed an amazing example of this the day I bought my house.

My goal for years was to own a home. Living in a house of my own had been impractical for me both in the parish ministry and in the military chaplaincy. Finally my life was stable enough to establish a home. After months of searching for the right house, followed by weeks of negotiations, applications, and inspections I was finally ready to close. I was too excited to concentrate on anything else, so I took the entire day off work even though I did not have to be at the title office until the afternoon.

I went into an appliance store to look at things I was going to need for my kitchen. A salesman approached me and offered to help. All I said was that I needed to look at kitchen appliances, and he said, "So you're going to finally get that house you've been wanting." I could not believe his insight. The salesman made light of his intuition, saying that when a man looks at stoves on a weekday, he's just bought a house. He told me that a good salesman knows his customers.

Jesus "heard" the silence of the deaf man's world and understood him even though he had a speech impediment. The crowd was amazed and could not keep quiet about the fact that the deaf man was healed. But I suspect that the man was amazed more by Christ's compassionate touch and attention. Being healed was no greater miracle than truly being heard.

**For reflection and prayer:** *Consider how Jesus saw and heard more than the obvious. In what ways do you get beyond the superficial?*

**Sunday, September 4**                    Read Psalm 125.

This week we have thought about integrity. The psalmist adds another aspect to our thinking. Those who trust in the Lord are immovable as Mount Zion. The psalmist pictured the most stable thing in life: the hills around his beloved hometown of Jerusalem. We must remember that this psalm is not about human character. It is about the timeless and indefatigable love of God. Christian integrity always points toward God's steadfastness and away from ourselves.

When a young friend asked me to teach him to pray, I gave him a copy of *Disciplines* and agreed to be his prayer partner. We would read the daily lessons and pray, knowing that the other was doing the same. It became the most significant friendship of my life. I learned the importance of a disciplined devotional life. I learned what it is to pray in community.

I asked him to pray in all the important moments of my life. I believe our prayers made a difference. We prayed during my sister's pregnancy. Yes, the baby is a beautiful, healthy child, but our prayers were more than some sort of magic formula. Rather, they served to remind us of our God's steadfastness and our need to acknowledge the Creator in the ongoing creation.

Both my prayer partner and I moved to new cities, and we eventually lost contact. I miss knowing that we are together in prayer. But the experience has helped me to trust more in the God who does not ever move. I hope it did the same for him.

**For reflection and prayer:** *Consider asking someone to be your prayer partner. Then pray the Lord's Prayer and thank God for the prayer partners you already have.*

September 5–11, 1994 **F. Gates Vrooman**✛
**Monday, September 5** Read Mark 8:27-28.

The people knew what a messiah should look like, but Jesus did not fit the picture. However, they did think he had the characteristics of the forerunner. So, while they didn't see the salvation before them, there was hope; but it was off in the future. What about us?

Mortar shrapnel tears into the chest of a soldier. A hollow-eyed child with a distended stomach stares blankly out from a newsmagazine. A twelve-year-old runaway girl joins a prostitution ring. A husband assaults his wife and walks out on the children. Sophisticated weapons replace obsolete ones. A drunken driver runs a stop sign and kills two people.

There is so much pain, suffering, and sin that it is easier, sometimes, to believe that a messiah *will* come rather than believing that one *has* come. After all, if the messiah has come, shouldn't things be much better?

Perhaps that's part of the reason belief in the second coming of Christ always gets more attention when times are tough. The desire for a messiah intensifies. And we do hope for Christ's coming in final victory.

Perhaps, then, we're not so different from those people who thought Jesus was only the forerunner. We're still waiting too.

**Prayer:** *Thank you, God, for having already sent us Jesus, your anointed one. Help us realize what that means for us and others. Amen.*

✛Co-pastor, The First United Methodist Church, Sycamore, Illinois.

**Tuesday, September 6**                    Read Psalm 19:14;
                                           Mark 8:29-30.

Peter answered, "You are the Messiah" (TEV).

Even though our radio is tuned into Mark's station, we seem to pick up Matthew's account of what Jesus said in response to Peter: "Blessed are you, Simon Son of Jonah! For flesh and blood has not revealed this to you, but my Father in heaven" (Matt. 16:17). But neither Mark's nor Luke's (9:18-22) version of the story contains Jesus' commendation of Peter.

Peter seemed to understand—but did he? He had not yet witnessed the crucifixion or resurrection. His use of the title "messiah" may have been correct, but Jesus had yet to define the term for the disciples. So instead, the disciples are ordered, or charged, not to tell anyone what Peter has said.

The verb translated "ordered" is also translated "rebuked" in verses 32-33. It implies strong negative judgment. Jesus tells the disciples that he will be rejected and killed. Peter, showing now his misunderstanding, rebuked Jesus for saying these things. In turn, Jesus rebuked Peter in strong terms, saying, "Your thoughts don't come from God but from [humanity]" (Mark 8:33, TEV).

What about us? Do we let Jesus be who he is, or do we slap a label of our own making on him? Can we really describe the divine in human terms with our limitations of thought and language? If all our language is necessarily metaphorical, then what we say about God is that God is *like* something we already know—*like* a father, *like* a mother, *like* a friend.

For us to say what Jesus is like still requires some encounter and relationship with him, some fresh, contemporary, firsthand experience. Then we can begin to answer the question, "But who do you say that I am?"

**Prayer:** *Be still and center yourself. Be receptive to God. Let God do the speaking and revealing. Amen.*

**Wednesday, September 7**                    Read Mark 8:31-32.

In Daniel 7:13, "son of man" refers to a symbolic representation of Israel (a faithful remnant) who is finally vindicated after extensive suffering and hardship. (See RSV.) If this is what Jesus meant by the term, then the "son of man" is a corporate entity that certainly would include the disciples. They too would suffer much, be rejected, and put to death. No wonder Peter reacts negatively! Not only should the messiah not suffer like that, Peter doesn't want to either. Are we disciples of our time any different?

Another interpretation of "son of man" is based on the prophet Ezekiel. The term is applied to Ezekiel innumerable times. Ezekiel used it to describe himself as one commissioned by God to serve in lowliness and suffering on earth and later to see glory in a restored temple and land.

The parallel to Jesus' life is striking. "Suffer," "rejected," "death," "rise"—three negative strokes and one positive. Notice the ratio. Three acts of downward mobility and one upward.

Why is it, then, so many of us expect that the ratio should be reversed once we are baptized or converted or enter full-time Christian service?

We are not merely passive recipients of salvation. We are incorporated into the Son of man, a faithful remnant, and through our baptism we are commissioned, as was Ezekiel, to take up a ministry involving suffering service. Whether we are laypersons or clergypersons, how does our Christian life and ministry measure up?

**Prayer:** *Lord, if there is faithful suffering for me to do, show me where and how. Stand by me, for I am often weak and fearful. Amen.*

**Thursday, September 8**                    Read Psalm 19:7-13;
                                                    Mark 8:32-33.

The same destructive force that Jesus exorcised from the Gerasene demoniac (Mark 5:1-13) is rebuked in Peter. There is the same cosmic scope and danger as when, under a darkened sky, the howling wind and raging sea threatened to swamp the disciples' boat (Mark 4:35-41). Jesus knew he had again encountered Satan because it was a temptation to thwart his ministry by perversion of the divine power that was his.

How insidious evil can be! One might have expected it among the tax collectors of prostitutes or in the rantings and ravings of a demagogue. Certainly one would not expect it in the reasoned cadences of one's best friend, who, after all, only has your best interests at heart.

Could that evil still be tempting Jesus' disciples today? Doesn't it speak its treachery by an inner voice cautioning us against "risks" and "rash actions" for the sake of Christ? Doesn't it infect our will, making us want earthly security, praise, and promotions? Doesn't it pervert our highest goals and noblest intentions so that consciously or unconsciously our self-interest is served? Doesn't it hide in our best plans so that when they are implemented, they leave injustice and wounded people in their wake?

**Prayer:** *Savior God, humble me; make me more aware of my sin and your saving power. As the psalmist prayed, so I pray, "Create in me a clean heart, O God, and renew a right spirit within me." Amen. (Psalm 51:10, KJV)*

**Friday, September 9**                    Read Mark 8:34-37.

Pictured is a procession of condemned criminals with rope restraints around their necks, marching off to Jerusalem where they will be crucified. Now it is clear. To be a disciple means not only walking with Jesus but dying with him too. It is a paradox of Christian faith that we'll find our lives as we lose them for Christ and his kingdom.

Jesus' dramatic language does not permit us to think of inconveniences we encounter or our picayune trials as cross-bearing. Cross-bearing is a voluntary act, a personal choice, done for the sake of Christ and the kingdom of God, not merely to please friends or to comply with cultural norms or niceties.

Toyohiko Kagawa was a Japanese Christian missionary. During World War II he had risked his life to nurse and bind up wounds of American pilots shot down over Tokyo. Following the example and teachings of Jesus, he loved his enemies. He also worked with tuberculosis victims until he, himself, caught the disease.

One evening, while speaking at Princeton, his voice was broken and unclear. Kagawa gave his talk and sat down. Two young students, obviously disappointed, commented to each other: "He really didn't say much, did he?" "No, and what he did say was hard to understand."

Overhearing them, an older woman spun around and said, "Young men, when a person is nailed to a cross, he doesn't have to say anything at all!"

**Prayer:** *Dear suffering Son of man, make my discipleship more than words; make it committed action for you and your kingdom. Give me the courage to deny myself, take up my cross, and follow you. Amen.*

**Saturday, September 10**          Read James 2:1-5, 8-10.

Does a church gain anything if it shows partiality? If it does, is it not in danger of losing its soul? (See Mark 8:34-37.)

The pastor notices the distinguished visitor in the worship service: the honorable John Doe, state senator, a man of considerable means. If he joined the church, he could make a pace-setting pledge for the annual finance drive. He could also bring leadership skills, business contacts, and status to the congregation. After church, the pastor introduces him to all the "right people" who heartily welcome him.

During the same worship service, a young couple and their children are also visitors. They're new in town. He's a machine operator in a factory. She stays home with the children but wants to find part-time work to help make ends meet. Nobody notices them that day, though they feel conspicuous because he lacks a suit coat and her dress isn't finely tailored. They decide this church is too rich for their blood; they never return. Ironically, the Honorable Doe doesn't either—at least not until shortly before the next election.

James says to show no partiality on the basis of cultural or class distinctions. The church as an outpost of the kingdom of God is to be the true classless society.

Some church-growth advocates teach that greater growth occurs when new members are recruited from the same socioeconomic class as the majority of church members. The principle seems to work. But what do we do with James 2:1-5, 8-10?

**Prayer:** *Dear God, receive me into your kingdom and let me see through your eyes the inestimable value of every human being. Amen.*

**Sunday, September 11**                    Read Psalm 19:14;
                                            James 2:14-17.

We hardly need to be reminded. Faith and works are complementary; they must go together. Paul and James are not in conflict. We are saved *by* faith through Jesus Christ. We are saved *for* deeds of love and justice. Faith roots into the soil of God's love with the consequence that the plant bears the fruit of God's love.

Talk is cheap, but discipleship is not. There is a price to be paid. When people are in need, we are to help. It is as simple as that. We don't ask about their denominational affiliation or their national allegiance or their reputation in the community.

Much of what passes for Christian spirituality today is faith without works of charity. Service and simplicity are just as much spiritual disciplines as are prayer and meditation. Discipleship is not just walking alone in the garden with Jesus. It can be just as spiritual an act to march for nuclear disarmament as it is to go to church. If it is genuine, faith will boldly express itself in social service, social witness, and social action. And even when that is done in love, a price will be paid.

Mother Teresa was awarded the Nobel Prize for her humanitarian work. The irony is that they gave it to her for doing what all of us are called to do. She is doing what Jesus would do if he had her opportunity today. Are we doing what Jesus would do if he had our opportunities?

**Suggestion for meditation:** *Be still and prayerful. Let Jesus show you where in your life you need to take some faithful, loving action. Ask for his help and listen for his reply.*

## CHOOSING LIFE WITH GOD

September 12–18, 1994
**Monday, September 12**

**Paul L. Escamilla✢**
Read Proverbs 31:10-31.

Proverbs 31 is a strikingly vivid picture of a woman who is, in her own right, a "renaissance woman" of sorts. Securing food, growing produce, making wool and linens, trading, merchandising, clothing her family, discharging orders for her household staff—this is a woman of some means.

But clearly her means are not merely material. Her success derives from an inner sensibility or character rather than from an outer set of resources. The text profiles this character beautifully.

First, the woman's hands (mentioned seven times) figure prominently as an extension of her inner intentions and motives. Not only do they craft and sew and plant and reap; they also clothe and feed and respond to the poor, always exuding self-assurance and confidence. Not to be missed is the fact that they serve the woman's own needs as well as those of her household and the needy (vv. 17, 22).

Other verses demonstrate the balance and well-roundedness of this woman as well. She has dignity in her person but also laughter (v. 25). She is wise but also kind (v. 26). She seeks opportunities for generosity no less than for gain (v. 20). She is clearly a beautiful person, but charm or physical appearance are irrelevant to her beauty (v. 30). Finally, she knows the dimension of life from which all other dimensions derive their meaning: knowing God (v. 30). Indeed "her works praise her."

**Suggestion for meditation:** *Think on the life of this person in Proverbs as a model of virtue.*

---

✢Pastor of First United Methodist Church, Heath, Texas.

**Tuesday, September 13**                    Read Psalm 1:1-2.

The first verse of Psalm 1 introduces us to a word that has not appeared to this point in the Hebrew scriptures: *blessed.* We've seen words like *bless* and *blessing* before, of course, but those particular Hebrew words refer to the act or experience of anointing, affirming, or exalting (for example, Gen. 48:8-22). This word, *blessed,* has more to do with an outlook or disposition toward life. The closest translation for the word is probably *happy.*

*Happy* is about as washed out, watered-down, overused, and undernourished as a word can get. Yet Psalm 1 lifts it up and applies it with remarkable freshness, substance, and depth. And what is the source of this state of happiness? It takes a while to find out, following the sentence to its conclusion; but the search leads us here: "Blessed are those . . . whose delight is in the law of the LORD."

The psalm, which serves as a prelude or preamble to the whole psalter, spells out in simple terms the way a good life evolves: happiness is a matter of finding good instruction (while avoiding poor instruction) and living by it.

As it turns out, the good instruction is not a package deal. No formulas or "secret steps to happiness" apply. We could translate "The law of the LORD" as "The LORD's instruction," which clarifies something extremely important about the biblical understanding of happiness: it involves being in relationship with God, who teaches, guides, and directs our paths. Happy are those who delight in their teacher and whose teacher's name is the Lord.

**Prayer:** *God, I wish to know you in all your delightfulness and to learn your instruction that my life may be blessed. Amen.*

**Wednesday, September 14**                    Read Psalm 1:3.

If verses 1 and 2 of Psalm 1 explain the means to happiness in God, then verse 3 has something to say about its effect on our lives. In essence, to be related to God is to become as trees. This metaphor occupies the whole of the third verse.

The trees depicted here are not cut down for firewood, used up once, and discarded as ashes. A person of faith is meant for greater and repeated resourcefulness—a lifetime of giving, serving, growing, and prospering. That these trees are planted by streams of water suggests that not only do they nourish others, but they receive nourishment. Further, their fruit bearing is seasonal, rhythmic, and natural; not erratic, hyperactive, then finally, spent. Trees are not fruit factories but fruit bearers. The fruit they yield is not an unrelated "product" but an expression of their own organic makeup.

Of course the trees envisioned by the psalmist are grounded. By their nature, they will reach outward and upward, toward water and sunlight. And in season, their boughs will bend earthward with the weight of their fruit. But not all their activity is so visible to the eye; at the same time, they always will be developing roots deep down, drawing continual nourishment from both earth and stream.

Nourishing and drawing nourishment. Giving, yet maintaining identity. Growing and reaching, yet firmly grounded. Persons whose lives are rooted in God's presence and instruction reflect these characteristics.

**Suggestion for meditation:** *Think of yourself in terms of Psalm 1: I am like a tree, and my life is grounded and watered. I am reaching, providing shade, and bearing fruit; for I delight in God's instruction.*

**Prayer:** *O God, you are rain and sunshine, river and soil to the tree that is my life. I rest in your provision and delight in your care. Amen.*

**Thursday, September 15**          Read Psalm 1:4-6.

Verses 1-3 painted the blissful picture of a life of happiness in God in all its substance, creativity, and beauty. Verses 4-6 draw the contrast. And for this purpose, the psalmist employs another metaphor, this one based on chaff.

The hues and tones of this metaphorical picture are somber and bland. Gone are the images of streaming sun and the shade of boughs of green leaf and robust fruit, flowing stream and cool, sweet-smelling earth. Here we have chaff—weightless, tasteless, void of substance or texture or color. The only thing said of it is that the wind drives it away. At winnowing time, its only value is its absence.

The psalmist's artistry becomes clear. Even as the lessons of the good life; that is—life within God's instruction—are being spelled out, two pictures have been painted that affect our senses in very different ways. Life with God tastes sweet, savory; it is joyous and abundant. Life apart from God—that is, lived to oneself—is husklike, bland, and dry; in other words, it is tasteless.

Likewise, the sense of footing differs in the two pictures. The "way of the righteous" is well-grounded, even while allowing for growth and movement. The "way of the wicked" is shifty, flighty, and completely without bearing.

In terms of contrasts, we could draw no greater. Of course, life does not always present such obvious differences between choosing life with God versus life on one's own. That is precisely why Psalm 1 is so valuable; it sees with a clear, spiritual eye the way life with God and life on one's own really are. Then it invites us to choose life with God.

**Prayer:** *Guide me, O God, in choosing always that which is good and worthy and deeply delightful over that which is banal and tasteless and dry. Amen.*

**Friday, September 16**                    Read Mark 9:33-37.

We know Mark as the hard-driving evangelist. Just reading his first chapter without pause can leave us nearly breathless. By the time we get to this point in the Gospel, not only have many, many actions been recorded but the word *immediately* has been peppered throughout. This is no sit-down story. Jesus is on the move—healing, teaching, exorcising demons, feeding the hungry, and on and on.

Then something happens to bring it all to a halt. Is it a run-in with Pharisees? a scrape with the Sanhedrin? Is it fatigue or weariness or disillusionment? It is none of these things. In the middle of chapter 9, which is the middle of the Gospel, everything comes to a halt because Jesus perceives that his disciples are talking about their own greatness. Jesus sits down—one of the few times in the entire Gospel—and teaches his disciples.

It is very important to notice that the one thing that slows down the pace of this Gospel is the evidence of selfish ambition on the part of Jesus' disciples. Who is the greatest? Who is the best? Who is on top? Who is more special? When Jesus sensed that this was the subject of their conversation, he sat down.

Think for a moment about what makes you "sit down." What leads you to set aside whatever you are doing and look the other person in the eye? For Jesus, it may have been his concern that the very heart of his teaching and witness might be misunderstood, overlooked, or forgotten.

Jesus sat down, called the twelve, and said to them, "Whoever wants to be first must be last of all and servant of all." This is important; this is critical. In a nutshell, this is discipleship.

**Prayer:** *O God, grant me ears to hear this word of Jesus. Beginning now, and throughout this day, give me courage to live it! Amen.*

271

**Saturday, September 17**                Read Mark 9:30-37.

The Gospel text for this week is a centerpiece for the whole Book of Mark, a focal point for the portrayal of Jesus' fate at the hands of his enemies: he is to suffer and die before he is raised up again. It is the second of three prophecies in which Jesus foretells his own fate. (Mark 8:31-33 and Mark 10:32-45 are the other two.) All three of these passages share a common external structure as well: the anticipated suffering of Jesus is followed by evidences of the lofty ambitions of certain of Jesus' disciples.

In each case the inappropriate response to Jesus' prophecy appears to be completely unwitting. In the first instance, Peter simply expresses a protectiveness related to his own ambitions for Jesus (8:32); in the third, the prophecy appears to go over their heads (10:35 and following). In today's reading, confusion and fear drive the disciples to a different subject (v. 32).

Different, but not unrelated. Greatness is the common denominator of both Jesus' words and the disciples' miscast responses. But the disciples can think of greatness only in terms of self-filling, while Jesus speaks of a greatness based on self-emptying. The disciples' gaze is rather high up in the clouds; Jesus looks upon the weakest, smallest, lowliest example around and demonstrates the meaning of true greatness.

"Whoever wants to associate with me, and even with God, is so invited," Jesus in effect says; and we all look up, dreaming of the possibilities of such greatness. Meanwhile, Jesus stoops down and takes a child in his arms.

**Prayer (to pray throughout the day):** *Lord, reveal to my eyes and to my heart the truly great things, that I may seek them and, having found them, learn to love them. Amen.*

**Sunday, September 18**                    Read James 3:13–4:3.

Not one to mince words, the writer of James spells out some very plain matters in a very short space. Are you wise? This is how we will know: your good life will show works that are carried out with gentleness. On the other hand, if your hearts are occupied with envy and selfish ambition (see this week's Gospel readings), then this is how we will know: disorder and wickedness of every kind will be in evidence. James calls this wisdom too but of another sort (v. 15).

And what exactly does "wickedness of every kind" mean? Exactly that: everything from disagreements to murder (4:2). It is difficult to imagine murder's being an actual issue in the life of a congregation; but if the Letter of James is anything, it is realistic. James knows well that when it comes to the struggle to become holy, compassionate, and wise, Christians are by no means out of the woods simply by virtue of their name. "Envy" and "selfish ambition" (referred to twice in this text) often find abundant soil in Christian climates.

But let us go on to the next characterization—that of wisdom, which comes from above. This description, rather than the one we have just looked at, is the real heart of the text. It reminds us in many ways of the characterization of the blessed person in Psalm 1: fruitfulness and a willingness to yield—another use of the harvest metaphor. The passage names other qualities: purity, peaceableness, gentleness, mercy, and the absence of partiality or hypocrisy.

James teaches us that wisdom is far more than simply head knowledge. Wisdom gives texture to every dimension of our life and serving. And it is one thing more; it is a gift from above.

**Suggestion for meditation:** *Meditate on the qualities of wisdom from above. Begin to seek these in prayer and in practice.*

# *1995*

## Is just around the corner!
## Now is the time to order your copy of
## THE UPPER ROOM DISCIPLINES 1995

*Year after year, The Upper Room Disciplines continues to appeal to more and more Christians who, like yourself, desire a more disciplined spiritual life. Be sure to order your copy today, while the 1995 edition is still available.*

---

### THE UPPER ROOM DISCIPLINES 1995
$6.95 each; 10 or more $5.91 each
(PLUS SHIPPING AND HANDLING)
Ask for product number UR692.

**TO ORDER YOUR COPIES —**

**CALL:** 615-340-7284
Tell the customer representative
your source code is 95D.

**WRITE:**
Merchandise Products
Upper Room Books
P.O. Box 856
Nashville, TN 37202-0189

**SHIPPING and HANDLING:**
On **prepaid orders** include
$2.00 for handling. We pay
postage.
On **"bill-me-later" orders** we
will add $2.00 for handling plus
postage to your account.
**Payment must accompany all
orders under $10.00.**
Please make all payments in
U.S. funds.

THE UPPER ROOM DISCIPLINES 1995
*is also available at most bookstores.*

September 19–25, 1994                  **W. Douglas Mills✝**
**Monday, September 19**               Read James 5:13-20.

The responsibility of the individual to the community and the community to the individual is a recurrent theme in Christian thought. If one in the community is sick, the whole community is weakened. The whole community, led by its elders, should pray for healing for the one and for the whole. If one member commits a sin, the whole community is weakened. We are to confess our sins to one another so that the one and the whole can be restored.

The community and its members are held together like a fragile spider web. A ripple in one place can be felt throughout. And if the web is broken at one juncture, the whole thing may collapse.

In his program from "Lake Wobegon," Garrison Keillor used his stories to communicate this truth. All of his characters in this town were intricately connected, and their stories were held together in these fragile connections. In his painfully humorous way, Keillor reminded us that one weak link can break the whole chain of community. If one commits adultery, what is to stop another from selling rancid sausage? At that point, there is no accountability and no sense of responsibility.

The Christian community has a different set of expectations. Our lives are intertwined. We rejoice together, confess together, sing together. And most of all, we pray together.

**Suggestion for prayer:** *Pray the Lord's Prayer.*

✝Pastor, New Covenant United Methodist Church, Farmington, New Mexico.

274

**Tuesday, September 20**                    Read Esther 1–3.

What are we to do with the Book of Esther? Some have said that it should not even be in the Bible. The Essene community of Qumran did not regard it as canonical. It is the only Old Testament book not represented in the Dead Sea Scrolls. Few Christians find anything in it that is edifying. Martin Luther even wrote that he wished it did not exist.

Some have argued that the Book of Esther has little theological value. It does not mention God, though it does speak of the King of Persia some 190 times. It does not acknowledge the Law of the Covenant. There is no mention of sacrifice or the Temple. Some readers have even thought it teaches values opposite to love, kindness, and forgiveness.

Still, here it is in our Bibles. The Council of Jamnia included it as canon in A.D. 90. Josephus paraphrased the Esther story in his volume *Jewish Antiquities XI*. It was included on the canonical lists of Origen, Clement of Rome, Ruffinus, Augustine, and others. It was included in the Septuagint (Greek) version of scripture. And it is in every English version!

Not every book of the Bible has to be as profound as the Book of Job or Paul's Letter to the Romans. Not every book has to be as instructive as the letters to the Corinthians, Timothy, and Titus. Some books—such as Esther—need make only one point: the people of God belong to a community; and though the people may be far from God, God is never far from them.

**Prayer:** *Be near this day, gracious God, especially in the reading and studying of your word given to us in scripture. Amen.*

**Wednesday, September 21**                    Read Esther 4–6.

During one of his drinking parties in his capital city of Susa—a party not unlike a fraternity party in the movies—King Ahasuerus summoned his queen, Vashti. For whatever reason, Vashti refused to appear, and Ahasuerus had her summarily deposed. After a lengthy and broad search, a beautiful woman named Esther (a Jew, though the king did not know it) was chosen to be the new queen.

Some time later, a palace plot was hatched to assassinate the king. Esther's adopted father, Mordecai, heard of it and reported it to Esther. She, in turn, reported it to the king. Thus Mordecai, a Jew, saved the life of King Ahasuerus.

Though the king became indebted to him, Mordecai had enemies inside the palace, most notably the prime minister, Haman. Because Mordecai would not bow before him, Haman slyly convinced the king to issue an edict declaring that the enemies of the king should be killed—to which Haman appended the name of Mordecai and all Jews.

If you did not know that you were reading this story in the Bible, you might think you were reading contemporary history. During the first half of the twentieth century, Jews have been persecuted to the point of death by Russia and Nazi Germany. The German persecution was so great that about one-third of all Jews were killed and others tortured—and this not by the ruse of the prime minister but at the explicit direction of the supreme Nazi leader.

Like King Ahasuerus, we need to read our books of records (6:1), lest we forget the sadness of our past and the hope of our future.

**Suggestion for prayer:** *Say a prayer of forgiveness for this nation and all nations.*

**Thursday, September 22**     Read Esther 7:1-6, 9-10; 9:20-22.

Had it not been for Esther and Mordecai, the Jews would have been destroyed. As it was, Esther used her position to thwart the plans for destruction. From that day to this, Jews have remembered this story with rejoicing at the feast of Purim.

Esther 4:14 is worth review. If Esther had kept silent, "relief and deliverance" would come from another place—that is the assurance from God. But on the other hand, maybe she was given her position for "just such a time as this." Even from her place of prestige and power, she had a responsibility to her primary community, the people of God.

In *The Book of Worship* of The United Methodist Church, the prayer "For the Nation" asks that God teach us "to see every question of national policy in the light of our faith." This is the message of the Book of Esther.

We must not trivialize our positions or the positions of others. We must do our work with competence and expect that others will do the same. And those who are close to the king, the president, the legislator, or the mayor must act in faith, not as citizens of this town or country but as citizens of God's kingdom.

**Prayer:** *Teach us, God of every nation, to see every question of national policy in the light of our faith, that we may check in ourselves and in others every passion that makes for war, all ungenerous judgment, all promptings of self assurance, all presumptuous claims.\* Amen.*

---

\*"For the Nation," #515, *The Book of Worship*, © 1992 by The United Methodist Publishing House.

**Friday, September 23**     Read Mark 9:38-41.

"Who is part of our group?" the early Christians asked. Down through the centuries the question has been asked again in many forms: Who is authorized to teach? to preach? to cast out demons? And who authorized them?

The truth is, we are suspicious of others who do not do things the way we do them. We are suspicious even of other Christians—those who act in Christ's name (v. 38) but not necessarily with our label. We may like the preaching of Baptists but question their view of sanctification. We may like the liturgical worship of Episcopalians but have reservations about their loyalties. We may like the singing and the politics of United Methodists but have deep reservations about their commitment to the fundamentals.

To make matters worse, a whole new breed of "nondenominational" folks also claim to be acting in "Christ's name," and they are reaching the unchurched by focusing on the needs of people in today's society and often by providing definite, easy-to-understand answers to issues of faith.

In all these cases we see amazing things happen. People's lives are being changed. Miracles occur. The grace of God in Jesus Christ is proclaimed. And still, in the back of our minds, the question lingers: Should we stop them?

Jesus' answer is, in part, to broaden our definition of community. Don't look so much at labels; look more at action. To borrow a thought from another Gospel (Matt. 12:33), "the tree is known by its fruit."

**Prayer:** *Open our eyes, gracious God, to the wonders of your work; let us not judge; instead let us rejoice. Amen.*

**Saturday, September 24**                    Read Mark 9:42-48.

Living in community carries certain obligations and restrictions. Jesus' instructions to cut off a hand or a foot or to pluck out an offending eye can be read in at least two different ways. To speak of parts of our own body as if they were autonomous is part of the language custom.

Following this Jewish line of thinking, the hand and the eye may tempt us toward adultery, and the foot may take us there. Similarly, other parts of ourselves may bring different kinds of temptations. Our jobs may tempt us toward injustice. Our hobbies may tempt us to neglect responsibilities. Our obsessions might hold us back from love, kindness, or even from going on to perfection. If they are leading us into temptation, cut them off. In all of these cases, the community may be tempted to look the other way.

Jesus was not suggesting literal self-mutilation. Instead he was speaking of the costliest of sacrifices. The body should be treasured, but God should be treasured more. God is more important than even the most important parts of our own bodies. We should be willing to deny any part, to "cut it off" if it keeps us from following God's will.

In another vein, we may read these verses as if we as individuals are members of one body, the body of Christ. In this sense, then, we must not allow one member of the body to bring down the whole. We may exhort, reproach, and forgive, yes. But we have the responsibility to protect the community from any who might lead it astray. We are accountable to others and to the community at large. We can be neither victim nor victimizer.

**Suggestion for meditation:** *What part of yourself is your greatest temptation?*

**Sunday, September 25**                    Read Mark 9:49-50.

The ancient world could not have survived without salt. It preserved food from putrefaction. It also cleansed the sacrificial offering in the Temple. Today, we likewise use salt as a preservative. Some meats are preserved this way still. And salt is used to improve taste as well as for other helpful purposes: to keep water from freezing on highways and to lower the temperature in our ice cream freezers.

In our world, though, we can also buy salt substitutes. These products have the look, the feel, and the taste of salt, but they have none of the preservative or purifying qualities.

The requirements of discipleship are demanding. To respond and then forsake them is a great loss, akin to salt's losing its saltiness. Disciples have a responsibility to the immediate community and also to the greater community to be the world's salt.

Perhaps all of us have partaken in that U.S. custom of "church shopping." We visit different churches until we find one that "stocks" the programs we are looking for—the music, children's ministries, small groups—and then we become a regular customer there. When our perceived needs change, we may church shop again.

At some point, radical discipleship requires us to stop and consider that *we,* not the programs of any given church, are the stuff—the salt, if you will—that this church stocks. The responsibility and the choice to be a purifying presence wherever we are is ours. And no substitutes will do.

**Prayer:** *Lord God, in your great mercy, pour out upon your people your Spirit, that strengthened by your blessings, we may hold fast to the gift of faith as salt unto your world. Amen.*

September 26–October 2, 1994        **Deborah Lynn Drash✚**
**Monday, September 26**                      Read Job 1:1, 9-10.

A protective fence in the land of Uz and a perfect man of integrity living there sets the stage. The reader suspects that it is just a matter of time before Job will be set up for the inevitable. Soon Job's life spins miserably out of balance.

Inspirational author Og Mandino, in *The Greatest Miracle in the World,* has a dialogue reminiscent of the complex theodicy in Job's plight. Mandino asks an old man, "Aren't you trying to play God?" He responds, "I am not playing God. What you will learn sooner or later, is that God very often plays man. God will do nothing without man and whenever He works a miracle it is always done through man."* We do not know exactly what will happen to Job or what the final outcome of his story will be. How will Job fare?

Though Job's situation may differ from our own, we each eventually face the challenge of dealing with suffering. It is as if some are enrolled in the "Intro to Suffering I" class and find that, at least for now, they pass with easy marks. Others, such as Job, discover they are in life's "Advanced Suffering Comprehensives" class without even willingly registering for the course!

**Suggestion for meditation:** *How can we address suffering in our lives and the lives of others?*

---

✚Pastor, First and Vacherie United Methodist Church, Thibodaux, Louisiana; author, spiritual retreat leader.

*Og Mandino, *The Greatest Miracle in the World* (Bantam Books, 1975), p. 18.

**Tuesday, September 27**                    Read Job 2:1-10.

In Job's era, organized religious life was changing. At one end of the spectrum, Jewish faith affirmed God's definitive action in human history. However, sometimes that God-action was interpreted as a personalized punishment for sin. Misfortune and suffering were explained as natural outcomes. Hence, we hear more laments than hymns of praise in some of the psalms. The feelings and experiences chronicled in Lamentations, Job, and Jeremiah reveal a preoccupation. At the other end of the spectrum, individual songs of complaint began finding new voices.

When one experienced a calamity, it was believed that retribution for sin must be made to achieve restoration. The ancient Israelite mindset began to articulate movements away from feelings of total hopelessness and alienation toward developing expressions of confidence and trust and songs of praise.

A new balance seemingly was being reached as the conscious spiritual soul-self in complaint began to differentiate between external and internal circumstances. In Job we see an exciting new theology emerging which in part affirms the notion of mercy in the midst of suffering and injustice—especially for God's suffering servants. The sin/punishment motif was giving way to the new paradigm of hope.

Today our faith asserts that Christ's love is ever present, even when shifting internal or external circumstances and suffering become our lot. Jesus is the author of new paradigms and possibilities! Through every change he will remain faithful.

**Prayer:** *Lord, when life begins to shift, some say you are tester, tyrant, punisher. Be for me a ballast, redeemer, and advocate as I seek to live in the life of the Spirit. Amen.*

**Wednesday, September 28**                    Read Psalm 26.

Our parsonage neighborhood has lots of children, pre-adolescents, and young adults who enjoy riding their bicycles around the area.

Coming home after a worship service that had been a deep blessing for me, I sensed the Spirit's movement alive and vibrant within our congregation and in the joyful events earlier that day. Reviewing the worship service and pondering the mysteries of the Holy Spirit's involvement in human lives, I neared home.

One of the neighborhood kids passed by on her bike. She was trying to balance a gym bag almost as big as she was! Her bike hit an uneven rocky portion of the road, sending bicycle, gym bag, and bulging contents into an ominous wobble. Struggling to regain control, the little girl headed for a smooth, more even place in the road. Gliding to a stop she paused there. Shifting the load, finding a new balance, and resting, she then continued on.

In Israel during the time of the psalmist, and still today, the rocky terrain of that country challenges one to look for "even places" (KJV). Throughout salvation history, God provides many sources of integrity and elements of grace so we may regain spiritual footing in rocky places. We renew, recenter, and rejoice in finding a spiritually solid even place.

How many times in our own lives and journeys do we overload, hit a rough spot, and soon feel things wobble a bit? When we are willing to make and take time to spiritually pause and look for the even place, the Holy Spirit helps us take stock of things, enabling us to fully glide toward a new balance in our lives and congregations.

**Prayer:** *God of the even places, balance us anew this day. Amen.*

**Thursday, September 29**                    Read Psalm 25.

God's love never lets us go even when our lives are out of balance. The New Testament reminds us that all have sinned and fallen short of the glory of God. Verses 7 and 8 in today's psalm echo similar thoughts of reorientation: "Do not remember the sins of my youth or my transgressions; according to your steadfast love remember me, for your goodness' sake, O LORD! Good and upright is the LORD; therefore he instructs sinners in the way."

None is exempt from suffering, sin, and transgression. Healing, wholeness, shalom are possible and viable when God is the way. Christ invites us to immerse ourselves in learning "the way" that leads to God's eternal grace and salvation in Jesus Christ.

Discipleship is learning the intricacies and the pathways of Christian living and forgiveness. Disciples learn to love one another as Christ loves and abides in us. It is a lifelong process.

Similar to John Wesley's notion of going on in Christian perfection, we hope and yearn to be made perfect in God's agape love; if not in this life, then in the next. God's love is a love that will not let us go! *Hesed* is an Old Testament Hebrew word suggesting God's loyalty, remembrance, and everlasting faithfulness. This word, *hesed*, also reminds me of the New Testament notion of agape love. Our discipleship and our conviction is our response.

**Prayer:** *Lord, balance us and our often sluggish human inclinations. Through the Holy Spirit quicken our imagination and vision! Speak to us the truth we long to hear. Amen.*

**Friday, September 30**                    Read Hebrews 1:1-4; 2:5-13.

The land of Israel holds many powerful images, places, and memories. One such place is the ancient fortress, Masada. Jews under seige desperately chose self-death over imprisonment and torture by their would-be captors. While we were touring Masada, a black bird closely followed our group, eyeing us curiously. The bird stayed and perched near us, as we shared worship and devotionals at the Masada synagogue site. The bird began cawing a plaintive cry that sounded very much like "remember."

Disciples can never afford to forget the many cruelties and shortcomings of human experience. Neither can we ever afford to forget God's mercy and all-encompassing agape love. God remains steady and faithful in the midst of life's changes, sufferings, or imbalances. God remembers even when people forget!

Aren't there some things that will be imprinted forever in our rememberings and in our hearts? I know I will never forget some things. I am persuaded we can remember the delightful taste and smell of just-baked communion bread; cradling a squiggly newborn baby; seeing the earnest, outstretched hand of mission and caring; hearing Hurricane Andrew and tornadoes it spawned roar through our town; and most powerful of all, hearing the voice of God calling us by name in the night. And we respond, "Here I am Lord. Here is your church. What would you have us be and do?"

**Prayer:** *God of more excellent names and ways, your forgiveness and memory are complete and infinite. Our ways are different, incomplete, and finite. God whose name is Remember, help us to call upon you and hear your word of grace today. Amen.*

**Saturday, October 1**                    Read Mark 10:2-16.

It has been said that suffering is viewed as "the lint" in the fabric of life. Reba* seemed to have more lint than woven warp and woof in her life's fabric. The phone rang on Saturday night and a strained voice began, "You don't know me; I don't even live in your town. I saw the church ad and your name in the phone book. Please don't hang up." At about 10:30 P.M. we were just sitting down to supper.

She continued, "I need some scriptures and a word of hope and comfort about divorce." (Silently I wondered if the two things could be compatible.) My mind raced to form a response. Flipping through the Bible to Mark 10, I began to listen to her needs, hear the story unfold, and ask questions. It was okay that dinner got cold.

This Markan passage became chillingly real for me. During their entire marriage, Reba's yearning had been to share life in the Spirit and a church with her husband. Reba's husband had taken up with a "live-in" lover. He had been neglecting the babies to whom he and Reba had given life. He had gotten in trouble with the law over a fight concerning his lover and was now in jail. Reba was displaced, relying on family and friends for survival. Disgust and rebuke were her husband's common responses, according to Reba's side of the story.

We talked, we read the Bible; we prayed, laughed, and cried. This woman still loved him in spite of everything. She knew she was in a troubled marriage but did not know her options as a Christian. She wanted a blessing and a Christian family life for her children.

**Prayer:** *O God of options and blessings, when children suffer, help us to see and respond with Jesus' eyes and compassion. Amen.*

*Her name has been changed.

## October 2 (World Communion Sunday)

Read Mark 10:2-16.

### An African Model for Group Bible Study*

1. One person reads this passage aloud slowly.

2. Each silently recalls the word or phrase that catches his or her attention (one minute).

3. Each person briefly shares his or her chosen word or phrase aloud with the group.

4. In a mixed group, have one person of opposite gender/race read the passage out loud again.

5. Think or write your response to this question: Where does this passage touch my life today? (Take about 3–5 minutes.)

6. Each person shares his or her answer to question 5 with the group. (Allow ample time.)

7. Silently read the passage again.

8. Each meditates or writes a response to the following questions: From what I have heard and shared, what does God want me to do or be in the immediate future? How does God invite me to change? (Take about 3–5 minutes.)

9. Each shares his or her answer to question 8 aloud, beginning with the word *I*: "I . . ." (Allow ample time.)

10. Each person prays aloud for the person on his or her right, naming what that person shared in #9. Covenant to pray that same prayer for him or her until the group meets together again.

**Prayer:** *Almighty God, on this World Communion Sunday, generously bless your body of Christ throughout the earth. Balance us with your gifts of Spirit and the Holy Word. Help us live in integrity. Amen.*

---

* Lumko Missiological Institute of South Africa via the Bible base communities of South America. This model of Bible study was brought to Louisiana by Bishop William B. Oden. It was used at the 23rd session of the United Methodist Louisiana Annual Conference.

October 3–9, 1994                    **Charles R. Brown✢**
**Monday, October 3**                 Read Job 23:1-4.

*About God*

He was a good man, a family man. The record indicates not a bad word was said about him. He dealt honestly with others. If we had lived in his community, we would have wanted our children to meet him.

Yet this blameless and upright man named Job was faced with devastation. He lost his possessions, the people who worked for him, his family, and his good health.

Job's response? Did he fall to the ground, legs kicking, fists pounding the dirt? My reaction perhaps—but not that of the man from Uz. Yes, he did fall to the ground, but scripture says, "He fell to the ground in worship" (1:20, NIV). He did not charge God with any wrongdoing.

Then came the comforters, those who would sit with Job and cry with him. However, Job's devastation must have intensified when his visitors opened their mouths. His counselors' thorny words and apparent misunderstanding about God may have stimulated further struggle with all that happened.

"If only I had known. . . . " "If only I had. . . . "

Through all the potential misunderstanding surrounding him, with all the legitimate questions invading his mind, Job remained focused. He knew where to find the answers—yes, he knew *who* had the answers. (See Job 23:13-17.)

**Prayer:** *Great God of all understanding, increase ours. When the maze of life has us confused, cause us to find our way in you and rest. Amen.*

✢Land title customer service representative; elder and worship leader, Bible Fellowship, Riverside, California.

**Tuesday, October 4**     Read Job 1:1-17; Psalm 22:1-2.

*About darkness*

I turned off the engine and the lights, rolled down the window, and told the kids to listen. The quiet starlit night covering the country road was refreshing to my city-cluttered ears. We were there less than a minute when one of the boys asked, "Are we gonna go now?"

What I found to be solitude the children thought of as spooky. That which was irresistible to me was insecurity to them. In the dark, especially as children, we do not rest.

Job was in the dark spiritually. A heavy, thick darkness had fallen upon him. He was afraid. The psalmist echoes the trembling voice of Job: "O my God, I cry out by day, but you do not answer, by night, and am not silent" (NIV).

Darkness. How do you handle those ink-stained days; days none of us are immunized against? As a child I stared into the night, unable to sleep. Sometimes in desperation I cried and cried and cried. Like my son on the country road, we as adults tend to say to God when the shroud of darkness blinds our eyes, "Are we gonna go now?"

Would it have seemed strange to hear Job ask that same question? In the dark I am frightened. Are we gonna go now, Lord? I have lost those dearest to me. Are we gonna go now? All the wealth of a lifetime has been snatched away. Are we gonna go now? Lord, are we going to move on away from this place of ruin? Are we gonna go now?

But Job seems to have been blessed with night vision for his journey. Somehow he caught glimpses of light beyond the shadows of death. Through it all, Job was a man of hope.

**Prayer:** *When darkness overwhelms me, Lord, may I find hope in the Light of the world. Amen.*

**Wednesday, October 5**                    Read Mark 10:17-21.

*About eternal life*

Throughout the play *You're a Good Man, Charlie Brown,* Charlie Brown is ridiculed, embarrassed, dumped on, frustrated, and generally criticized by everyone, including his dog Snoopy. In the end, Lucy, of all people, offers him great affirmation. "You're a good man, Charlie Brown."

There *are* lots of good men and women in the world—people like the young man who asked Jesus about eternal life.

Jesus' answer read like a qualification list for admission to heaven. The wealthy young man was quick to respond. Ever killed anyone? No. Unfaithful? No. Swindled anyone? No. Testified falsely? No. Dishonored your parents? No. By now he was feeling good, thinking, *If this is what it takes, I'm in.*

But one more area needed to be considered. The challenge before the young man was to compare the treasure in his wallet with the treasure in heaven.

Look at what you have. Sell it all, Jesus tells him. Take the money and give it to the poor. The exchanged promise was treasure in heaven. Christ's final word to him was to change his whole lifestyle and follow him.

*But I have accomplished so much in these few years,* the young man thinks. *Look at all the money I've made. Look at the potential influence that is mine.*

Jesus did look but not at the young man's treasure. He looked at his heart, spoke the simple truth to him, and loved him. He offered him eternal life if he would walk the path that would lead him to new understanding—the path of Christ.

**Prayer:** *Giver of life everlasting, remind us often that it is not our goodness but your grace, not our sufficiency but your sacrifice, not our riches but your righteousness that opens heaven's gate to life eternal. Amen.*

**Thursday, October 6**                    Read Mark 10:22-31.

*About wealth*

My hands trembled as I opened the registered letter from Publishers Clearing House. Finally after all these years, after all the stamps and returned envelopes and all those subscriptions, I was a winner. My heart raced as I considered all the things I wanted to do with the $6 million about to be deposited into my bank account. Change vocations. Travel. Buy a condo in Palm Springs. Buy a car for my daughter. Smother my wife with flowers and gifts.

Suddenly I'm yanked from my fantasy when the thought of giving it all away crosses my mind. Would I do that if I really did find myself wealthy? Just what would my attitude be toward my treasure?

When the young rich man was encouraged to sell all and give everything to the poor, he didn't exactly leap for joy. The Bible says, "At this the man's face fell. He went away sad, because he had great wealth" (NIV).

Jesus seized the opportunity to give the disciples, who had witnessed this encounter, a minifinancial seminar. They were amazed when he told them how hard it is for a rich person to get into the kingdom of God. It was as if they were asking, "What's it going to take? We have left our work, our families and friends."

Then came Jesus' faithful reminder that nothing can buy access into the kingdom. Hearing this, we are reminded that "By grace you have been saved, through faith—and this not from yourselves, it is the gift of God—not by works, so that no one can boast" (Eph. 2:8-9, NIV).

**Prayer:** *God, grant us your perspective when it comes to money and your great kingdom purpose. Amen.*

**Friday, October 7**                    Read Hebrews 4:12.

*About God's word*

I became a serious collector in the fourth grade. I proudly displayed a large suitcase full of treasures and invested hours poring over my unique assortment of bottle caps.

My hobby involved regular visits to soda vending machines. I would come home with pockets bulging, sometimes with bags full of bottle caps. Like the person who wants canceled stamps with the least amount of markings, I looked for bottle caps with little or no bends in them.

I met a young man who told me his hobby was the Bible. He knew about more people, places, and events in the Bible than I even knew existed. I sensed a bit of pride in himself as he carried his knowledge of Bible stuff.

As a high school student, I was bothered that he seemed to know so much more than I did. After all, I had been going to church all my life, and I felt I should have had a little better handle on spiritual things.

However, I came to realize that for him this really was just a hobby. He knew much *about* the Bible, but it soon became evident that he was not acquainted with the spiritual things revealed through a relationship with Jesus Christ.

The writer of Hebrews says, "The word of God is living and active" (NIV). *Living and active.* The Bible is more than just a passing pleasure to be enjoyed when we are in the mood.

A look at Jesus' life puts flesh to the printed word. Living and active. Walking. Praying. Healing. Preaching. Loving. Teaching. Weeping. Giving. Caring. Holding. Blessing. Jesus is our example.

**Suggestion for meditation:** *What is one way that I might allow God's word to be living and active through me?*

**Saturday, October 8**                    Read Psalm 22:1-15.

*About rest*

Some cannot rid their minds of awful childhood memories of parental abandonment. Some of us remember a time on the playground when the other kids left us all alone. Or you may remember that summer trip your friends were so excited about, but you were not asked to go along. It's difficult to rest when ugly memories haunt us.

Today's psalm reaches across centuries to be repeated at Calvary. It is there that we are given a picture of total abandonment. The psalmist reviews the mystery of God's forsaking him. Still, in the midst of it is a call to rest.

Consider the psalm, rewritten somewhat, as it serves as a litany of your heart.

> My God, my God, why have you forsaken me?
> Yet you are enthroned as the Holy One.
> Why are you so far from saving me. . . ?
> You are the praise of Israel.
> O my God, I cry out by day, but you do not answer.
> In you our fathers put their trust. . . and you delivered them.
> O my God, I cry out by night, and am not silent.
> They cried to you and were saved; in you they trusted and
>     were not disappointed.

I have often thought of how easy it was for me to accept Christ as my Savior, to put my trust in him for all eternity, yet I find myself constantly struggling with the time given me. I rest in the forever that is to come but am restless with the day to day.

**Prayer:** *God of Calvary, when I feel restless, even forsaken, calm the turmoil of my heart, and let me rest in you. Amen.*

**Sunday, October 9**                    Read Hebrews 4:12-16.

*About Jesus*

No matter what their background, most people will admit that Jesus was a good man. Some would even say he was a great man, perhaps the greatest man to have walked the earth. He was a rabbi whose life demanded the respect of his contemporaries. Many in the world freely call him the Savior of humankind. Some acknowledge him as the Son of God.

The writer of Hebrews says he "is a great high priest." But he is more than one who would hear our confessions of weakness.

The astounding thing about this one we call high priest is the fact that he was so much like us. He faced disappointment, betrayal, and heartbreak. He was confronted with false accusations (Luke 23:1-12). The Prince of Darkness offered him the world in exchange for his worship (Matt. 4:8-10). He experienced the death of a loved one (John 11:28-37).

What a mystery is our God! Holy Man; wholly man. Holy God; wholly God. The Bible says he was tempted just as we are; tempted in every area of life. Yet, with all that was put before his eyes, all that was offered to his flesh, he did not sin.

We began this week with Job. When his counselors pressed him with hard questions about God and about life, Job held firmly to his faith and experienced God's mercy and grace in his time of need. In the darkness, Job knew to whom he must give an account. He knew there was nothing about him that could be hidden from his Creator. In sackcloth and ashes, everything about his life was laid bare.

Like Job, we know that nothing about us is hidden from God. But we do not approach the throne of grace in fear; we approach it with confidence because Christ is our great high priest.

**Prayer:** *Thank you, Father, for the blessing of access to you through your Son, our Savior, the Lord Jesus Christ. Amen.*

# GLORY AND GREATNESS

October 10–16, 1994 **Lonni Collins Pratt**✢
**Monday, October 10** Read Hebrews 5:1-6.

*The glory of Jesus*

The trouble with any kind of priesthood is that its existence points to our estrangement from God. We need priests primarily to help bring reconciliation between fallen humankind and their holy Creator.

This need for a priesthood—any one of the many, and often complicated, clergy structures found among the denominations—is my reminder that I am not what I pretend to be, and I have fallen short of who God created me to be.

Jesus steps in as priest. But what is different is that he is not just a priest. No, he is *the* Priest. He represents the end of the work of one order and the beginning of another.

The new order combines the roles of king, prophet, and priest. The new order offers only one sacrifice—for all time. It is superior because it does not just appease; it settles once and for all the matter of my relationship with God. That is the work of the King of Peace. There will be no repetition of the sacrifice.

In this passage, we see the glory of Jesus; we see the glory of the office of eternal priest, king, prophet. Humanity enters the glory and greatness of Jesus by entering into the sacrifice. We become saints with scars as we identify ourselves with the sacrifice of our Christ.

**Prayer:** *God, most people will not comprehend the kind of glory that involves sacrifice. Such a sacrifice reminds me that I too often take my sin lightly. Have mercy on me. Amen.*

---

✢Writer, Lapeer, Michigan.

**Tuesday, October 11**  Read Hebrews 5:7-10.

*The glory of humankind*

Every intelligent person struggles with a drive to establish her or his own significance. It is part of humanity's nature, the willful side that still reaches for dangerous fruit rather than finding identity in God.

The importance of Jesus Christ's humanity becomes evident in these lines of scripture. The author reaches back to Gethsemane, where we come face to face with the very real struggles of the Messiah.

These verses hold no incredible mystery. We hear humanity crying, "Let this cup pass from me!" (Matt. 26:39) We understand faltering friends and shuddering confessions of trouble that overwhelm. We have experienced suffering and almost unendurable pain and anguish. God and humanity are on level ground now. By becoming human, God is doing what God could never do in divinity—die a tortured, human death.

Here too we see the ultimate glory of humankind. We see what humanity is made for—humble dependence upon God. In spite of all the pain, quiet and strong submission to the mysterious, glorious way of God working in our lives comes in the end. Eden reversed. Not mine, but Yours.

God, working in Jesus, has hit the wall. This is the place where humanity failed before. Here we are in a garden again. The cosmos stops to listen; here it culminates; here Jesus determines to move past human ambition into God's way.

There is no attempt to bypass or discount the human experience with rebellion. Christ tackles it and walks from the garden, willfully ready to redeem humankind.

**Prayer:** *O God become human, in great anguish you prayed in Gethsemane to "let this cup pass" from you. But in the end you made the once-and-for-all sacrifice. I am grateful and humbled. Amen.*

**Wednesday, October 12**                    Read Psalm 104:1-9.

*The glory and greatness of God*

Hallelujah! This psalm vibrates with the telling of God's majesty and works, chorused from one generation to another: "Bless the LORD, O my soul. . . . Clothed with honor and majesty. . . . You set the earth on its foundations."

God is so far above me that when confronted with God's total Otherness, I can do nothing but stand silently, awestruck and aware of how little I know, how limited my wisdom, how very different from me God is.

This early movement in Psalm 104 evidences the stirring of human senses by God's creative work. And in that creative work, we discover a little about who we are.

Our own creative ability, our drive to use tools and become makers, is one of the most obvious of human traits. We identify so strongly with what we make that it tells us who we are.

Look at this wondrous instinct in action from childhood. We produce something, and others—parents, teachers—stand back and say, "Hmmm, it's good." In those words we echo the Master Creator, who pronounced over all of creation, "It is good."

Whether a child with artwork, a student with an essay, a teenager with a poem, a writer with a story, a carpenter with a house, or a cook with a meal, we reflect God's majesty. God remains wholly Other and yet mysteriously, joyfully we are wrapped up in the strands of God's creativity and are even defined by it. God is all glorious. We are slivers of that glory, scattered like gold dust on God's great work.

**Prayer:** *Master Maker, in some small way, let me reflect your glory. It is not important that others stop and notice but that what I build today is built as a monument to your glory rather than to my cleverness. Amen.*

**Thursday, October 13**          Read Psalm 104:24, 35*c*.

*Confronted with countless glory*

Because I am often aware of my capabilities, my limits do not scream at me. When I read here, "How countless are your works" (JB), I feel drawn into holy mystery. I am like Job, perhaps, wrestling to comprehend how God is different than I. What are the ancient understandings and rules spinning my universe, and how does my presence enter into it?

When I scramble and sort, looking for something to fill the place where only awe belongs, it all turns to crumbs. Mystery itself defines my relationship with God because who God is defines our relationship, not who I am.

When the sorting and figuring is over, our relationship is one of Maker and product. I am the product of God, the craft of God, God's handiwork. Something of God is in me.

It is like when I make bookshelves. Those bookshelves reflect something of myself because they reflect what I like and do not like in wood, how many books I own, and where I want to store those books. But the bookshelves do not become me. The bookshelves remain completely distinct from me.

Yet I find myself building, hoping that in the process I will find out who I am and who God is. My significance and the significance of the work of my hands rests squarely on God's reality.

**Prayer:** *You who remain Countless, teach me to see you in the world where you place me. In my bean counting, let me pause long enough to see you in earth-prone days. When I am scrambling for definitions of Deity, let me find one in the ocean, in a friend's laughter, in a child's tears, in a note from my sister, in a stone shaped by forces in time I cannot even comprehend. Teach me to stop counting and start enjoying. Amen.*

**Friday, October 14**                    Read Job 38:1-7, 34-41.

*Obscuring purpose*

The Lord answered Job, "Who is this that darkens counsel by words without knowledge? I will question you, and you shall declare to me." If tallied, chances are that I have spent years of my life debating God. When I really think about it and enter into God's presence, I can reach only one conclusion: all *is* trivia. Yet I am fascinated, often obsessed, with trivia.

Now it is natural to think, *Well, all is not trivia.* What about world hunger, injustice, inequality, racism, poverty, institutional evil, sin?

When I call God to task over such issues, I am revealing my separation from God. God did not create these things. God did not make these things happen. I did. You did. When my angry human voice screams for explanations and answers, God responds by calling me to become an answer. If I am actively pursuing opportunities to become God's answer, I will find little time for debates and meaningless words.

Solutions are not the product of human wisdom, education, scholarly debate, conferences, committees, or anything else external. Solutions happen when the perfect partnership of God and mortal extends itself to a suffering race.

Everything else obscures the purpose. Everything else is trivial.

**Prayer:** *God, so often I hide myself from the truth, and your purpose is obscure to me. I stand before you weary of the trivial. Help me seek purpose. Amen.*

**Saturday, October 15**                    Read Mark 10:35-40.

*Human greatness*

Christians are called to identify with Jesus. Human glory is based on God's glory as revealed in the person of Jesus Christ. Greatness, as defined by Jesus, is when we "drink the cup that I drink."

When his disciples came to him, asking for greatness and status, Jesus did not tell them not to seek after greatness; instead, he warned them about the road they were setting out on.

Contrary to conventional ideas, the road to greatness begins and ends with the purposes of Jesus Christ. Greatness receives and drinks his cup, seats itself with him, is crucified with him.

Against our climbs to the top, Jesus calls out, "Whoever wants to be great among you must be your servant"—everyone's servant.

Less is more, last is first; it is an upside down, totally other view of greatness and glory that once more points to how wholly other God is from us. This image has no thrones, only crosses, tombs, servanthood.

There is a cheap imitation of greatness for those who would rather not bother with a bloody Christ. Rooted in and driven by personal ambition, this imitation relentlessly makes slaves of those who decide to chase after it.

Perhaps the really tragic individual is the one who has neither the guts to follow Jesus nor the leaning to absolute self-indulgence.

**Prayer:** *How do I begin sorting my self-centered ambitions from your paradoxical purposes, O God? Do I have the ability to know when I have done this? Release me from the high-walled place of personal ambition to follow you joyfully. Amen.*

**Sunday, October 16**                    Read Mark 10:41-45.

*Enabling others to greatness*

What did they really want from Jesus, these who were so upset that others in the group might dare to step from the crowd and take greatness on themselves? Were they afraid of being left in the dust?

This passage makes me uncomfortable. I hear my own voice in this crowd muttering, "Who does she think she is?" This passage unapologetically reveals bare human motivation. It teems with the truth about you and me. We don't mind others succeeding, within reason. We just don't want them to be more successful than we are.

As Jesus moves toward Jerusalem, he is surrounded by puny thought and pathetic talk. This Holy One walks with open eyes toward the great act of self-emptying while his followers, daft, thickheaded, and self-centered, argue about who gets to be first and who among them will be the greatest.

Christ will enable their greatness; these doltish disciples will soon become saints. Linger near and watch as sacrifice enables the birth of saints.

When we bristle at others' ambitions, Jesus calls us to enter his greatness and pour ourselves out. In this picture of twelve power-zealous men, we count ourselves. Jesus is leading them into greatness, and they do not even know it. Not yet.

For Christian leaders, the message of Christ is unmistakable. We enable great disciples when we are willing to give ourselves completely to loving them.

**Prayer:** *God, this picture of leadership requires more of me than I can easily give. In walking with you, I walk with greatness. In leading the way you lead, I enable others to greatness. Help me see how you lead—and then to follow. Amen.*

# FAITH ACTIVELY SEEKS CHRIST

October 17–23, 1994          **Mary Roodkowsky**✢
**Monday, October 17**          Read Hebrews 4:2.

The good news of Christ surrounds us, and we have numerous opportunities to listen and believe. When we do, we may enter into that rest which God provides.

But that rest and eternal salvation which come from belief in Christ cannot be pursued for their own sake. To do so is to set them as idols that replace what should be our true goal—a life in Christ. Jesus, through his life and death, has made that peace available to us. We cannot create it anew since it already exists! But Jesus does not direct us to seek our own salvation. He merely states, "Follow me." He does not say that we should seek truth in itself; he does say, "If you continue in my word, you are truly my disciples, and you will know the truth, and the truth will make you free" (John 8:31-32).

When we live in Jesus and become his disciples, we live a life of justice. For all our sisters and brothers who do live to bring God's justice to all persons, that life sometimes seems rocky—and certainly not very peaceful! But the kind of peace that we might seek for ourselves does not compare with the eternal rest that comes only as a result of profound belief in the way of Jesus Christ.

**Prayer:** *O God, if I seek peace as an end in itself it will elude me like a shooting star. When my faith in you grows and I agree to follow you, real peace will be mine. Help me grow in that faith. Amen.*

✢Acting Director, Boston Industrial Mission, Cambridge, Massachusetts.

**Tuesday, October 18**                    Read Mark 10:46-47.

Bartimaeus didn't hesitate to call out when he heard Jesus was nearby. "Jesus, Son of David, have mercy on me!" He was not afraid to call attention to himself or to ask for the help he needed—especially when he knew that the one who could help him was so close by.

Sometimes it is easier to ask for help for other people that to ask directly for ourselves. We can spend time or energy on the needs of our family, our friends, or our church or make donations to causes in which we believe. Yet, when it comes to our own problems, we are reluctant to ask others to spend their energies on us—even when it means our own work and ministry suffer as a result.

Bartimaeus was not shy. Jesus was very famous, and a large crowd surrounded him. But that did not stop the blind beggar. He knew that Jesus could cure him, and he knew, too, that his problem was important to Jesus.

Because we are human we often need support or advice. Requesting it is a sign of strength, not weakness. Even Jesus before his crucifixion asked his friends, Peter, James, and John, to stay with him.

**Prayer:** *Dear God, open my eyes wide enough so that they can see the boundaries of my vision. Encourage my arms to swing so freely they can feel their limits. When I can see no further and reach no longer, give me the courage to ask others to see for me and to stretch their arms where mine cannot touch. Then we shall work together by combining our strengths. Amen.*

**Wednesday, October 19**            Read Mark 10:48-49.

When Bartimaeus called out to Jesus, the crowd shushed him. They wanted to see and hear what was really important—Jesus— and couldn't be bothered with the lowly pauper in their midst.

But Jesus, when he heard Bartimaeus, immediately focused his attention on him.

This crowd thought it was seeking Jesus and his word. They pushed close to him to hear; yet their zeal was not for the real Jesus. In turning away from the one who called for help, they were also turning away from Jesus. Christ's ministry is one of attentiveness to others. If we constantly shut out those who call to us, we cannot participate in that ministry.

The French philosopher Simone Weil said that Christian love consists simply of paying attention to other persons, to really place oneself in another person's position, to fully understand what other persons are going through. And most especially we must listen carefully to the voices of those who are disenfranchised from the mainstream, who must, like Bartimaeus, call from the wayside.

Yet, how often are we deaf or blind to these needs? Whenever we close our eyes to urban decay; whenever we do not listen carefully to the voices of the underdeveloped countries as they describe their plight or suggest solutions; whenever we decide that trying to learn about some—or even one—of these issues is too tiring or boring; then we, too, are silencing the calls of those who are hurting in today's world.

**Prayer:** *Dear God, strengthen in us the energy to seek those who are oppressed in our society, and open our ears to hear their voices and to respond. Amen.*

**Thursday, October 20**                    Read Mark 10:51.

When Bartimaeus, blind and left to sit like a lump on the road-side, called to Jesus, everybody knew what he was after. Why, then, did Jesus ask him so directly, "What do you want me to do for you?"

Certainly it would have been simpler for Jesus just to declare Bartimaeus healed, rather than belabor the obvious. Instead, Jesus waited, allowing the beggar to speak for himself.

How often do we assume that we are qualified to decide for others without consulting them! Service to others—whether counseling, in community affairs, in matters of social policy—often creates rules which supposedly will help another without any dialogue between the two parties. Sometimes this leads to results disastrously opposite to those desired.

Programs to feed hungry people sometimes fall into such traps. One group of scientists developed a nutritious kind of wheat to be used in protein-deficient parts of Latin America. But although they promoted this new product, people refused to use it. The flour made from this wheat contained many nutrients but would not hold together to make the local bread! The scientists had never conversed with the people to find out what they needed and how they might use the scientists' expertise.

Jesus' attitude models ideal ministry. Christians need never impose themselves on anyone. The power of Christian ministry rests in respect for all God's creatures and creation and in seeking to use skills carefully for others' needs.

**Prayer:** *Thank you, God, for the gifts you have given me. Guide me in their care-full use for others and for the glory of all creation. Amen.*

**Friday, October 21**                                Read Mark 10:52.

A young woman was once helping her friends construct a new building. Each board in a stack of plywood needed trimming. As she sawed each one, she became increasingly aggravated. The saw seemed to drag along its path, making her arm ache. Toward the end of the cut, the board always broke off, leaving an ugly ragged edge. Yet when people walked by and asked how she was doing, she would say, "Fine."

Finally she asked another builder about this problem. "It doesn't need to be so hard. You need a little help—someone else or maybe a sawhorse—to support the end of the board. Then it won't pinch your saw, and the wood won't break by its own weight."

At first, she had sawed away, half pretending that there really wasn't anything wrong, half convinced that the sawing difficulty was due to personal faults (whereas she actually was experiencing a problem common to carpenters). Not only did this lead to second-rate woodwork, but it made the task much harder.

As long as we remain convinced that the current state of affairs—in our lives, our societies—must exist as it now does, nothing will change. As long as we remain convinced that we alone will tamper with whatever is awry, the *status quo* will prevail.

Jesus Christ offers us liberation from this desolate and isolated world view. He can transform our lives and our relationships: with others, with the physical world, with our social institutions.

**Prayer:** *O God, may I have the faith of Bartimaeus: that beyond what I can now see there is always the chance to change, to live more fully, and to create a more loving world. Amen.*

**Saturday, October 22**                    Read Jeremiah 31:8-9;
                                            Psalm 34:4-5, 19-22.

Who are the people of God?

We are all God's people, gathered "from the farthest parts of the earth."

God makes certain to include all, most especially those most likely to be forgotten: the blind and the lame, the pregnant women and the women in labor.

These are folks it would be easier to leave behind. Going on a long journey—as the prophet Jeremiah envisioned—was hard enough, trudging miles by foot or with pack animals. It might seem more reasonable not to bother with those who will be a burden to all. They might make it harder for all; with them, how can the goal be reached?

Today's journeys often leave people behind, as earthly tasks are pursued. High employment rates might slow overall corporation growth, so many people go without jobs. Some industries use overly high levels of toxic materials which cause illness in workers, but health regulations might slow down production.

It is easy in industrialized culture to desire efficiency. But Christians must remember that such efficiency comes second to a higher goal: love, which means living on behalf of *all* people.

When efficiency helps to do good for more people, or to work for others more powerfully, it is a virtue. But pursued for its own sake, efficiency turns into an idol which encourages us to exclude others for our own greater benefit. Efficiency must serve justice, not vice versa. God will never leave any of us behind; we can try to do no less.

**Prayer:** *All of us are your people, O God. You will always support me in my journey; remind me that my journey is undertaken along with and on behalf of my sisters and brothers. Amen.*

**Sunday, October 23**                    Read Hebrews 4:3-10.

Sometimes the gospel stretches clearly before us, and sometimes its direction seems foggy or its path rocky. Yet our journey of faith does not need to be a lonely path. Guides and scouts surround us if we do not harden our hearts in disbelief at their challenge.

Harvey Cox suggests that saints are such guides, living the gospel before us. Studying their lives can help us discern where that path lies. Contemporary saints illumine the way especially well—not because they are faultless people, but on the contrary, because they grapple successfully with tensions and situations similar to the ones we know.

Dorothy Day, for example, lives the Beatitudes in New York's Bowery, running a soup kitchen and clothing room. The simplicity of her life bears witness against material excesses, for she and her community own only essentials and share as many goods as possible. Martin Luther King's life and death push us on the climb to the mountaintop. They also clarify something about what that rest in God's peace really is—not earthly comfort, but something deeper and far more lasting. Many other prophets and saints surround us. Closing our ears to their voices makes walking the gospel road more lonely and difficult. Being open to their example can guide us in the ways of living in Christ's justice. Perhaps when we, too, are firmly directed, we may ourselves serve to bring peace to others.

**Prayer:** *O God, we thank you for giving us saints to guide us. Help us to seek true prophets of your word. Remind us they are no different than we are. We can, with your help, meet their challenge and join them in your rest. Amen.*

# DEVELOPING A RIGHT RELATIONSHIP

October 24–30, 1994                    Tommy Cresswell✠
**Monday, October 24**                    Read Mark 12:28-31.

*First things first*

In the New King James Version, the scribe asks Jesus, "Which is the first commandment of all?" While other translations opt for the words *most important* or *greatest*, I like to think of Jesus' response as setting forth the first of all God's commands. In fact, a quick look at Exodus 20:1 and following confirms that the first three commandments deal with (a) who God is and (b) what a person's right relationship with God entails. This right relationship includes no other gods, no worship of graven images, and no taking of God's name in vain.

However, Jesus' response to the scribe actually comes from the first verses of the Shema (from the Hebrew word for the first word of the text: *Hear*) found in Deuteronomy 6:4-9. Rabbis of old required a daily recitation of the *Shema* as a sort of pledge of allegiance. Judaism offered the world a religion founded upon belief in the one true God. Understanding that "the LORD our God, the LORD is one" was and is primary to understanding the significant, distinguishing truth that Christianity offers to a world in need.

The God we worship is One. And God requires the number one spot in our lives. We are living in a time that some consider to be the New Age. Secular "spiritual growth" seminars offer experiences in crystals, channeling, past-life regression, astrology, self-enlightenment, and a veritable plethora of "spiritual" alternatives. Some of us still cling to money, toys, and other earthly riches. Which god is *first* in your life?

**Prayer:** *Lord God, in the midst of the busyness of this life, help me to remember that you are first in my life and that my relationship with you should be my first priority. Amen.*

---

✠Professional actor and licensed attorney; certified lay speaker in The United Methodist Church.

**Tuesday, October 25**     Read Mark 12:28-34.

*Burnt offerings and sacrifices*

At Monteagle, in full view of Interstate 24, there are still vestiges of good ol' Southern "gospel" messages that I recall adorning the highways of my youth more often than Burma-Shave signs (ask someone forty or over what Burma-Shave was). One of those signs still entreats the passerby to "Get Right with God." When Jesus affirmed that loving God with all of one's heart, soul, mind, and strength and loving one's neighbor as oneself were the greatest commandments, the scribe responded by declaring (a) the truth of Jesus' words, and (b) that to live out these commands was more important than worldly offerings. Jesus said, "You are not far from the kingdom of God."

Who of us would not want to be close to God's kingdom? The scribe knew that loving the one, true God and one's neighbor capsulized the truth of Judaism. He also knew the significance of loving with one's heart, soul, mind, and strength. What else is there after all that? Totally committing one's self to God and God's commandment of love is far greater than any burnt offering or sacrifice we can make.

Who has not sat fretting over a pledge card or an offering envelope? Yet by fretting over that matter, we distance ourselves from God as we ponder what is most important to us. God only asks one thing of us: God asks that our commitment to God be as total as is God's to us.

In this day, we elevate the concept of self. We find it difficult to "commit," difficult to love others as we do ourselves. Consequently, our challenge is to focus outwardly and accept the responsibility that comes from being loved by One who loves us totally, unconditionally, and committedly. Today's reading encourages us to "Get Right with God," to get closer to God's kingdom, by living The Great Commandment.

**Prayer:** *Loving God, teach me to love. Help me to love you and others with the same commitment I make to myself, that in doing so I put you and others first in my life. Amen.*

**Wednesday, October 26**                    Read Hebrews 9:11-14.

*More than burnt offerings*

Yesterday's reading focused on God's commandment to love and the realization that God calls us to give of ourselves totally. Today's reading helps to put that total commitment in perspective. Why should we commit to God? Because Christ gave himself to "purge your conscience from dead works" (NKJV) or from "acts that lead to death" (NIV).

Developing a right relationship with God requires that, in our daily living, we not lose sight of the great truths of Christianity: There is but one, true God, and God loved us so much that God gave God's son to suffer and die upon the cross for our sake. In doing so, Christ has saved us *from* death in sin and saved us *for* life eternal with God. Now, just how important is that missed phone call, that broken antique, that designer dress, that rare *object d'art*, that investment opportunity?

What is important? You are. God made you, loves you, and was willing to suffer death for you. And your neighbor is important. The person next door, that woman in the office, the fellow on the street corner. God loves them and died for them too. God did not make a representational sacrifice of goats or calves. Jesus' blood was spilled in the war with Evil for control of your life.

Is it not hard to think of any worldly gift you give to the church or to another as a sacrifice, when you think of the price Jesus paid for the gift he gave you?

**Prayer:** *Precious Savior, strengthen my commitment to you. Keep me ever mindful of the great gift you have given me and the price that was paid. How can I not do what you ask? I renew my pledge today to love you and my neighbor as myself, without reservation. I will hold nothing back. Amen.*

**Thursday, October 27**                    Read Psalm 146.

*Beginning and ending in praise*

Psalm 146 is considered a hallelujah psalm because it begins and ends with the call to praise. In between, the psalmist explains why we should praise God.

Reading this psalm reminded me of a community of believers in a small Methodist church in rural Mexico. The worship and other devotional services began with significant oratories, followed by hymn after hymn, sung with great "vim, vigor, and verve"—as my grandfather used to say. When a member of our missionary team had the temerity to ask about the informal nature of the services (as opposed to the more refined, structured services to which she was accustomed), the lay leader of the congregation responded:

"We come to church, first, because God is God and worthy of our praise. We begin our services by acknowledging that God is great, awesome, and supreme. We offer honor because God is God. Then, and only then, do we continue our worship by expressing our thanks, by celebrating what God means in our lives, and by setting forth our petitions of concern for ourselves and for others. No service is complete without this celebration."

Our Mexican friend echoes the psalmist who warned of trusting in persons or things of this world. A person is only truly happy whose hope is in the Lord, Creator of all things—the One who frees the prisoners, raises up those who are bowed down, and watches over strangers.

As we strive to develop a right relationship with God, let us celebrate God's covenant with us. God has reached out to us in love through Jesus. *Happy* is the believer in the great I AM. Remember to praise God, first, last, and in between.

**Prayer:** *Merciful and loving God, I come to you because you are. Help me to be mindful of the joy that is mine through you and Christ Jesus. And help me express that joy in a celebration of life, by praising you in all that I do and in loving others as you have called me to do. Amen.*

**Friday, October 28**                    Read Ruth 1:1-14.

*When troubles shake the foundation*

In the first 14 verses of Ruth, we encounter a Bethlehem family that is trying to escape famine. Soon Naomi's husband dies, and then her sons meet untimely deaths. Naomi loses hope, and she puts forward this understanding of her situation: "The LORD's hand has gone out against me!" (NIV)

How many times have all of us—though we want to develop a right relationship with God—allowed a disappointment, a hardship, or a serious trial shake our belief? What misfortune in your life have you rationalized away as some sort of divine punishment, the ill-begotten gains of some wayward predilection?

How does this kind of thinking pervert our understanding of a loving, redemptive God? What are we suggesting about God when we understand the consequences of this world as a heavenly reckoning? What effect does this view have on others? Orpah finally took Naomi's advice and returned to her "foreign" home and gods, leaving the God she had come to know and worship for over ten years in Naomi's home.

If we fail to establish a close, right relationship with God, not only is our own faith foundation inadequate but we negatively influence others whose faith either is not yet strong or is nonexistent.

**Prayer:** *Loving and merciful God, help me to grow in my faith and understanding of your ways that I may learn to trust in you and not weaken when the obstacles and troubles of this world challenge me. I ask this for myself and for those whose lives I touch and influence, that they may not fall away from you because of my weak resignation. Amen.*

**Saturday, October 29**                    Read Ruth 1:15;
                                             Psalm 146.

*Setting the standard of conduct*

"Everybody else is doing it." Who of us has not either offered or received that flimsy reasoning as an excuse or justification for a particular activity or course of conduct? Naomi says to Ruth, "Look, your sister-in-law is going back to her people and her gods. Go back with her" (NIV).

That consequence is more severe than it first appears. Most readers give Naomi credit for not wanting to subject her daughters-in-law to a life of widowhood and hardship. But for Ruth, going back to her people, the Moabites, meant returning to a culture that did not know God. The Moabites worshiped Chemosh. (See Num. 21:29; 1 Kings 11:7.)

Ruth had lived with Naomi and her sons for ten years. During that time she had come to believe in the one, true God. What favor was Naomi doing for Ruth to return her to a society founded upon a false religion? Most women would have taken Naomi's advice—Orpah certainly did.

Is that the standard by which we live? When life becomes difficult, do we go back to the familiar, the safe, or the comfortable? Go ahead and do it; everyone will understand. In fact, everyone else is doing it. Does not this reasoning explain, in part, the prevalence of drugs, divorce, and the general decay of morals in Western cultures that attempt to establish social order and ethics without God and God's word as the underpinning?

What strife and hardship are you or your loved ones facing? Do you tell yourself or them that it is okay to leave God and return to former ways? that others are doing it? The psalmist reminds us not to trust in things of this world but in the true God who is a God of truth forever.

**Prayer:** *God of creation, love, and hope, as we endeavor to establish a right relationship with you, strengthen our trust and understanding so that our faith does not waver. Amen.*

**Sunday, October 30**                    Read Ruth 1:1-18.

*A firm resolve*

Ruth's statement of commitment is so moving and beautiful that it deserves the place it receives in so many wedding ceremonies. If only we could affirm this same devotion: to God, to spouses, to friends, and to those whom God calls us to serve. Ruth makes this pledge, "May the LORD deal with me, be it ever so severely, if anything but death separates you and me" (NIV).

Persons often use the story of Ruth (in its entirety) as an allegory of God's redemptive love in the everyday lives of ordinary people. Some use the story to show how God's covenant knows no cultural boundaries. Ruth, a Moabite and Gentile, becomes an ancestor of David and hence, of Jesus. (See Ruth 4:13-22.) Others speak of how Naomi's plan provided for her Gentile daughter-in-law.

I like the story because of the way Ruth's pledge of devotion affected Naomi's life. Prior to Ruth's loving resolve, Naomi had declared herself cursed by God. Ruth's faithful commitment strengthened Naomi to go on to Bethlehem.

When we have become strong in our faith, when we have drawn near to the heart of God and sought God's will, we do more than realize God's unconditional love and have the comfort that such a realization provides. We are enabled to offer that same unconditional resolve to others: I will not desert you; I will be there for you; God deal with me if I let you down; you can trust and depend on me.

Does someone in your life need your encouragement? Whose faith might you restore by letting him or her know of your love, faithfulness, and devotion?

**Prayer:** *Faithful God, as you draw near to me, help me draw near to you and to others in need of your loving care. I will seek to love you with my heart, soul, mind, and strength, and others as myself. Amen.*

## A HOME BUILT WITH HEARTS, NOT HANDS

October 31–November 6, 1994        **Eradio Valverde, Jr.✝**
**Monday, June 6**        Read Ruth 3:1-5; 4:13-17.

Home is where the heart is, or so goes the popular adage; and indeed love is one key ingredient that makes a house a home. A home is where kindred hearts share and strive together to meet all basic necessities for one's well-being. Thus it was in a patriarchal society that Naomi, the loving Hebrew mother-in-law to Ruth, instructed her daughter-in-law in a Hebrew custom that would help Ruth find a new home for herself. Guided by God, Naomi advised Ruth to act before their home would be no more and Ruth would find herself alone, a widowed Moabitess in Judah—an undesirable status. Ruth's faithful love to Naomi is rewarded in this greater way, the love that gives and frees and expects nothing in return. Naomi sees beyond her needs to the needs of her loved one.

The reward of faithfulness to Naomi's counsel was one that cannot be measured easily. In Ruth's marriage, the new home included a grandson named David who became king; and as Matthew testifies, an even greater grandson, Jesus, the One who showed the ultimate selfless, self-giving love. Is our love like Naomi's?

**Prayer:** *With all that happens in my home today, let it be love that happens spontaneously among those who live with me and share my heart. In the name of Jesus. Amen.*

---

✝Pastor, Iglesia Metodista Unida El Mesias, Mission, Texas.

**Tuesday, November 1**                    Read Isaiah 25:6-9;
                                           Revelation 21:1-6*a*.

Among some Latino people, this day marks the day before *El Dia de Los Muertos*, the Day of the Dead, a day in which people remember with fondness and joy those who have passed on to another life. The cemeteries become parks with picnicking families, and bright, colorful streamers and other decorations dot the tombstones and fences. In parts of the United States and in Mexico and other Latin countries, candies in the shape of skeletons and other images associated with death are part of the celebration. This celebration does not make this day frivolous, though the emphasis might be hard for many to understand. The day becomes not a macabre event but an almost joyful celebration of victory over death. It is a time to remember the life that has gone beyond not with sadness but with joy. The presence of those who once filled homes with love and laughter lives on in the memories. Death may have brought a setback, but ultimately death is no more.

Today's texts speak of the same assurance and hope: Isaiah speaks of a great celebration of life in the presence of God with the climax being the ultimate destruction of death and mourning. John's vision in Revelation affirms this. The eschatological image is of a new home promised by God and revealed by Jesus to John. This new home, the setting of the reunion among saints, will be a place where death becomes a memory because death will be no more. The images also bring hope and inspiration for the earthly saints to continue meeting the challenges of life until that day.

**Prayer:** *Gracious Lord, may the memory of those saints gone before be a joyous one. May that memory serve to inspire me to live life abundantly as promised to me by Jesus. Amen.*

**Wednesday, November 2**                    Read Psalm 127.

The scripture images of this week have been those of a home built not with hands but with hearts, that is, homes based on God's love for us and on God's love reflected in and through us. Today's psalm describes that image in a deeper way. Many couples have approached their marriage date and their clergyperson with stars in their eyes, certain that their marriage, unlike any before, will be special and eternal. When questioned as to why they have the belief, they respond as if the question were incredulous, "Because we are in love!" The marriage service and the counseling prior to the wedding should share the psalmist's belief that unless the Lord is at work in any effort, including an effort of love, all can be in vain.

We place our trust in God, who will bless our efforts. Our prayers and lives should reflect a faith in a loving, active God at work in our hearts, minds, and spirits and in the lives of those whom we love. What, asks the psalmist, could be better than a safe home and a large family when seen as gifts from God? The fruits of a family, if a family so chooses, are children—ideally, children created out of love and raised with love, to be loving members and participants in our homes and later in our society.

As a "pilgrim's song," probably sung on the way to Jerusalem, Psalm 127 was meant to remind us to be thankful for all we have, especially the love and comfort of a home and the love and fellowship of a family—truly, gifts from God.

**Prayer:** *For the blessings of home and of love from and to loved ones we are thankful. We are also mindful of those without the emotional shelter of a house or home. Bless them, Lord, and use us as that blessing! Amen.*

**Thursday, November 3**     Read Hebrews 9:24-26*a*.

Yesterday's psalm, we said, was a pilgrimage song, most likely sung on the journey toward the Holy City. The journey to Jerusalem was a faith builder taken in the presence and fellowship of other believers. Usually a family affair, the trip served as instruction for the children. It was on one of these pilgrimages that Jesus was left behind in the Temple. Having arrived in Jersualem, the pilgrims participated in the celebrations and sacrifices associated with feast days. The high priest would enter the holy place of the Temple to offer the sacrifice. The Temple, the beautiful, handmade, earthly house of God, was a replica of what surely must represent the sanctuary or presence of God in heaven. Using the blood of the sacrificed animal as the atonement for sins in the presence of God, the priest, serving as the bridge between God and humanity, would offer up the prayers of forgiveness and ritual. It was an important ceremony in the pilgrim's spiritual life.

Today's text says that Jesus has now entered into the sanctuary of heaven, not into a replica made with hands, but into the actual house of God, where he is appealing on our behalf. And Jesus does not have to do this repeatedly, year after year, like the high priest. He has done it once and for all on behalf of those who believe. For the writer of Hebrews, this role of Jesus was important to share with the Hebrew audience, for it showed that Jesus was above the role of the Jewish priest. Jesus was and is the High Priest for all people. What he offered, he offered for you and me.

**Prayer:** *Gracious Lord, accept my thankfulness for Jesus, who serves as priest between you and me. Let me also serve to bring others to you. Amen.*

**Friday, November 4**                    Read Hebrews 9:26b-28.

Christ's appearance and purpose was to redeem humanity from sin and from death. For the writer of Hebrews, no better message or loving act was ever performed for all humanity. Jesus gave of himself once and for all as the Lamb of God. His body and blood were poured out for the sake of humanity. Jesus' crucifixion defeated death and judgment for all who would believe and accept. The writer says Jesus offered himself once and will return to earth to save those who are waiting for him eagerly.

Our second child had the privilege of staying home with her mom for her first year, but when she was two she went to a daycare center. At about three-thirty each afternoon, while her classmates played on the playground, she sat with hands glued to the chain-link fence, looking out for us. Her internal clock told her it was time for us to arrive. She knew that if Cathy or José left before she did, we were late, and that would not do. While she did play with her classmates and did enjoy that setting, it was not home. The writer of Hebrews says the same thing. Through Jesus, God has showed us love, and we look forward to the ultimate fulfillment of a love without end.

**Prayer:** *Lord of all life, we are thankful for Jesus and for the way you showed love through him to the world. Guide us to love others and to share with them the hope found in Jesus Christ. Amen.*

**Saturday, November 5**                    Read Mark 12:38-40.

Who were the scribes that they merited the notoriety Jesus gives them in this passage? What exactly was Jesus accusing them of? We do know they were a religious order of men who gave their lives to the study of scripture. They were the only ones in Jesus' time who could choose not to marry because of their vocation. Yet in this passage, Jesus says that people should beware of the scribes. What was their sin? They dressed in long robes. A violation of fashion law? They enjoyed public recognition and privilege. Is that a crime? Among the greatest accusations seems to be that they "devour[ed] widows' houses." While the meaning is not exactly clear, the idea that a religious person would take advantage of the  hospitality of a widow, in any manner, is serious. The abundance of material things was uncommon in the home of a Jewish widow. And for anyone, especially one of the scribes who should be concerned about the well-being of people, to take away a widow's home—that is sinful. Jesus is saying that the abuse of hospitality, especially when one receives that hospitality because of position, is not to be tolerated. And to follow that action by a long prayer fools no one, especially not God, except perhaps the one who utters it.

Are we mindful and respectful of the needs of others, especially those who are powerless in our society? Or have we at times abused our position and trust: What would Christ have us do?

**Prayer:** *Gracious Lord, show me today the ways in which I can care for the powerless and be a part of their home by showing them love. Amen.*

**Sunday, November 6**                    Read Mark 12:41-44.

Jesus has led his disciples to the temple treasury, where worshipers could deposit their offering. Many did. Here was an object lesson. Jesus and the disciples could see the rich putting in large sums of money. It must have been quite a sight, and quite a sound, with the loud noise of many coins being deposited. Along came the poor widow who put in two coins that made up one penny. In any currency system, the penny enjoys the same, small purchasing power. One could suppose that ushers and finance committees around the world make a universal grimace when a penny makes its appearance in a church's offering plate. Imagine a system where it takes two coins to make one penny! The half-cent coin must have been popular, though its true purchasing power then is not fully known.

The lesson, Jesus says, is that while the rich people have given out of their abundance, the widow out of her poverty has "put in everything she had, all she had to live on." Again, the lesson focuses on the widow's poverty and how, even though she may have been taken advantage of, she continues to put her whole trust in God. Out of that faith she gives all. The key is that the rich are contributing to the treasury, while the widow is giving to God.

Have we not at times given out of duty and not gratitude? And certainly, we have given out of our abundance simply as a contribution rather than as a love and trust offering to God.

**Prayer:** *Gracious God, we are thankful for your endless faithfulness. May we learn from that faithfulness and give as we should, putting our faith and trust wholly in you. Amen.*

# THE SHADOW OF GOOD THINGS TO COME

November 7–13, 1994                         **Anna H. Bedford**⁜

**Monday, November 7**                     Read 1 Samuel 1:1-11.

She had married into an excellent family. She had a devout husband who loved and indulged her. But she was depressed and had no appetite. She cried all the time. She wanted a son, but she could not conceive because "the LORD had closed her womb."

Hannah understood that her problem was not medical but spiritual. So on her family's annual visit to the Temple, she released her pent-up pain and confusion in bitter weeping that culminated in a solemn vow to God: "Give to your servant a male child, then I will set him before you as a nazirite."

Consider this extraordinary pledge. With the taunts of her rival, Peninnah, still ringing in her ears, Hannah placed her confidence in God's power. Her prayer of complaint became a prayer of promise. She set apart her as-yet unconceived son for God's purpose.

When Hannah dared to make a covenant with the Almighty, could she have imagined that her son would become the anointer of kings? Could she have guessed that he would become the instrument by which God's people would move from undisciplined tribal groups to a cohesive political power? Elkanah asked, "Why do you weep? . . . Why is your heart sad?" By looking deep within to find an answer, Hannah became an agent of God's intended future for Israel. Today, also, honest answers to these questions can bring the clarity that allows God to use us to reshape history.

**Prayer:** *Almighty God, caught as we are in the web of our own small stories, may we never forget that we are part of your wide purpose for all creation. Amen.*

---

⁜Associate editor of *Horizons*, the magazine and Bible study of Presbyterian women in Louisville, Kentucky.

**Tuesday, November 8**                    Read 1 Samuel 1:12-20.

She did not see the priest, but he saw her. He watched her lips moving silently and thought she must be a drunk. But Hannah was pouring out bottled-up emotions, not wine. She did not ask for help or comfort; she did not explain the problem. She simply told him, "I have been speaking out of my great anxiety and vexation." Her words captured all the misery of being childless in a culture that measured a woman's worth by the number of her offspring, all the humiliation of watching a second, less-loved wife's family flourish. Eli believed her and blessed her. "Go in peace," he said. And she did. Eyes bright with hope, Hannah went home and ate a good meal with her husband.

How could she do it? She could do it because she offered her pain to God and experienced the release of letting go. Hannah no longer felt abandoned and helpless. In the same spirit that Israel gave the first fruits of harvest and livestock back to God, she offered her extraordinary sacrifice—the promise to let the child go for God's purpose. And, in so doing, she was affirmed by Eli. Hannah's new-found confidence rested on an unbeatable combination—confession, covenant, and confirmation!

For us, too, God's transforming power creates new personal possibilities. Perhaps, like Hannah, you are beginning to actively take charge of your life and cocreate your future with God. Or perhaps God is calling you to fill Eli's role, not to solve others' problems but to stand with them, never doubting.

**Prayer:** *God of love, help us to remember that no story, no sorrow is too small for your tender attention. Help us to keep the promises that we make to you, and teach us how to nurture and support those with whom you are working to bring about change. Amen.*

**Wednesday, November 9**                    Read 1 Samuel 2:1-10.

A stunning reversal of fortune—stock-in-trade of the teller of tales—here explodes into song. Hannah was not the first Hebrew woman to couch her victory in terms of a battle triumph. Think of Miriam (Exod. 15:20-21) and Deborah (Judg. 5). But into her rich imagery of defeat of enemies (v. 1), wisdom (v. 3), life and death (v. 6), and creation (v. 8*b*), Hannah wove the gentle narrative of the birth of a child (v. 5*b*).

Not just any child. Her miracle baby would be a king maker and king breaker who would change the role of Israel forever. In Hannah's day, fertility in childbirth was not only a personal and social event, but also a political and religious one. Appropriately, her hymn of praise to God closes with a prophecy of the coming king (v. 10). As her painful relationship with Peninnah comes to an end, so will Israel's painful relationship with the Philistines. Not only was Hannah's worth, her dignity, her rightful place with her husband restored, the life and future of Israel was ensured through her.

Centuries later, Mary echoed the ancient victory carol (Luke 1:46-55). And the songs of these women are sung by the church today. No matter how desperate the present predicament may appear, Almighty God is still in control. The world cannot sink into chaos. God's cosmic power is invincible. This same wondrous Lord of the universe is intimately concerned about our personal distress. The lowliest ones have a part to play in the grand scheme of things.

So join the song. We can even add another verse, for we know that Christ has broken the power of death, the ultimate enemy. Sing!

**Prayer:** *Lord, sometimes we don't feel like singing when so many things within and around us seem all wrong. But I know you hold the future, and I will trust in your unfailing love. Amen.*

**Thursday, November 10**                    Read Hebrews 10:11-14.

A television commercial extols the merits of one kind of fast food over another: "Same, same, same, same—DIFFERENT!"

The writer to the Hebrews makes a similar point with the image of a priest's repeating over and over again ritual acts that have no power to change lives. Not so with Jesus who came to earth to do God's will. In Christ, something entirely new has taken place. His offering of himself consecrates every single believer to God—once, for all time.

How does Christ's death bring life? The unknown writer of a letter to a group of Christians in an unknown place does not explain. The writer assumes that the readers would accept the premise that sacrifice is at the heart of faith and life, a concept that is hard to grasp today. Sacrifice was central under the covenant God had made with Moses and the people of Israel. That is still true, the writer claims, with the new covenant God made with believers in Jesus Christ.

We can scarcely imagine how radical these words must have appeared to the original readers of the Letter to the Hebrews. After all, sacrifice of crops and livestock had worked pretty well for 2,000 years. To say that these were no longer necessary took a giant step in faith. Christians take for granted the centrality of the life, death, resurrection, and ascension of Christ. Why, then, do we find it so hard to live in the light of that knowledge? "He has perfected for all time those who are sanctified." Perhaps it is difficult because we realize that sanctification is both gift and goal; it begins with rebirth and ends in heaven's glory. It is the divine gift of perfect love. We become holy when we participate in God's love. We receive it, and we choose to live in it day by day.

**Prayer:** *Source of the world's gladness and bearer of its pain, grant that I may live in your love this day with eyes open to the need of others, ears to hear their cries, and heart full of compassion to do your will. Amen.*

**Friday, November 11**                    Read Hebrews 10:15-18.

Forgiven! Listen to the Holy Spirit's whisper, "I will remember their sins and their lawless deeds no more." God utterly forgives and utterly forgets. That is the heart of the new covenant prophesied by Jeremiah (Jer. 31:33-34) and quoted here by the writer of the Letter to the Hebrews. Such amazing love requires no appeasing sacrifices, not even the refusal to forgive ourselves that many of us lay on the altar on a daily basis.

Why is it so hard to accept forgiveness? Perhaps it is hard because receiving pardon disturbs us to the depths of our personalities. We constantly exhort ourselves to be good; and just as consistently, we fail. To be forgiven means that someone has accepted the worst of us—and that is like a kind of death. How difficult it is to receive the truth that we do not need to fight our own worst selves anymore. We justify ourselves and ask our forgiver, "How dare you accept me as I am and not condemn me?" We want to set conditions for our forgiveness: "If I...then, you..."

Even more than human forgiveness, God's forgiveness through the new covenant in Christ is unconditional. It is like a rushing river that sweeps our little boat along in its mighty flow. We grasp at rituals—weak reeds—to keep some kind of control. Do we dare let go? To let go completely is to die. But this we must do to find life.

**Prayer:** *Merciful God, prepare me for death, the final letting go, by holding me in your forgiving love today. Amen.*

**Saturday, November 12**          Read Hebrews 10:19-25.

Drawing on the historical faith memory of Hebrew readers, the writer evokes the image of the solemn, once-a-year entrance of the high priest into the curtained holy of holies. The incarnation of Jesus can be compared to the tearing down of the curtain that separates us from God. Christ has become the living way to God's presence (v. 20). The only appropriate response we can make to such grace is to live a grace-filled life.

So theological discourse gives way, as it always does, to practical application. Right living holds equal place with right thinking in the writer's view. Three imperatives are laid upon those of us who know that we are forgiven through Christ's sacrifice. First, we are to approach God with the assurance that comes from baptism and a clear conscience (v. 22). Second, trusting God's promise, we should keep on steadily confessing our faith, no matter what (v. 23). Third, we must be active members of the Christian community, challenging one another in ministry and mission (vv. 24-25).

For the writer of the Letter to the Hebrews, the Christian life is a journey of transformation toward being in communion with God and with others. Persecution will come, but we are to persevere in faith, hope, and love. And for this we will need the encouragement and support of the community of believers. We begin with the local congregation of which we are a part, however imperfect. But we cannot end there. Christ's sacrifice is for all people everywhere, and our lives must reflect a breadth of compassion for all who suffer, especially those who do so because of their faith in Christ.

**Prayer:** *Lord, show me where love and hope and faith are needed, and use me to bring them to those places. In Jesus' name, I pray. Amen.*

**Sunday, November 13**                    Read Mark 13:1-8.

It might have been made for TV: Long shot of Herod's magnificent Temple atop Mount Moriah, its 40-foot white stones gleaming in the sun. Camera pans the pre-Passover crowds, buying, selling, milling around. Move in to a strong figure, framed in a gilded archway. It is Jesus. As he emerges from his final Temple visit, an anonymous follower comments, "Teacher, what large stones and what large buildings!" Close-up of Jesus' face as he flings out his arms and declaims, "All will be thrown down." There is a rumbling from the crowd.

Cut to the Mount of Olives. Gazing across at the Temple, Jesus relaxes over a lunch of fish sandwiches with four close friends. In confidential tones they ask him, "When will all this be, and what will be the sign?" Images flash across the screen as Jesus tells them to watch out for false messiahs, for national calamities and natural disasters. All these and more will be signs of the new age.

Fast forward to the Roman Christians to whom Mark wrote. How comforting was this apocalyptic vision to a little company beset by fear. The eastern frontier of the Roman Empire was eroding; earthquakes rocked the reigns of Claudius and Nero; Roman soldiers had torched Herod's Temple; Christians were being persecuted. But all was bearable, for, if Jesus' forecasts of disaster had been fulfilled, so would be the promise of salvation. The assurance of God's purpose sustained their hope.

And so for us. As countries with nuclear power proliferate, trusted religious institutions appear to be disintegrating, the world's "misery index" continues to rise, and we too take comfort in knowing that everything created has its term and God's steadfast love keeps us safe forever (Ps. 40:11).

**Prayer:** *Lord, I need to keep things in perspective. I get so engrossed in my own ups and downs that I forget that you hold the whole world in your hands. Just for today, help me see a larger perspective. Fill my heart with a daring and dangerous hope. Amen.*

# THE GOD WHO KEEPS HIS WORD

November 14–20, 1994                                    Ira Gallaway✝
**Monday, November 14**                             Read 2 Samuel 23:1-4.

As David comes to the end of his life, he witnesses to a God who speaks to and through those who are God's chosen people. David's words come from a long life of hearing and responding to the one God who is in communication with the people. When Samuel anointed David, we read in First Samuel 16:13 that "the spirit of the LORD came mightily upon David from that day forward." David had learned that God's Spirit would guide him as he was open to the Spirit in all kinds of circumstances. He had felt the leading of the Spirit in his combat with Goliath (1 Sam. 17). He has felt the judgment of the Spirit as a result of his sin with Bathsheba (2 Sam. 11-12), and he had known the comfort of the Spirit upon the tragic death of his son Absalom (2 Sam. 18:33–19:8). All of us can learn from the life of David.

Though David had been anointed by God's Spirit and was a man "after God's own heart," he experienced human frailty and so did not always listen to God. But David had learned that when he turned back to God he would find a God who communicated with him through word and Spirit.

God often uses the pain in our lives to get our attention. And even when that hurt and pain is a result of our own actions, God will not abandon us when we turn back to our Creator.

**Prayer:** *Lord, in my own situation today enable me to listen for your word and respond to the leading of your Spirit. Amen.*

---

✝United Methodist pastor, author, teacher; currently Director of Leadership Development, Four Corners Native American Ministry, Shiprock, New Mexico.

**Tuesday, November 15**                    Read 2 Samuel 23:5.

In spite of the trials and tribulations of his life, as he came to the end, David was sure that he had served a God in whom he could place absolute trust. While David knew that he had not always been trustworthy, he knew even more surely that God had never broken the divine covenant with David and the people of Israel.

We need to know and trust this experience of God's love and forgiveness in our lives today. Personally, I must confess that when I face great adversity, danger, or hurt in my own life, and when I look to the future, I find it difficult to trust in the goodness of God's providence for me. When I am asked, "Do you believe in God's guidance and providence for your life?" I often respond, "In prospect I have difficulty, but as I look at my life in retrospect, I do firmly believe in the goodness of God's providence in my life."

As with David, after living three score years and ten, I have learned that you can trust God. God's word is always faithful. Though we often fail God, God never fails us. Sometimes it is our pain and suffering which enable us to hear the word of God and respond to the leading of God's Spirit.

Paul knew this when he penned the words in Romans 8:28: "And we know that all things work together for good for those who love God, who are called according to his purpose." Paul did not say that God is responsible for hurt or evil in our lives. But when we turn to God and place ourselves in God's hands, whatever our condition, God can and will work good in our lives. God's love and covenant with us is everlasting. We can count on that!

**Prayer:** *Lord, I affirm today in my life that you are in control, that you are a good God who loves me and undergirds me with your forgiveness and Spirit. Please Lord, let it be so. Amen.*

**Wednesday, November 16**                    Read Daniel 7:13-14.

Daniel lived in the time of exile for the people of Israel. Though Israel was in captivity, God had not deserted them. It was Daniel's calling to witness to the continuing power and love of God through his personal life and his prophetic insight.

Daniel foresaw the coming of the One who would return Israel and establish the kingdom of God upon the earth. In a time of near hopeless circumstance, Israel needed to hear this word. Our God will come and save us.

But this message of God to and through Daniel is a stretching and extension of the traditional message of salvation as Israel had understood it. This kingdom, this dominion was to be for all people upon the earth, people of every nation and of every language, and not just for Israel.

Oh, how we need to hear this message today! In a time when we have heard the awful call for ethnic cleansing, when Christians are killing Muslims in the name of Christ, and when Christians are killing Christians in the name of Christ, we need to hear about a God who will come and save.

As Christians, we believe that the "Son of Man" spoken of by Daniel is the Son of God who came and died for the sins of all people. He came to establish God's kingdom of love and forgiveness that would transcend all ethnic and language barriers. This is a salvation which is universally offered to all who will become disciples.

As we profess Christ as Savior and serve him as Lord, we become a part of that kingdom of mercy and justice, love and forgiveness which transcends all kingdoms of this earth.

**Prayer:** *O God, give us the vision and trust to walk into your kingdom through faith in Jesus Christ our Lord. Amen.*

**Thursday, November 17**                    Read Psalm 93.

Since the beginning of time human beings have been tempted, and even prone, to place their hope for meaning and security in temporal structures. Earthly kingdoms, or political power, have been a primary center of that hope for many. Then on the other hand, in our modern culture of science and technology, an even more prevalent hope for security has come in the form of material wealth and financial security. Many people tie their hopes to a modern corporation or an industrial giant.

And yet, as we look at history the lesson seems to be clear. Hitler dreamed of a Third Reich of a thousand-year rule. Lenin and Stalin established the Soviet Union which was to be the political utopia for all humanity and which would last until the end of time. All of us know what has happened to those secular dreams which became nightmares for many. And who would have believed twenty years ago that there would be no Pan-American Airways or Eastern Airlines? No, there is no ultimate security in political power or material wealth.

The psalmist sees God as holy and sovereign, the source of ultimate power and the only hope for security. God's strength is more than the strength of the waters of the flood, or of the principalities and powers of this world. One cannot read the psalms devotionally without hearing over and over again about the everlasting nature of God's kingdom and the eternal benefits of God's love and forgiveness. The psalmist knows that the only thing in the world that is "firmly established" is the kingdom of God. This we must relearn in our day.

**Prayer:** *Dear God, it is so easy to be bound by the false security of the things of this earth. Free us to trust only in your love and grace for our security! Amen.*

**Friday, November 18**                    Read John 18:33-37.

Pilate had asked Jesus, "Are you the King of the Jews?" Part of the reply of Jesus was to state that his kingdom was not of this world. Christians are often charged with having an other-worldly religion; and, of course, this can be true. But there is a real sense that the heart of the Christian faith is spiritual, for true faith is centered in a relationship with Jesus Christ. If you have the King in your heart, then, and then only are you a citizen of his kingdom. And while that relationship should impinge on all that we say and do temporally, it is not primarily a temporal matter but an eternal matter.

On December 22, 1982, about 12:30 P.M., I was being interviewed by a T.V. reporter, when the station manager interrupted to say, "Dr. Gallaway, your house is on fire!" My wife, Sally, and I immediately returned to our home to find it engulfed in flames with the fire department out in full force. We lost not only our home but over 90 percent of our possessions. We learned many things from this tragic event in our lives. First of all, we were shown great love and support from our staff, the members of our church, and many other friends in the city of Peoria, Illinois. It was Christmas time, and truly we were surrounded by much love. In many ways it was the most love-filled Christmas of our lives.

During the next week, someone asked me this question: "What have you learned from the fire?" My reply was almost spontaneous: "We have learned that the things of life are eternal!" This is the truth to which Jesus bore witness.

**Prayer:** *Dear Lord, let us bear witness to your eternal truth: that we have a God who died for us and lives in us. Amen.*

**Saturday, November 19**                    Read Revelation 1:4*b*-6.

In yesterday's devotion we talked about being citizens in God's kingdom, which was not of this world. In today's passage, we read where we are called to be a kingdom of priests to the God and Father of our Lord Jesus Christ. As Protestant Christians, we are not especially comfortable with the term *priest*, and we do not as a rule affirm the vocation of a priest. And yet, along with the affirmation of salvation by faith alone, the designation of all Christians as a priesthood of all believers serves as the very foundation of the Reformation and the clarion call of the great reformer Martin Luther.

The author of Ephesians refers to the gifts of the Spirit as being given to equip all the saints of God for the work of the kingdom (Eph. 4:11-13). And in First Peter 2:9 the author designates Christians as a "chosen race, a royal priesthood." What does it mean to be a priest to the God and Father of our Lord Jesus Christ?

This is where the kingdom which is not of this world impinges upon the world in which we live. If we are called to be priests of God, the primary way we live out that priesthood is in relationship to the others in our lives. A priest is a mediator and channel of God's grace and love to others. Therefore, a husband is called to be a priest to his wife, and a wife to her husband, parents to their children, and, in turn, children to their parents. This is the stuff of grace and love, mercy and justice, in all our relationships. And that is only possible as we make room in our individual hearts for the Son of God, who is God's eternal Mediator of grace and love to all humanity.

**Prayer:** *Dear God, we cannot be your channels of grace and love without the presence of your Spirit in our hearts. Please be with us in the NOW. Amen.*

**Sunday, November 20**                    Read Revelation 1:7-8.

Today's scripture in a real sense wraps up all that we have been saying this week about the God whose word is faithful, about the God of Covenant whose kingdom and dominion is forever.

When John writes that God is the alpha and omega, in my mind's eye I see a God who stands with the beginning of time in one hand and the end of time in the other. I see a God who was at the beginning of creation, who is in the process of continuing creation and re-creation, and who will bring creation to consummation in the end time of God's own choosing. I do not have to hold all the answers to this life in my own mind or understand the abounding ironies and complexities of this life. I can work at finding answers as best I can and then know that I trust a God who has the answers and that the answers will ultimately be good.

When I see all around the decline and decay of nations, and the ultimate failure of all economic systems to bring real and satisfying meaning to life, I find great comfort in believing in "the Lord God, who is and who was and who is to come, the Almighty."

Humanity seems destined to pit race against race, nation against nation, and creed against creed. If we are ever to work our way out of the divisions and hatreds which divide the world today, we must come again to believe in an almighty God, who is greater than all the other powers in the world.

**Prayer:** *O God, it is often so difficult to believe truly in you and your great love for us. Help us, Lord, to believe. Amen.*

# RESTORING LOST HORIZONS

November 21–27, 1994                    Roy I. Sano⚜
**Monday, November 21**             Read Jeremiah 33:14-16;
                                              Luke 21:25-28.

"The days are surely coming. . . . " (Jer. 33:14).

"They will see 'the Son of Man coming. . . . '" (Luke 21:27).

Latin has two words for the future. One is *futurus* and the other *adventus. Futurus* suggests an "unfolding" in the future of developments from the past; *adventus* points to something quite different "coming" into our world that we could not anticipate. Advent begins a new Christian year because the coming of Jesus Christ, whether then or now, surprises us with changes we did not expect.

One of the sad ironies in Christianity today is that the most ardent advocates for biblical Christianity hold God hostage. While they appeal to the Bible, they actually restrict our focus to the summaries of God's word in the doctrines and dogmas that come from our heritage. While these summaries of the faith may teach us much about some portions of God's word, they do not disclose all that the Bible says about God. While we cannot excuse theological illiteracy about our tradition, those less captive to that tradition are among the most attentive to hear God speaking in the lectionary beyond doctrines and dogmas. They are likely to recognize and welcome the fuller advents of God and to recover the lost horizons of possibilities today.

**Prayer:** *Dear God, as you give me the humility to learn from my predecessors in church history, also keep me open to hear your divine calling in new ways from the Bible. Amen.*

---

⚜Resident Bishop, the Los Angeles Episcopal Area of The United Methodist Church.

**Tuesday, November 22**  Read Psalm 25:1-10.

*Pray to know God's ways*

"Make me to know your ways, O LORD; teach me your paths."

When people in the Bible passed on what they learned about God, they inevitably told stories. When the early church summarized its faith in the creeds, it essentially retold what the triune God does. Powerful witnesses occur today when we share what God has done in the course of specific developments in our own life or when we describe what God is doing despite awesome developments in our time. Why do we use stories when we share our faith?

The reason is simple. God is a living God. Describing a living God with abstract concepts or symbols alone cannot convey who God is. We must finally say what God does. Stories express best who God is and what God does. To know this God fully, therefore, means we live the story by participating in what God is doing (see Jer. 9:24; 22:16).

We tell two stories in our witness. At one level we describe the directions that developments are taking us even if the outcome is dreadful. At another level we bear witness to the acts of God in the midst of this course of events, and therefore, we also witness to what we can do and be. "In the world you will have tribulations; but be of good cheer, I have overcome the world" (John 16:33, NKJV).

Therefore, we pray for help so we can recognize the "ways" God moves in this world. Then we can bear witness to the hopeful "paths" or the course of action that God pursues in the midst of our frightful developments (Psalm 25:4).

**Prayer:** *Dear God, help me see your promising activities in the difficulties I now face and join you and others in the sacred story you are staging even in secular developments. Amen.*

**Wednesday, November 23**                    Read Psalm 25:1-10.

*Our Lord rectifies wrongs.*

"The LORD is our righteousness" (Jer. 33:16c).

Martin Luther made a grand discovery. At one point he detested the phrase "the righteousness of God" (Rom. 1:17). It depicted for him a stern God making unrealistic demands and then punishing those who failed to meet them.

Luther played with the phrase. He looked at it in the light of what followed. "The righteousness of God is revealed through faith for faith." Reference to faith prompted memories of those warm moments when he prayed the psalms with humility and trust. Such faith changed him.

He therefore experimented with the phrase by using "righteousness" to describe God's loving actions rather than to describe the austere actions of a tyrant. He read "righteousness of God" as "a God who makes righteous." Seventeenth-century Puritans translated "the One who makes righteous" into a "right-wiser" of all the wrongs we have committed. One might say that "The LORD is our righteousness" means that this God is our "Rectifier" of all that has gone wrong.

The psalmist made the same point in other words. "Good and upright is the LORD." Furthermore, this Lord, or Sovereign Savior, is unswerving in accomplishing what is good, in reaching the right ends. "The paths of the LORD," the courses of action that this God follows, "are [characterized by] steadfast love and faithfulness" (v. 10a). The Lord whose Advent we celebrate is therefore the One who is the gracious and unrelenting Rectifier of all that has gone wrong.

**Prayer:** *"Come, Lord Jesus!" Come and sustain us in our struggles to make right all that has gone awry because of the wrongs we have committed. Amen.*

339

**Thursday, November 24**                Read 1 Thessalonians 3:9-13.

*A loving holiness*

"May the Lord make you increase and abound in love. . . . And may he so strengthen your hearts in holiness that you may be blameless . . . at the coming of our Lord Jesus."

The work of God the Rectifier appears in individuals who are "blameless in holiness." Holiness again has become a major concern among a variety of people. Since women and people of color around the world have felt violated, they are struggling to restore the sanctity and holiness of God's image within them. So too are the youth and the elderly, persons with handicapping conditions and those with different family structures.

In careless moments, strident advocates among these valid pursuits often place the blame excessively on white males. For them, white males are a curse on humankind and the scourge of the earth. While white males may have contributed immensely to evils in this world, we can still support those white males who are struggling without self-pity or self-indulgence to restore their own sense of worth.

Permeating all of these movements is a deep longing for holiness, a yearning to recover the sanctity of the divine image God planted in us. Blamelessness in holiness, however, is much more than a shrill affirmation of our self-worth as we ventilate hostility toward those who have violated us. Because we too have violated others, we need God's forgiveness, which generates love (see Luke 7:47). We, therefore, hallow our lives authentically as we "increase and abound in love" toward others and God as well as ourselves (see Matt. 22:37-40).

**Prayer:** *Establish me, dear God, in a blameless holiness that increases and abounds in love toward others and you, as I increase in love toward myself. Amen.*

**Friday, November 25**                    Read Jeremiah 33:14-16.

*The broader sweep of salvation*

"He shall execute justice and righteousness in the land. In those days Judah will be saved and Jerusalem will dwell securely."

As we have seen, the Rectifier who comes executes righteousness by nurturing a loving holiness in persons. John Wesley described it as "faith active in love" (see Gal. 5:6). He had in mind our trust in God's grace, which forgives us, renews God's image in us, and perfects us in love. We speak of these three steps in the "order of salvation" as justification, sanctification, and perfection.

The Rectifier also executes justice in addition to righteousness. The Wesleyan societies and classes addressed injustices primarily through acts of charity. We can never trivialize the quiet but powerful impact they exercised in early eighteenth-century England.

At the same time, we have a lot to learn about justice from the late eighteenth-century democratic revolutions. From the perspective of the Bible, these advances lead us to place the "order of salvation," which primarily promotes righteousness in individuals, within the context of the broader sweep of the "history of salvation." In the history of salvation, God executes justice and makes Jerusalem a safe place. The history of salvation (see Jer. 32:36-41) is as integral to God's saving work as the "order of salvation" (see Jer. 31:33-34). We, therefore, profane the work of God if we do not see God's saving mission in efforts to promote better housing, safer streets, stronger schools, opportunities for gainful employment, and equity in salaries.

**Prayer:** *Dear God, help me restore the struggle for justice in the horizon of your saving mission. Amen.*

**Saturday, November 26**                    Read Luke 21:25-28.

*Our redemption is drawing near.*

"Now when these things begin to take place, stand up and raise your heads, because your redemption is drawing near."

Jesus predicted that great earthquakes, pestilence, and famines would occur among the people. What they held most dear and most sacred would be desecrated, he said. Powers in the heavens would be shaken. People would faint with fear and foreboding. Turmoil among the family of nations would lead loved ones to betray one another (Luke 21:10-26).

"Now, when these things begin to take place," Jesus said, "stand up and raise your heads, because your redemption is drawing near" (v. 28). In the midst of such traumatic times, Jesus promised that "they will see the Son of Man coming" (v. 27).

While we are vividly aware of frightful developments, Jesus urges us to look to the broader horizons of God's work because our "redemption is drawing near." We, therefore, light Advent candles as the nights lengthen and the days shorten because we hold out hope when hearts grow faint with fear and foreboding.

The coming redemption is comparable to the ones that launched several major rounds of God's "history of salvation" in the Bible. We see it first in the exodus from Egyptian bondage, then in the deliverance from Babylonian captivity, and finally in the liberation that Christians anticipated from the domination of the "new Babylon" (Rome). The same redemptive actions of God reappeared in the American Revolution, in the struggles for independence from classical European colonialism after World War II, and most recently in liberation struggles from neocolonialism, East or West.

**Prayer:** *Come, Lord Jesus, who redeems us and rectifies what has gone wrong! Amen.*

**Sunday, November 27**                    Read Luke 21:29-36.

*Take heed.*

"Be on guard so that your hearts are not weighed down with dissipation and drunkenness and the worries of this life."

A lot of messiness accompanies our struggles for a loving holiness. Recovery of God's image in us after we have marred it with sinful habits brings with it a lot of backsliding and, thank God, new starts.

We also see a lot of messiness in the long journey to a just society and safe environment after independence from historic European colonialism and liberation from the more recent domination of the conflict between the superpowers. As the old orders crumble, ancient tribal and ethnic rivalries produce bloodshed. As we challenge or overturn old tyrannies, we discover an environment ravaged by consumerism and turned into a dumping ground for nuclear waste.

Therefore, we are overwhelmed easily with "the worries of this life" in our personal sojourn toward a loving holiness! It is easy to "be weighed down with dissipation" in our broader struggles for justice in society and health in God's creation! (See also Mark 4:18-19.)

Taking heed, therefore, applies most directly to ourselves. Lest we are weighed down with cares, we vow to God in our demanding journeys, "To you, O LORD, I lift up my soul. O my God, in you I trust" (Psalm 25:1-2a). By God's grace, we will not lose our focus on the coming Lord, whatever else we may face.

**Prayer:** *"You are the God of my salvation; for you I wait all day long" (Psalm 25:5). Amen.*

# EL CAMINO REAL

November 28–December 4, 1994                    **Wendy M. Wright**✠
**Monday, November 28**                              Read Luke 3:1-6.

When I was a little girl growing up in coastal California, a familiar sight along the highways on which my parents and I traveled were the historical markers that kept alive the memory of the Spanish colonial inhabitants of that region. Streets, towns, and monuments bore lyrical names like *Cabrillo*, *Escondido*, *San Juan Capistrano*, and *Santa Maria*. One of my favorite markers, discovered at intervals up and down the coast, bore the name *El Camino Real*, The King's Highway. The placard marked the major artery of transport and travel up and down the Pacific coast. It had been marked out and named by the first Spanish explorers who, wherever they went, claimed the land for the king of Spain.

*El Camino Real* had to be constructed wide, safe, and free enough of obstacles to allow large quantities of supplies and entire regiments of soldiers to be transported on it. It had to be a road fit for the entourage of the king.

The liturgical week that leads up to the second Sunday of Advent celebrates another royal road or king's highway, the metaphorical road of our lives on which Jesus, the Promised One, will arrive. John, son of Zechariah, describes the road for us in the Gospel of Luke. It must be direct and obstacle-free for the King to pass along it. This week we have the opportunity to reflect on the ways we prepare the road of our lives for the entry of the King.

**Suggestion for meditation:** *Imagine your life as a road upon which God wishes to travel. How easy will it be for God to make that journey? What are the hills and valleys of your life that might make the journey difficult?*

---

✠Roman Catholic laywoman; assistant professor of theology at Creighton University, Omaha, Nebraska.

**Tuesday, November 29**  Read Luke 1:67-79.

This canticle, spoken by Zechariah, father of John the Baptist, is one of several ancient hymns of the Christian community that can be found in the Gospels. It is traditionally known as the *Benedictus*. In it Zechariah raises up his son as a prophet who will go before the Lord and prepare a way for him. He places John in a long line of holy ones who have prophesied the advent about to take place. It is as though the royal road that John proclaims reaches back through time into the hearts of generations of those who seek God.

Part of our preparation for the coming of Christ at Christmas involves a remembering, a looking back. On the one hand, we look back at the past year or at the past phases of our lives to discover there what we would change or nurture. What have we done that either does or does not allow us to welcome our God?

On the other hand, our looking back can also be deeper and more communal. We look back and see that our own most poignant longings that we associate with the promises of God are not simply our own. They belong to all God's people; for generations they have been sung and longed for. Our Advent hope is a hope that connects our fragmented church across time and denominational boundaries. The royal road is walked by all of us together.

**Suggestion for meditation:** *Imagine yourself in the company of Christians from an earlier era. Vividly conjure up their dress and style of worship. Allow the commonality of our Advent hope to enter your prayer.*

**Wednesday, November 30**  Read Luke 1:67-79.

Most of us who live in cities and who function in a round-the-clock electrically lighted world have little appreciation for the power of the sunrise. Unless we are camping in the mountains or have the opportunity to rise before dawn to catch an early-bird plane flight, we rarely see the sunrise in its full magnificence. But for the people of Jesus' day the rising of the sun was a daily event of significance. Because of their ability to illuminate the night only weakly, the people welcomed with joy the coming of the sun with its warmth, clarity, and promise of nurturing light.

In the *Benedictus,* Zechariah speaks of Jesus as the rising sun who by the tender mercy of God will come to visit us. The canticle points us toward the future and helps us lean into a part of ourselves that can believe in fullness, fruition, and peace.

Part of our Advent preparation involves a turning toward the future, an imaginative entry into both a personal and communal life that corresponds to our deepest dreaming. The *Benedictus* captures our future imaginations exactly when it promises the rising of the sun that will give light to those in darkness and the shadow of death.

All of us find ourselves in darkness of one kind or another. Certainly as a species, humankind finds itself in the somber specter of its own capacity to create weaponry that can destroy creation many times over. Our habits of exploitation endanger the ecological balance of life itself. The *Benedictus* invites us into a dawning reality that can turn fierce shadows like these into a radiant new day. The royal road stretches out into infinity with this dawning.

**Suggestion for meditation:** *Imagine a sunrise that reveals a world transformed. What would it look and feel like? Thank God for this hope of ours.*

**Thursday, December 1**                    Read Philippians 1:3-5.

What was the last letter you wrote? Was it a business memo, a Christmas form letter, a thank-you note for a gift received? Before the invention of the telephone, letters were the only means that people had of keeping in contact with one another. They were the expression of the intangible part of ourselves that extends beyond body and ego boundaries and connects us with one another.

I think it a curious human delusion that our identity, our self, is defined primarily over and against other selves. Actually, we are part of an interconnected network of selves, our identity in part made up of those to whom we belong and those who are given to us. This is clearly true for us in the Christian church. Beyond our identity as husbands, wives, children, parents, workers, citizens, friends, we are members of the body of Christ. We belong to a network of persons interconnected on levels so complex and deep that our reality as church has been termed a mystery.

In his letter to the Christians living in Philippi, Paul extends his greeting and his love. He acknowledges his shared identity with them, recognizing them as kin who share in the good news preached by Jesus. It might be helpful for us during this Advent season to acknowledge our shared identity with our brothers and sisters in Christ. The royal road of our lives onto which the King will enter stretches not only into the past and future, it spans wide in the present as well. Part of our Advent preparation might be smoothing the rough places between ourselves and our brothers and sisters in Christ.

**Suggestion for meditation:** *Bring to mind someone in the Christian community you would call "stranger" or "enemy." Encircle him or her in the light of Christ. Ask God that you may know that person as a brother or sister.*

**Friday, December 2**                    Read Philippians 1:6-11.

I am always struck, reading Paul's letters to the Christian communities he served, with how deeply he cared for his brothers and sisters in Christ. This letter to the church at Philippi exudes an air of care and concern that is most remarkable.

Throughout his writings Paul emphasizes the importance of community. For him the various churches are not simply discrete groups of the faithful. Together they make up the body of Christ, that mysterious spiritual organism that lives and breathes in unison and union with Christ.

Paul sees the body as more than a fellowship, more than a unity joined by its shared purpose and work. The body is also a *formative* reality. By this I mean that being part of it gives one the opportunity to grow, to change, and to become more responsive to the life that animates the whole. This is clear in the prayer he sends with his greetings to the Christians at Philippi. He prays that their love for one another might increase, that their knowledge might improve in order to prepare them for the day of Christ.

The point here is that preparation takes place not only individually but also within the context of community. Our friends, our families, our fellow parishioners, our co-workers help form us. Our Advent preparation cannot be done alone in the solitude of prayer. Preparing also means attending to the quality of our relationships and practicing active love. It may mean confronting patterns of abuse or neglect that have crept into our dealings with one another. It may mean rethinking our attitudes toward the poor, toward strangers, or the marginalized. Whatever it means to each of us personally, the preparation we do to ready *El Camino Real* involves one another.

**Prayer:** *Gracious God, you give us one another to care for, to love as we have been loved. This Advent may we be given new eyes to see into our relationships and to invite them into the light of your promise. Amen.*

**Saturday, December 3**     Read Malachi 3:1-4.

Have you ever planned with someone who is a professional painter or wallpaper hanger to repaint or wallpaper an older house or apartment ? If you are like me, you leap right to the thought of the finished product. You imagine that the process basically involves smoothing on a fresh coat of paint or whipping out a roll of something like contact paper. Your professional friend will have a very different view of the matter. He or she will assess the surface onto which the fresh decor must go. Perhaps it needs extensive scraping and sanding, perhaps earlier layers of paper have been carelessly painted over, perhaps even new sheet rock must be laboriously put up. There is always more to the preparation phase than I can imagine.

The same is true when one builds a road, even a highway of the heart like the one we are preparing during Advent. There is always extensive digging and leveling to be done before the surface of the road is laid down.

The fiery words of the prophet Malachi make us aware of this truth. The Hebrew prophet foretells the arrival of the messenger— John the Baptist. And he speaks of Christ's subsequent coming in vivid and fearsome terms. He uses images of scouring and refining, of a purification that is less like gentle cleansing than stripping and transformation. He also suggests that it is the divine action that will initiate such a radical change.

Perhaps to truly prepare for the King we must be willing to let God undertake the laborious, foundational work of readying us, leveling and planing the contours of our lives so that we may truly become roads on which the Promised One might travel.

**Prayer:** *God, you who are both Gentle Shepherd and the One who winnows the chaff from the grain, give us the courage to allow you to genuinely shape our lives so that we might be welcomers of your promise. Amen.*

**Sunday, December 4**                    Read Luke 3:1-6.

There is something persistently compelling about the figure of John the Baptist, that wild-eyed locust eater wrapped in animal skins roaming about on the margins of the civilized world, crying out, pointing an accusing finger at the complacent of his day. How very uncivilized he was. His message was not artfully packaged to attract the attention of the average consumer, and what he preached certainly was not a user-friendly product. I think it is important not to let our familiarity with the Gospel narratives dull us to the striking, counter-cultural wildness of this man who, we are told, heard and preached the word of God.

John's ministry was in the wilderness. While he drew followers from all over, including the residents of the cities, he was first and foremost a man of the margins. And he spoke as a voice from the wilderness.

It may be possible, as we prepare for the coming of Christ this season, that the voice that inspires us and instructs us in straightening the paths of our hearts may very well be a voice from the wilderness.

Perhaps it will be the voice of the stranger: someone with AIDS; someone racially, ethnically, or religiously different from us; someone battered, abused, or forgotten. Perhaps it will be the voice of a marginalized part of ourselves crying out to be attended to, heeded, healed.

Whatever the voice, John's eccentric person, the radical insistence of his call, invites us to begin our preparations at the margins, in the wilderness of our lives. God meets us there, not as familiar friend but as unexpected invitation, as a beckoning call to fill the valleys and level the mountains of our lives so that Christ the King might enter by the long, wide, level road of our hearts.

**Prayer:** *God of surprise, God of the wilderness, give us ears to hear the cries of the forgotten and marginalized of our world and of our own hearts. Amen.*

# FUTURE HOPE, PRESENT JOY

December 5–11, 1994                           **Richard H. Summy✝**
**Monday, December 5**                        Read Luke 3:7-14.

John the Baptist gets the week off to a fierce and frightening start. He hisses a verbal assault, unleashes a spoken slap. "Vipers," he says, to the very crowds that approach him for baptism.

And he's not only sharp but quick. Anticipating their response to such a belittling label, he reacts before they can voice their defense, briskly cutting it from beneath them. No status of birth matters a whit to the God who is eager to wield an axe at the feet of the fruitless, says John.

"Vipers," John calls them, but it is repentance to which he calls them, a repentance that bears fruit worthy of turning one's life around. He cites concrete examples (vv. 10-14).

Several years ago a TV commercial featured sleepy faces being slapped awake by a certain aftershave. The response was a surprise: "Thanks, I needed that." John the Baptist is an Advent slap-in-the-face that does not harm but rather serves as a wake-up call for sleepy Christians. May we respond to his call with a renewed commitment to ethical actions—and an expression of thanks as well!

Our encounter with John the Baptist is not a joyful encounter initially but a necessary one, one that refreshes our hope for the future.

**Prayer:** *Dear Lord, wake us when we fall asleep to our Christian commitments, that we might turn to you and give thanks that you continue to call us. Amen.*

---

✝Pastor, St. Michael's Evangelical Lutheran Church, Sellersville, Pennsylvania.

**Tuesday, December 6**                    Read Luke 3:15-18.

Advent is a season of expectation. But perhaps we have grown too comfortable, too familiar with what we expect: sweet baby Jesus, wrapped in swaddling cloths and cooing cutely in a manger; Mary standing serenely by; Joseph somewhat confused but nevertheless passively resigned. The picture pastoral—all is calm, all is bright.

John's expectation differed from ours. He anticipated One more powerful, a baptism of wind and fire. He expected a winnowing fork—the wheat to be gathered, the chaff to be burned.

But Jesus was not exactly what John expected either. To be sure, he was much more than the helpless manger babe he is so often portrayed to be at Christmas. Jesus could overthrow tables in the Temple and was certainly capable of making the unsettling remark. But he was also the one who spared the woman caught in adultery (John 8:1-11), the one who healed the man born blind (John 9:1-12), the one who forgave Peter his denial and replaced it with love and a call to serve (John 21:15-19). He was the one who gave his life for his friends, for the world, for us.

John's preaching was good news, Luke says. Yes, he pointed to the one to come. It is good news too that this more powerful, pointed-to One, the thong of whose sandals we are not worthy to untie, is often found when we don't expect and least deserve it, washing our feet, so to speak, giving himself yet again in humble service.

We may not know exactly what to expect, but we can trust the One whom John said was to come after him, who did indeed come, and who comes still to serve and save.

**Prayer:** *Gracious Lord, we don't always know what to expect from you. Help us to live trusting that what you will do will be good news. Amen.*

**Wednesday, December 7**                    Read Zephaniah 3:14-20.

Much of this short prophetic book speaks of judgment and condemnation. The refrain of "on that day" resounds throughout the first two chapters and the opening lines of the third. "That day" is a day to dread. It will be a day of wrath, distress, anguish, ruin, devastation, darkness, gloom (Zeph. 1:15).

A graduate school friend, a person of great faith and good humor, once gave me some advice about praying on the day of exams. "If you've studied well, you pray for justice. If you haven't studied very well," he said, "you pray for mercy."

When a prophet warms up with "I will utterly sweep away everything from the face of the earth, says the Lord" (Zeph. 1:2), you know that the justice deserved is judgment. You pray for mercy.

Early in chapter three the tone changes dramatically with the promise of a faithful remnant. The door to hope is cracked open. Then, suddenly, the judgments are removed. Mercy reigns. Singing, rejoicing, and exultation are the order of the day. The prophet declares that the Lord is in the midst of the people. They now are told not to fear "that day," and they hear a new promise for the future. "On that day" becomes "at that time." It will be a time when the Lord will gather his people and bring them home.

Sometimes it is simple. No studying required. We deserve judgment. We receive mercy.

That brings joy in the present. The Lord is in our midst! It gives us hope for the future. Without fear, we look forward to the time when the Lord will gather us and bring us home.

**Prayer:** *Caring Lord, help us to work for justice and pray for mercy. Amen.*

**Thursday, December 8**                    Read Zephaniah 3:14-20.

Here's the story:
Who? The Lord God.
What? Joy.
Where? Babylon.
When? Sometime after 586 B.C.
Why? Because God does not abandon God's people.
How? Love.

Most scholars agree that this passage originated during Israel's exile. The people had been sent packing from the promised land. The Temple had been destroyed. They had become slaves in a foreign country. There was cause for despair and certainly no apparent reason for joy.

But the prophet says to sing aloud. Rejoice! Why? He proclaims it not once but twice. The Lord is in your midst—even in exile, even with the Temple destroyed, even enslaved. Even so.

The prophet's promise stands true for us, too. Even when dilemmas bedevil us, when life's load is burdensome, God is in our midst, renewing us with his love, exulting over us with loud singing. Imagine that! God singing a song of joy to us! (Sounds like Christmas!)

As we prepare to celebrate the birth of Emmanuel, the ultimate gift of God with us, we can be joyful no matter our circumstances. For the God who traveled into exile with Israel not only will never abandon us but also promises to reverse the very brokenness that we feel. The lame will be made whole. The outcast will be welcomed in. Shame will be transformed into praise.

The Incarnation fulfilled the promise God made to Zephaniah—present joy. Someday, the kingdom will dawn in all its fullness—future hope.

**Prayer:** *Lord, the gift of your presence among us brings us joy. Regardless of circumstances, help us to hope for the day of wholeness still to come. Amen.*

**Friday, December 9**                    Read Isaiah 12:2-6.

In a short story entitled "Trust Me," John Updike tells about a boy named Harold and what happens when he jumps into a swimming pool for the first time.

His father is already treading water, encouraging him to jump in, telling him everything will be fine. At first, the youngster is skeptical, frozen by fear; the water looks deep and dangerous. But his father's encouragement convinces him. His father can be trusted, he thinks. Harold jumps.

He sinks like a rock. He is certain he is drowning, is sure he will die. But then, after what seems an eternity, a hand pulls him up out of the water to safety.

In language reminiscent of the psalms, today's reading encourages us not to be afraid, to put our trust in God. To do so requires a frightening leap of faith, a leap that will not always be easily or obviously rewarded. A leap that we sometimes simply will refuse to make. A leap that we, now and again, will hurry past without consideration.

There will be mortifying moments when we are sure we are going down for the last time. There will be too-confident moments when we will be tempted to go ahead and try to swim away on our own (which will certainly lead into dangerous waters). There will be impatient moments when we will not wish to wait for the Lord to lift us to safety.

Isaiah assures us, however, that God is our strength and our salvation, that God can be trusted. And the prophet promises that those who so trust will not drown in but will draw water from and drink deeply of the wells of salvation.

**Prayer:** *Lord God, help us, again and again, to take the leap of faith and trust solely in you. Amen.*

**Saturday, December 10**                    Read Philippians 4:4-7.

Don't worry. Be happy.

Sure.

Well intended, but for many persons I know, including myself, impossible advice from the twentieth century. At first glance, Paul might be accused of dispensing similar advice from the first century: "Do not worry about anything . . . . "

It is an interesting imperative from a person who is sitting in prison, waiting to go on trial. How can someone who suffered as much hardship as Paul (shipwreck, persecution, the thorn in his side) be such a Pollyanna? How can we slap on a silly, smiley face while the world, perhaps our own lives, seems to be in such trouble?

Well, Paul was no Pollyanna. A "but" in the middle of his "do not worry" sentence brings a proper perspective and a suitable hope (v. 6).

Paul's sentence does not promise a benign and blissful happiness. Nor does it blithely guarantee simple, satisfying answers to our requests. But through prayer, supplication, thanksgiving, we acknowledge the One greater than we, who is always appropriately addressed and worthy of being thanked and praised.

Paul does say "don't worry." However, his is not an attitude to be put on like a button but a prayerful posture of life that both puts us in our place and allows us to rejoice in being there. We are to rejoice, not in some happiness that comes from a good attitude, but in the Lord. Our joy is the gift we receive when we realize whom we are to trust.

**Prayer:** *Faithful Lord, true happiness comes from trusting in you. No matter what our circumstances, may we rejoice in your great and precious gift of life. Amen.*

**Sunday, December 11**                    Read Philippians 4:4-7.

As he begins to conclude his letter to the Philippians, Paul writes, "The Lord is near." We can interpret this simple sentence in at least two different ways. He might have meant, of course, that Christ was coming soon. That seems to have been Paul's conviction.

On the other hand, Paul might have meant that the Lord was at hand, was already present somehow. Paul's marvelous sense of the mysterious peace of God that reaches deeper than human comprehension and guards—like an ever-vigilant sentry—our hearts and minds, reveals a strong sense of an abiding presence.

Perhaps Paul was purposely vague. Perhaps he wished to allow for more than one meaning in his words. It is impossible to know. But whatever Paul intended precisely, both meanings are true.

Certainly God is ever-present, is with us always. That's the awesome beauty of the Incarnation. But the Incarnation is not yet complete. The glimpses of God's presence that we experience now—in a mirror dimly—give us courage to look forward to that day when we shall see God face to face.

Advent has a sense of absence about it that eagerly awaits an arrival. It is a "not yet" season on its way to a "now," a season with an edge-of-the-seat expectation awaiting fulfillment. In a way, that fulfillment comes at Christmas. We celebrate God's presence in Christ. But in another way, Advent continues. We still await the final fulfillment of God's plan.

**Prayer:** *Stir us up, Lord. As we celebrate your presence with joy and look to the future with a pregnant hope, grant us your peace that graciously surpasses our feeble understandings. Amen.*

## WEAVING SALVATION'S TAPESTRY

December 12–18, 1994 **Loretta Girzaitis**✢
**Monday, December 12** Read Psalm 139.

It would be difficult to understand Jesus' role in our salvation unless we look back at the faithlessness of the Hebrews once they entered the promised land and hear the message of the prophets who tried to draw them back to God.

The regularity and persistence of the Hebrews' obstinacy and incorrigibility brought thundering challenges from a handful of prophets. In their midst were also those who foretold the coming of a future leader who would free them from their sins. Yet, this was not what the masses wanted. Their fervent wish was for a political leader who would conquer all their enemies and free them for their own style of living.

This week we will meet Micah, a prophet whose strong faith compelled him to address the issues of the day. We will also meet the courageous young woman Mary and her aging cousin Elizabeth. We will visit with Hannah who, like Mary, could not keep her jubilation about her son's birth to herself. And we will examine God's motive for releasing Jesus to the human race.

How do we weave these various threads into a tapestry that reveals the beauty of salvation? Can we be reflective and prayerful enough to allow the Spirit to intertwine the various pieces into a distinctive portrait?

**Suggestion for meditation:** *As you read Psalm 139, use your imagination to its fullest, recognizing that you are a tapestry created by God. Recall that winter is a period of hibernation when nature withdraws from activity to rest and replenish its energies for new birth and growth. What do you need to do to permit God's spirit to merge with yours as you prepare for Jesus' birth?*

---

✢Spiritual director who facilitates workshops on spiritual growth; author; director of Victorious Spirit Enterprises, Saint Paul, Minnesota.

**Tuesday, December 13**                    Read Micah 5:2-3.

Micah is identified as a prophet, although the scripture says nothing about a specific call to prophecy. Neither did he have visions or receive oracles from the Lord. Instead, he preached with unusual directness about the needs of the poor, thundering against the social injustices of Jerusalem's religious and civil leaders who attempted to draw attention away from the needs of the poor. He was a poor person suffering with the poor rather than a wealthy one fighting for their rights.

Micah came from Moresheth, an insignificant outpost in southwest Palestine. He seemed to be connected with the people of the land who reached back to David and were loyal to David's family. He turned against the royalty of his time because he saw that they failed to fulfill the purpose of the Davidic dynasty.

Micah was sure that only someone of the Davidic line could change the destiny of the people, so he focused on Bethlehem Ephratha over Jerusalem when he promised that God would choose the one who would rule Israel from this smallest town of Judah's clans. He spoke of the mother who would give birth to a descendant of David, a descendant who would shepherd the flock with the strength of the Lord and gain renown to the ends of the earth. Early Christians easily made this connection with Bethlehem when they spoke of Jesus as this leader.

Micah was a forerunner of Jesus because of his lifestyle of poverty. He, like Jesus centuries later, was unafraid to challenge the rulers and clergy concerning their lifestyles. Choosing Bethlehem, the least of Judah's towns, rather than Jerusalem, the center of power, he underlined the importance of the lowly and insignificant over the wealthy and powerful.

**Suggestion for meditation:** *Are you more impressed with the poor and lowly or with those who are successful and powerful? Why? What is of Jerusalem and what is of Bethlehem in your life? Jesus was homeless at birth and again in adulthood. How do you identify with his homelessness?*

**Wednesday, December 14**                    Read Luke 1:39-45.

The angel's invitation to Mary to become the mother of the Son of God was a crucial event. The messenger knew he had to make the proposal while leaving it up to this teenage girl to determine whether she was willing to accept it. When Mary asked how she, a virgin, could conceive, the messenger's response was direct: "The Holy Spirit will come upon you and the power of the Most High will overshadow you." When Mary consented, the Holy Spirit surrounded her, supporting her through the torturous nine months. It was the Spirit who sustained her when not only the townspeople but also Joseph and her family doubted her.

Yet, during this painful period the Spirit filled her with joy, peace, patience, and love. It was during this time that she left her village to visit her aged cousin in the hillside outside Jerusalem. Somehow she sensed she had to carry the Spirit within her to the forerunner who was to introduce her son to the world.

The confirmation of Elizabeth's intuition took place when the child she was carrying leapt in her womb. This same Spirit also inspired Elizabeth, who proclaimed that Mary was blessed indeed.

Was Mary consciously aware of each step she should take during these nine months? Was the messenger prompting her to do this or that so that prophecies would be fulfilled or history could be written in a special way? God does not seem to work in that manner, rather God gives us the freedom to choose our response.

Mary must have puzzled intensely about the events swirling in her life. They did not make sense, but she must have had an openness and trust that pulled her forward as a magnet pulls its opposite pole. Something mysterious was happening; all Mary could do was let it take its course in spite of its absurdity.

**Suggestion for meditation:** *What seemingly absurd or impossible situations have you faced? How did you respond? What resulted? Were you aware of how the Spirit was present in any or all of them?*

**Thursday, December 15**  Read Luke 1:46-55.

What happens to Mary and Elizabeth as they greet each other? Two women, one beginning life and another close to its end, face each other filled with an exaltation beyond expression as they are captured in the awe of the moment.

Because both women are conscious of God's action in their lives, they must express this. Elizabeth blesses Mary and the child in her womb. Mary bursts forth with her own hymn of praise. In addition, the child leapt in Elizabeth's womb, foreshadowing the relationship the two boys will have in adulthood.

Mary's hymn focuses first on herself in relationship to God and then on God's relationship to humanity. She praises God as she rejoices in the fulfillment of God's promise. She also recognizes that she, the lowly mother, will be honored through all history because she is giving birth to the divine Son. As she acknowledges God's power in this conception, she also acknowledges God's power over all humankind.

Who are the rich and the arrogant whom God scatters? Who are the poor and downtrodden who are filled with good things? Each of us needs to identify with one or the other, examining our hearts to see if we are those who are to be put down or lifted up.

Can we see ourselves as poor, totally stripped of the possibility of living enriching lives unless we are open to God's gift of grace and presence? Can we understand how much we are dependent upon God's Son for our salvation? Do Mary's words foreshadow the work that her son will be doing among the poor and downtrodden in the years ahead? Yet the poor are blessed not because they are the have-nots of society but because in their emptiness they are open to the filling of the gift of salvation.

**Suggestion for meditation:** *Recall instances in your life when you were conscious of God's presence and found yourself overwhelmed with it. How did you express it? Through silence, tears, song, dance, or drawing? What does it do to you to recall the memory at this time?*

**Friday, December 16**                    Read 1 Samuel 2:1-10.

As we immerse ourselves in the Magnificat, Mary's hymn of praise and prophecy, it is helpful to see the parallels between this teenager and Hannah, a married woman living at the time of Eli.

Women in Old Testament times were perceived to be cursed by God if they did not bear children, particularly sons. Such was the lot of Hannah because of her barrenness. So she went to Shiloh and spoke to the priest Eli, promising him that if her prayer were answered and she bore a son, she would consecrate him to the Lord as a nazirite. She was so eager to have a son that she was willing to give him up to the Lord's service after weaning him. Eli prayed along with Hannah, not realizing that this newborn would eventually replace him at Shiloh.

The birth of Samuel was God's gift to an oppressed woman; she, in gratitude, returned this gift to the Lord after three years. She then chanted her hymn as she thanked God for the birth of her child and praised God's power and holiness. She also declared that the rich will be cast down and the poor raised up. Her hymn was not only an outpouring of gratitude but also a song of justice, inviting God to overcome the enemies of the poor.

There are differences between Hannah, the mature woman, and Mary, the young maiden. Hannah wants a son because of the derision others heap on her; Mary is not seeking motherhood but conceives and suffers derision because of it. Hannah offers a hymn of gratitude and justice; Mary, evidently familiar with the Hebrew testament, paraphrases Hannah's hymn into one of gratitude and mercy. Hannah dedicates her son to God's service after three years; Mary waits thirty years before her son determines his destiny.

**Suggestion for meditation:** *What in your life reflects Hannah's and Mary's dilemmas, not necessarily in pregnancy but in the poignancy of rejection and derision? Write your own hymn of praise or paraphrase either Mary's or Hannah's hymn in response to your own situation.*

**Saturday, December 17**                Read Hebrews 1:1-4.

The Letter to the Hebrews is more likely a sermon to a group of communities of conservative Gentile Christians than an epistle to Palestinian Jews. Scholars speculate that someone other than Paul may have written Hebrews, since the earliest mention of it comes late in the first century by Clement of Rome.

Hebrews focuses primarily on the life and death of Jesus rather than on his resurrection. Christ is highlighted as the word of God communicated to humanity in a very personal way because of his presence among us. Hebrews also emphasizes Christ as the eternal high priest who sacrifices himself through death. By that death he writes a new covenant that facilitates access to God in a new way.

In this sermon the author offers an insight into Jesus' understanding of God and so offers us a model for faith. This work integrates events in the Hebrew testament with the work of Christ.

As a work, Hebrews is an inspiration, since it addresses the problems that beset spiritual pilgrims in every age. It affirms that having problems does not indicate a lack of faith. Jesus' birth into human life makes him one with us in our humanity. Understanding his story and paralleling ours with his gives us a lifeline to God.

Jesus reflects God's glory, represents his Abba, and becomes the Word that guides us. His birth, presence, and death become our salvation. We need to follow the guidelines he offers us as his story unfolds from his conception until his return to Abba.

His name is Emmanuel, "God with us." The name is a promise that both the divine and the human will be with us until the end of time.

**Suggestion for meditation:** *What connecting link do you have to this Savior born in our midst? With what aspect of his story do you identify? How grateful are you for your birth at this time and in this place and of this particular set of parents? How do you feel about being the adopted child of God? What significance does your baptismal name have for you?*

**Sunday, December 18**                 Read Hebrews 10:5-10.

The Letter to the Hebrews lays out the qualifications for a priest that follow those outlined in the tradition of Aaron. A priest is one who has been called by God from among the people to be God's representative to them. So the priest acts on behalf of the people. As a mediator, he offers sacrifices not only for the sins of others but also for his own sins.

The high priest had the privilege of offering the cultic sacrifice annually in the temple, reminding the people that the scapegoat sent into the wilderness at that time symbolically took their sins away with him. Yet the burden of sin remained, since this sacrifice had to be repeated annually.

In time Jesus was born into our midst, called by God to be the high priest, but one different from the high priest of the Levite line. If we apply the Aaronic credentials to Jesus, we note that he is God's representative, acting as a mediator on the people's behalf. He offers the final sacrifice, becomes the final scapegoat so that the human race never needs another.

In today's reading the author contrasts the offerings and sacrifices of the Hebraic priesthood with Jesus' simple priestly declaration, "I have come to do your will." That becomes Jesus' priestly duty, and he lives it out to his final sacrifice. All we are to do is to recall the memory of his final sacrifice continuously so that we would never forget his total and uncompromising love. Recall that at his final meal, Jesus told his disciples, "Do this as a remembrance of me."

**Suggestion for meditation:** *Ask yourself, How am I called to do God's will? How does my response connect with Jesus' response?*

## ICONS OF CHRISTMAS

December 19–25, 1994
**Monday, December 19**

**Calvin D. McConnell**†
Read Psalm 96.

An icon is a painting of the type usually associated with Orthodox churches. It is impossible to make eye contact with persons who are portrayed. They are not present to us. Their eyes are fixed on the Divine. As we gaze meditatively upon them we are transported beyond their humanity to the mystery and reality of God. The many images of Christmas can serve as icons, leading us beyond what we see, do, and feel to the Divine reality of Christmas.

The psalmist sees beyond the evidence of things as they appear to the promises of God's presence in ways which make a difference. This ability to view life as an icon which reveals God's redemptive and recreative activity causes the psalmist to exclaim in astonishment and joy. All is not as it appears to be on the surface. There is newness to be seen through our icon vision.

"For awhile I was able to survive with my near vision," remarked an insightful person, "but it is not good enough for seeing the far world, the whole world." God is continuously creating in ways which make all the difference God wants and we need. Viewing Christmas as an icon into the purposes of God among us will cause us to sing a different kind of song.

**Prayer:** *We thank you, God, for this Christmas week. Enable us to view the images of Christmas icons which reveal your reality and greater purposes. Amen.*

---

†Bishop, Seattle Area, and President of General Board of Higher Education and Ministry.

## Tuesday, December 20

Read Isaiah 9:2-7.

*Floating on faith and driven by dreams*

It is a complex and dangerous world in which we live. The sometimes chaotic nature of our times is described by Flora Lewis when she says we are a people of idealism but also stridency, we are self-confident but hold deep resentments and hostility, we are generous but mean, and civic minded but communally greedy. With James Fowler we "long for eyes to see and hearts to respond to the moving shape of One who is our author and destiny." The prophet Isaiah provides us with a Christmas icon of such a Savior who can shape our lives and guide that of our societies. We respond with hope to the dependable leadership and personal companionship of this one who is a wise counselor and a mighty but peaceable God-like Savior.

While we may feel there are few lands of promise these days, this icon assures us that there will always be persons of promise, places which hold promise, and time pregnant with promise. "The zeal of the Lord of hosts will do this." In our attempts to govern ourselves and to create just, loving, and beneficial communities for all people, "the moving shape of One who is our author and destiny" is actively present.

Llewelyn Morgan is author of BARD, a legendary/historical novel of the Irish people. As the people set out in primitive boats from their ancestral lands along the coast of Spain to cross the unknown sea to what is now Ireland, the bard sings as history unfolds, "We are floating on faith and driven by dreams." With Isaiah's incarnational icon we can move into the future with confidence.

**Prayer:** *Grant us the grace to see in the icon of our times and places of darkness the eternal and trustworthy presence of the One who is our Way, our Truth, and our Life. Amen.*

---

*Practical Theology*, edited by Don Browning.

**Wednesday, December 21**                    Read Hebrews 1:1-4.

*The road past the view*

An icon is transparent. It compels us to see through it to the creating mind and loving heart of God. The writer of the letter to the Hebrews reminds us of this iconographic nature of Jesus. Reminding the readers that other icons had been given to their ancestors, God has now blest us with the supreme icon of the very Son of God. "He is the reflection of God's glory and the exact imprint of God's very being," the writer exclaims in excitement. This Son of God sustains all things and frees all humanity who will receive him from the debilitating power of sin. All this is through God who desires us to know the nature of the Divine Presence among us so that we might respond in life-transforming and saving ways.

"The Road Past the View" is the title given by Georgia O'Keeffe to two of her paintings. They are different interpretations of a road which travels through the foothills of a mountain range, rounds a corner, and disappears into a canyon. Our eyes tell us that the road has ended, but our minds know that it has only moved beyond our view. It continues, carrying travelers on to more commanding vistas. Her title provides us with another Christmas icon. God, wanting us to know more of the Divine nature which creates, sustains, judges, and nurtures us, moved beyond the view which humanity had understood up to that time. In Jesus the Christ we are challenged to travel this "Road Past the View" of what this Savior can mean to us. Traveling in the company of Jesus we will encounter great vistas of understanding which will enable us to view and do life in ways that will take us on journeys far beyond our present views.

**Prayer:** *For Your desire to be known and loved by us, O God, we give You thanks. O holy Child of Bethlehem, descend to us, we pray; cast out our sin and enter in, be born in us today. Amen.*

*From the hymn "O Little Town of Bethlehem" by Phillips Brooks.

**Thursday, December 22**                    Read Titus 2:11-14.

*Trying to climb your own belt*

The salvation God offers through Christ is not a pretty little Christmas gift whose wrappings are more attractive than the contents in the box. Paul makes it clear to Titus that the gift is a plain and practical one meant for hard, daily work. Look at the inscription on the gift card: "trains you to renounce impiety and worldly passion," "redeems you from iniquity and purifies you." That's a tough and rather unglamorous gift. Kind of like giving your wife a "Dust-Buster" hand vacuum on your wedding anniversary or giving your husband a new garbage can on his birthday. But we need that kind of tough love from God at times.

Nobel Prize poet Czeslow Milosz in his poem Winter" reflects:

> This hasn't been the age for the righteous and decent.
> I know what it is to beget monsters
> and to recognize them myself.*

While God's judgment may be harsh at times, we have the means of responding hopefully by the grace of a loving and very concerned Savior. The One who was humanity's Christmas gift lived and taught among us, died for us, and was resurrected as our promise of hope. The philosopher Hocking gives us a Christmas icon in his quip, "You cannot climb a rope that is attached to your own belt."

The longing of Christ is for "a people of his own who are zealous for good deeds" (v. 14). Our thank-you note for such gifting is to commit ourselves to being one of those persons.

**Prayer:** *"What can I give him, poor as I am?"** I give you my heart. Amen.*

---

*Collected Poems: 1931–1987* (Hopewell, NJ: Ecco Press, 1990).
**From the carol "In the Bleak Midwinter" by Christina Rossetti.

**Friday, December 23**                    Read Psalm 98.

*Balloons in the snow*

Now is the time for celebration, for balloons in the snow, and the creator on the earth. Fantastic. Miracle. Wonder. Surprise. Celebration. No word can contain it all. The creator is in the crib. The Lord is in my heart. A NEW ONE is on the earth. A new song is on our lips. A new spirit is in our minds. Christ is here in every color. We can see this with our Christmas eyes.*

We started this week with another psalm which opens with an identical exclamation, "O sing unto the Lord a new song." With our "Christmas eyes" we can view and do life differently. God's gracious caring for us, reflected in the manner in which the Christ dwells among us, brings a newness that is hope-creating. Tom Wilson of the Foundation of the Northwest told me recently that seven of the most helpful words that can be spoken are, "I didn't know I could do that." Because of the promise of the Incarnation, "a new song is on our lips, and a new spirit is in our minds." We are able to enter into our life and relationships in ways that were not possible before because of the "immeasurable greatness of his power for us who believe, according to the workings of his great power." (Eph. 1:19). So let us look forward to the year which is ahead with the resolve to "do what excites you a lot and scares you a little." For "now is the time for celebration, for balloons in the snow."

**Prayer:** *God of our history and future, our tradition and innovation, our memory and vision, bless us now as we create a useful future in company with your most blessed child, our Companion-Savior. Amen.*

*Used by permission of Sacred Design Associates, Inc., Minneapolis, MI 55343.

## Saturday, December 24

Read Luke 2:8-20.

*Shepherds glorifying God and telling everyone*

Tonight we participate in the mysterious and joyous celebration of Christmas Eve. As we hear again the shepherds' story, let us be attentive to an icon which might be overlooked. It is an act in two scenes. Scene one: After hearing the announcement of the angelic choir, the shepherds immediately departed for Bethlehem. Would you or I have responded in like manner? It would take a lot of discussion about this unusual announcement from a highly improbable source. Would you have risked it? How would you feel and what would people say if it were all a hoax? The shepherds, however, recognized a holy event when they saw one. They left immediately for Bethlehem.

The second scene follows their rewarding participation in the nativity, their place in history forever guaranteed. They returned to their homes and flocks. We would expect that. What is unexpected is what they did about what they experienced. They glorified God and told everyone they saw. They were the original evangelists—the first to announce that God-is-with-us in the Christ. That's an unusual response for us present-day Christians. Bishop Roger Heft's description of our Anglican friends in New Zealand in uncomfortably incisive: "If there is one commandment of Christ that Anglicans have kept with some degree of joy, it is Jesus' admonition to the disciples, 'See that you tell no one.' " The messianic secret is one we have guarded too closely. We have not been the evangelists God expects and others need.

The real celebration of Christmas is to be found in the other 364 days of the year. The icon of the shepherds sets the pace. All who journey with Jesus will shout the good news that God-is-with-us!

**Prayer:** *Go, tell it on the mountain, over the hills and everywhere, that Jesus Christ is born!*

---

\*From the Afro-American spiritual; words by John W. Work, Jr.

**Sunday, December 25 (Christmas)**          Read John 1:1-5.

*"No one knows enough to be pessimistic"*

The affirmation, "No one knows enough to be pessimistic," is Norman Cousins' best known quotation. It serves as our icon for Christmas Day, elucidating the prelude to John's Gospel. "In the beginning was the Word, and the Word was with God...What has come into being in him was life...the light shines in the darkness and has not been overcome." These declarations are "music making that shakes the earth, stirs the heart, and rattles the bones" (to quote symphony conductor Carlos Kleiber's response to Beethoven's Fourth and Seventh Symphonies).

Christianity has always associated Jesus Christ with light. What a contrast Christmas light is to the darkness frequently encountered in and through events and persons we encounter. It is Christological optimism assuring us that darkness cannot overcome the light of God's presence with us in Christ. Jean Vanier challenges us in a compelling way to claim that divine light and to let it shine in all our relationships: "Somewhere in each of us we are a mixture of light and darkness, of love and hate, of trust and fear. If your light touches my light, maybe we can get through it together. But if your darkness touches my darkness we have problems, big problems." Such Christmas light which shines the whole year through is something to sing about!

Our observance of this Christmas Day, and its celebration throughout the year in the witnessing and serving company of other people of the Light is the way to "shake the earth, stir the heart, and rattle the bones" of all whom we touch. Indeed, "No one knows enough to be pessimistic." Praise be to God!

**Prayer:** *May the God of hope fill you with all joy and peace in believing, so that by the power of the Holy Spirit you may abound in hope." Amen. (Rom. 15:13)*

# AT ONE IN GOD

December 26–31, 1994
**Monday, December 26**

**Phyllis Tickle✛**
Read Psalm 148:11-13.

The three days that follow Christmas Day are for me a holy gathering of time, a kind of bouquet of days within the Christian year. Historically, all three are "saints" days. That is, on each of them Christians for centuries have stopped to honor a particular hero of our faith: on the 26th, Saint Stephen; on the 27th, Saint John; and on the 28th, the Holy Innocents slaughtered by King Herod in his search for the Christ Child. And, historically, this is the only week of the year in which three days of such major remembrance follow each other one after another. How appropriate that they should fall within—and give sweet perfume to—this stilled time of waiting between God's birth and the new year's coming.

When I was a child, we always sang "Good King Wenceslas" on this day, my father's big hands stroking the keys of the piano as his deep, full voice boomed over ours. Good King Wenceslas going forth on the Feast of Stephen to perform acts of charity. But I was a child and had no thought for charity or for the first martyred deacon of my faith. I scarcely had faith at that age. What I had instead was joy, more joy than I could hold. So I sang; and Stephen's day became for me that day which lay beyond being happy. It became that day of a music which was beside itself, in which, as our psalm says, all the kings of the earth and all peoples—princes, rulers, young men, and maidens—all of necessity praise him whose splendor is over all.

**Prayer:** *O God, let me know and give joy today. Let me also stop and teach a child, as I myself was taught, how to release Christmas's joy into sweet music to thee. Amen.*

---

✛Writer; Religion Editor, *Publishers Weekly*; lector and vestry member in the Episcopal Church, Millington, Tennessee.

**Tuesday, December 27**     Read Colossians 3:12-16.

Saint John, whose day of remembrance this is, was the beloved disciple, the one who captured in the greatest detail the lessons and word of our Lord. It was also John who remembered and recorded his "comfortable words": "Peace I leave with you" (John 14:27), "Do not let not your hearts be troubled" (John 14:1), and John who understood the enormous love of God more clearly than the other gospel writers and who, having understood it so well, then preserved its perfect statement: "God so loved the world" (John 3:16).

The word of God, the peace of God, the love of God—we meet them first in John's books, meet them as treasures that each of us can receive. And then we meet them here again this week. This time they are in Paul's letters; and this time they are treasures that we as church receive, we as one body, we as the communion of Christ. For, according to. Paul, as surely as each soul is enriched, so too must it enrich and be enriched by the whole. Love is the bond that holds us in perfectness, and the peace of God is that to which we are called in one body. The word of Christ—that which was most central to John's understanding of his Lord—is to dwell in us while we, as creatures singing and full of grace, teach and admonish one another. It is scripture's most moving picture of "church" as church as in the beginning, and the one we must all hold most dear.

**Prayer:** *O God, our Father and Source of being, create in us a unity of all our parts that as family, friends, and Christians together we may be unto you a whole and blessed company. Guide, likewise, my own thoughts, that they may be in and of and about, from and for your community both on earth and in heaven. Amen.*

**Wednesday, December 28**
Read 1 Samuel 2:18-20, 26;
Luke 2:41-52.
Isaiah 49:13-21; Matthew 2:16-18.

Our scriptures speak rather infrequently of children in terms of some specific action of theirs or of some prophetic function, but today we remember three of the more powerful exceptions to that rule: the young Samuel in the sanctuary; the young Jesus in the Temple with the elders; and the children of innocence whose mothers, in their disconsolate mourning, fulfilled the messianic prophecy of Rachel weeping for her children (Jer. 31:15). Today, on the day of the Holy Innocents, it is appropriate that our readings should group the three stories together, for children serve as parents provide; and that is the incontestable lesson of all three.

Undoubtedly, Jesus would have found his way into the Temple even if Mary and Joseph had not established his habits by their own. But it is equally probable that Mary and Joseph were chosen as the holy parents because of their devotion and their reverent habits. The same things must also be said of Samuel, and of Hannah and Elkanah as they first prayed for, and then gave back to holy service, Israel's great prophet-judge. And the same things must be said for the agony of Rachel and the blood of her children.

Our adult assignment then, the stories seem to say, is not so much to force the faith upon our young as it is to stand centrally within the faith ourselves. The stories, in fact, seem rather pointedly to teach that we are to be to our young a door into spiritual and holy opportunities, not a superior tower above them. The call, in this as in all other aspects of our Christian life, is to be humble if we would be effective.

**Prayer:** *O God, grant that I may parent both my own and the children of others as I have myself been parented by you. And grant me the graciousness not to be terrified by that joyful obligation. Amen.*

**Thursday, December 29**                    Read Psalm 148.

As the three great days of Christmas week come to an end, so too do their major themes come to summary in the poetry of Psalm 148. How earnestly I loved that poetry when I was a child!

> Praise the Lord from the earth, ye dragons, and all deeps:
> Fire, and hail; snow, and vapour;
> stormy wind fulfilling his word:
> Mountains, and all hills; fruitful trees, and all cedars.
>
> (vv. 7-9, KJV)

My skin would crawl up my back at those images as well as at the potency of their sound and meter. Here, in sacred words (in parentally approved words!) were all the wonders of my imagination, all the delights of fairy book and medieval story, all the entertainments of my own lively interior. It was years before I even perceived that there was theology here as well.

It was years before I saw more than the cataloguing of every part of creation from angels to peasants and from sun and wind to trees and birds, years before I understood with a thundering epiphany that the union of all things is in their praisings.

Amen and amen.

**Suggestion for meditation:** *Read Psalm 148 aloud. Feel the exultation in the words. Add your own praises to those of the psalmist.*

**Friday, December 30**                    Read Luke 2:46-52.

Jesus at study. The young Christ at his lessons. This has troubled Christians since the days when Luke first wrote it down.

Who was Jesus at twelve? A boy with vague intimations of his own nature? Already God Aware and waiting for a body to mature into usefulness? A prepubescent struggling with an emerging self-awareness of both his natures—human and divine?

Who knows exactly? None of us, certainly; and though we may have opinions, we have no proofs for them, only a kind of grinding discomfort with the questions themselves. Yet the Boy/boy in the Temple is the incarnation of God. Far more than Christmas itself with its angels and prettified stables, the adolescent-to-be struggling before the elders with conflicting messages from heaven, parents, and ecclesial authority is the great, searing portrait of God-made-flesh. We cannot walk away from Christmas without it. We cannot have done with these days or call their promise our own until we have bowed to this one mystery: Who was the Boy in the Temple?

**Prayer:** *O God, Father, Son, and Holy Ghost, forgive my ignorance, my soul's confusion, my not-knowing, and hold me blameless, sanctifying my limitations into faith and me into a useful humility. Amen.*

**Saturday, December 31**                    Read Colossians 3:17.

There are few things in life as revealing as all our gibberish about New Year's resolutions. The very fact that we have so many choices of what to change in ourselves and so many options about how to perform our psychosurgery is proof of either too much largesse or too much distraction—or just possibly both.

A new year is not a "thing" anyway, certainly not an object or a tangible. It is a measure, as an inch is, or a half-cup, or a pound. That we are excited by one but not by the others speaks more to our impotence than to our good intentions; for we are all time's victims and its prisoners. Every part of us yearns to escape time, to control it, to have more of it. We damn it or steal it or celebrate it, but we cannot evade it; and like all good pagans, ultimately we celebrate what we feel ourselves to be exceeded by.

But Saint Paul would have the young Christians at Colossae to be built of sterner stuff. He would have, among them, all resolution contained, as in a burning prism, by a single focus:

"Whatever you do, in word or deed, do everything in the name of the Lord Jesus, giving thanks to God the Father through him."

**Suggestion for prayer:** *Use Paul's exhortation as your own heart's desire and prayer—Whatever I do in word or action, may I do all in the name of the Lord Jesus, remembering to give thanks to God the Father through Christ.*

# The Revised Common Lectionary 1994*
## (*Disciplines* Edition)

**January 1-2**
  **Epiphany**
Isaiah 60:1-6
Psalm 72:1-7, 10-14
Ephesians 3:1-12
Matthew 2:1-12

**January 3-9**
Genesis 1:1-5
Psalm 29
Acts 19:1-7
Mark 1:4-11

**January 10-16**
1 Samuel 3:1-10 (11-20)
Psalm 139:1-6, 13-18
1 Corinthians 6:12-20
John 1:43-51

**January 17-23**
Jonah 3:1-5, 10
Psalm 62:5-12
1 Corinthians 7:29-31
Mark 1:14-20

**January 24-30**
Deuteronomy 18:15-20
Psalm 111
1 Corinthians 8:1-13
Mark 1:21-28

*Year B–Christmas, Year C

**January 31–February 6**
Isaiah 40:21-31
Psalm 147:1-11, 20*c*
1 Corinthians 9:16-23
Mark 1:29-39

**February 7-13**
  **Transfiguration**
2 Kings 2:1-12
Psalm 50:1-6
2 Corinthians 4:3-6
Mark 9:2-9

**February 14-20**
  **First Sunday in Lent**
Genesis 9:8-17
Psalm 25:1-10
1 Peter 3:18-22
Mark 1:9-15
  **Ash Wednesday lections**
Joel 2:1-2, 12-17 (*or* Isaiah 58:1-12)
Psalm 51:1-17
2 Corinthians 5:20*b*–6:10
Matthew 6:1-6, 16-21

**February 21-27**
  **Second Sunday in Lent**
Genesis 17:1-7, 15-16
Psalm 22:23-31
Romans 4:13-25
Mark 8:31-38

**February 28–March 6**
  **Third Sunday in Lent**
Exodus 20:1-17
Psalm 19
1 Corinthians 1:18-25
John 2:13-22

**March 7-13**
  **Fourth Sunday in Lent**
Numbers 21:4-9
Psalm 107:1-3, 17-22
Ephesians 2:1-10
John 3:14-21

**March 14-20**
  **Fifth Sunday in Lent**
Jeremiah 31:31-34
Psalm 51:1-12
Hebrews 5:5-10
John 12:20-33

**March 21-27**
  **Passion/Palm Sunday**
Liturgy of the Palms
Mark 11:1-11
Psalm 118:1-2, 19-29
Liturgy of the Passion
Isaiah 50:4-9*a*
Psalm 31:9-16
Philippians 2:5-11
Mark 14:1—5:47
  (*or* Mark 15:1-39)

**March 28–April 3**
  **Easter**
Acts 10:34-43
Psalm 118:1-2, 14-24
1 Corinthians 15:1-11
John 20:1-18
  (*or* Mark 16:1-8)

**Selected Holy Week lections:**
  *Monday:*
  Isaiah 42:1-9
  John 12:1-11
  *Tuesday:*
  Isaiah 49:1-7
  John 12:20-36
  *Wednesday:*
  Isaiah 50:4-9*a*
  John 13:21-32
  *Maundy Thursday:*
  Exodus 12:1-4, 11-14
  Psalm 116:1-2, 12-19
  John 13:1-17, 31*b*-35
  *Good Friday*
  Isaiah 52:13–53:12
  Psalm 22
  Hebrews 10:16-2
  John 18:1–19:42
  *Holy Saturday:*
  Job 14:11-14
  Psalm 31:1-4, 15-16
  Matthew 27:57-66
    *or* John 19:38-42

379

**April 4-10**
Acts 4:32-35
Psalm 133
1 John 1:1–2:2
John 20:19-31

**April 11-17**
Acts 3:12-19
Psalm 4
1 John 3:1-7
Luke 24:36b-48

**April 18-24**
Acts 4:5-12
Psalm 23
1 John 3:16-24
John 10:11-18

**April 25–May 1**
Acts 8:26-40
Psalm 22:25-31
1 John 4:7-21
John 15:1-8

**May 2-8**
Acts 10:44-48
Psalm 98
1 John 5:1-6
John 15:9-17

**May 9-15**
Acts 1:15-17, 21-26
Psalm 1
1 John 5:9-13
John 17:6-19
  **Ascension Day** (May 12)
  Acts 1:1-11
  Psalm 47
  Ephesians 1:15-23
  Luke 24:44-53

**May 16-22**
  **Pentecost**
Acts 2:1-21
Psalm 104:24-34, 35b
Romans 8:22-27
John 15:26-27; 16:4b-15

**May 23-29**
  **Trinity**
Isaiah 6:1-8
Psalm 29
Romans 8:12-17
John 3:1-17

**May 30–June 5**
1 Samuel 8:4-20; (11:14-15)
Psalm 138
2 Corinthians 4:13–5:1
Mark 3:20-35

## June 6-12
1 Samuel 15:34–16:13
Psalm 20
2 Corinthians 5:6-10
(11-13), 14-17
Mark 4:26-34

## June 13-19
1 Samuel 17:(1a, 4-11,
19-23), 32-49
Psalm 9:9-20
2 Corinthians 6:1-13
Mark 4:35-41

## June 20-26
2 Samuel 1:1, 17-27
Psalm 133
2 Corinthians 8:7-15
Mark 5:21-43

## June 27–July 3
2 Samuel 5:1-5, 9-10
Psalm 48
2 Corinthians 12:2-10
Mark 6:1-13

## July 4-10
2 Samuel 6:1-5, 12b-19
Psalm 24
Ephesians 1:3-14
Mark 6:14-29

## July 11-17
2 Samuel 7:1-14a
Psalm 89:20-37
Ephesians 2:11-22
Mark 6:30-34, 53-56

## July 18-24
2 Samuel 11:1-15
Psalm 14
Ephesians 3:14-21
John 6:1-21

## July 25-31
2 Samuel 11:16–12:13a
Psalm 51:1-12
Ephesians 4:1-16
John 6:24-35

## August 1-7
2 Samuel 18:5-9, 15, 31-33
Psalm 130
Ephesians 4:25–5:2
John 6:35, 41-51

## August 8-14
1 Kings 2:10-12; 3:3-14
Psalm 111
Ephesians 5:15-20
John 6:51-58

**August 15-21**
1 Kings 8:(1-6, 10-11),
    22-30, 41-43
Psalm 84
Ephesians 6:10-20
John 6:56-69

**August 22-28**
Song of Solomon 2:8-13
Psalm 45:1-2, 6-9
James 1:17-27
Mark 7:1-8, 14-15, 21-23

**August 29–September 4**
Proverbs 22:1-2, 8-9, 22-23
Psalm 125
James 2:1-10 (11-13) 14-17
Mark 7:24-37

**September 5-11**
Proverbs 1:20-33
Psalm 19
James 3:1-12
Mark 8:27-38

**September 12-18**
Proverbs 31:10-31
Psalm 1
  (*or* Jeremiah 11:18-20
    Psalm 54)
James 3:13–4:3. 7-8*a*
Mark 9:30-37

**September 19-25**
Esther 7:1-6, 9-10; 9:20-22
Psalm 124
James 5:13-20
Mark 9:38-50

**September 26–October 2**
Job 1:1; 2:1-10
Psalm 26 (*or* Psalm 25)
Hebrews 1:1-4; 2:5-12
Mark 10:2-16

**October 3-9**
Job 23:1-9, 16-17
Psalm 22:1-15
Hebrews 4:12-16
Mark 10:17-31

**October 10-16**
Job 38:1-7, (34-41)
Psalm 104:1-9, 24, 35*c*
Hebrews 5:1-10
Mark 10:35-45

**October 17-23**
Job 42:1-6, 10-17
Psalm 34:1-8, (19-22)
Hebrews 7:23-28
Mark 10:46-52

**October 24-30**
Ruth 1:1-18
Psalm 146
Hebrews 9:11-14
Mark 12:28-34

**October 31–November 6**
Ruth 3:1-5; 4:13-17
Psalm 127
Hebrews 9:24-28
Mark 12:38-44
  **All Saints Day**
  (November 1):
Isaiah 25:6-9
Psalm 24
Revelation 21:1-6a
John 11:32-44

**November 7-13**
1 Samuel 1:4-20
1 Samuel 2:1-10
  or Psalm 113
  (or Daniel 12:1-3
    Psalm 16)
Hebrews 10:11-14
  (15-18) 19-25
Mark 13:1-8

**November 14-20**
2 Samuel 23:1-7
Psalm 132:1-12, (13-18)
  (or Daniel 7:9-10, 13-14
    Psalm 93)
Revelation 1:4b-8
John 18:33-37

**November 21-27**
**First Sunday of Advent**
Jeremiah 33:14-16
Psalm 25:1-10
1 Thessalonians 3:9-13
Luke 21:25-36

**November 28–December 4**
**Second Sunday of Advent**
Malachi 3:1-4
Luke 1:68-79
Philippians 1:3-11
Luke 3:1-6

**December 5-11**
**Third Sunday of Advent**
Zephaniah 3:14-20
Isaiah 12:2-6
Philippians 4:4-7
Luke 3:7-18

**December 12-18**
**Fourth Sunday of Advent**
Micah 5:2-5a
Luke 1:47-55 (or Psalm 80:1-7)
Hebrews 10:5-10
Luke 1:39-45 (46-55)
  **Christmas Eve**
  Isaiah 9:2-7
  Psalm 96
  Titus 2:11-14
  Luke 2:1-20

**December 19-25**
  **Christmas Day**
Isaiah 52:7-10
Psalm 98
Hebrews 1:1-4 (5-12)
John 1:1-14

**December 26–January 1**
  **First Sunday**
  **After Christmas**
1 Samuel 2:18-20, 26
Psalm 148
Colossians 3:12-17
Luke 2:41-52
  *or* **New Year**
  Ecclesiastes 3:1-13
  Psalm 8
  Revelation 21:1-6*a*
  Matthew 25:31-46

*Come, Divine Presence, and journey with us.*
*Interrupt our steps and surprise us*

Minerva C. Carcaño
*Disciplines 1993*